A NEW FACE FOR THE CHURCH

A NEW FACE FOR THE CHURCH

LAWRENCE O. RICHARDS

ZONDERVAN PUBLISHING HOUSE
Grand Rapids, Michigan

Grateful acknowledgment is made to the following:

ASSOCIATION PRESS for a quote from *Who's Killing the Church?* edited by Stephen C. Rose, © 1966.

EERDMANS PUBLISHING COMPANY for a quote from *The Church's Mission to the Educated American* by Joel Nederhoed, © 1961. Used by permission.

HARPER AND ROW PUBLISHERS for permission to quote from *The God-Evaders* by Clyde Reid, © 1966.

HIS MAGAZINE for quotes from Paul Fromer. Reprinted by permission from HIS, student magazine of Inter-Varsity Christian Fellowship, © 1968.

HOLT, RINEHART AND WINSTON, INC. for permission to quote from *Discussion, Conference and Group Process* by Halbert E. Gulley, © 1960.

INSTITUTE FOR SOCIAL RESEARCH, University of Michigan for a quote from *Studies in Social Power* by Dorwin Cartwright, editor, © 1959.

J. B. LIPPINCOTT COMPANY for a quote from the book *The Comfortable Pew* by Pierre Berton. Copyright © 1965 by Pierre Berton. Reprinted by permission of J. B. Lippincott Company.

MACMILLAN COMPANY for a quote from *The Secular City* by Harvey Cox, © 1965.

NATIONAL EDUCATION ASSOCIATION for material from *Group Development* by the National Training Laboratories, © 1961.

TEACHER'S COLLEGE, Columbia University for permission to quote from *Designing Training Activities* by Matthew Miles.

UNIVERSITY OF CHICAGO PRESS for permission to quote from *The Planning of Change,* Second edition, edited by Bennis, Benne and Chin. Copyright 1967 by the University of Chicago.

WESTMINSTER PRESS for permission to quote from *The Split-level Fellowship* by Wesley Baker. Copyright © MCMLXV by W. L. Jenkins, The Westminster Press. Used by permission. Also for permission to quote from *The Layman in Christian History,* edited by Stephen C. Neill and Hans-Ruedi Weber, 1963. Copyright © World Council of Churches, 1963. Used by permission.

JOHN WILEY AND SONS for permission to quote from *Personal and Organizational Change in the Church* by Schein and Bennis, © 1967, and also for material from *T Group Theory and Laboratory Method* by Bradford, Benne and Gibb, editors, © 1964.

A NEW FACE FOR THE CHURCH

Library of Congress Catalog Card Number 78-120038

The quotations from *The New Testament in Modern English* © 1958 by J. B. Phillips, are used by permission of the publisher, The Macmillan Company.

Printed in the United States of America

Contents

Foreword

"There's a new mood in the country," says a pastor friend who has just returned from two weeks of conferences at Hume Lake and the Firs. "A 'let's do it differently' mood. Which isn't necessarily right — but it is exciting."

It has been exciting for me these last three years to sense this new mood in response to a series of articles exploring renewal in evangelical perspective (articles which first appeared in *NAE's Action Magazine,* and which are included as the first eight chapters of this book). These years have been more than exciting, they have been a challenging period of personal change — change from a "traditional" Christian educator and churchman to one who is convinced that "let's do it differently" is both right, and necessary.

In this book I hope to share my reasons for this growing conviction, and also to share ideas. Ideas about *what* must be done differently, and *how* it can be done differently, today.

This is not supposed to be a definitive book — a book which presents "the answers." For the real answers to questions about the life of the church can only be found *in* life. They can only be *worked out,* by believers who are committed to the Lordship of Christ and subject to His authoritative Word, and are molded by His Spirit into a living fellowship. And this sovereign Spirit may well work out new patterns, structures, and faces, for a living and vital church.

At the same time this book is meant to do more than restate problems which all of us know only too well. I trust it will help to keep our evangelical focus on the truly basic issues facing Christ's Church today; that it will suggest directions — basic steps that can be taken on a local level to move toward renewal and revitalization; that it will encourage those who feel a need to do things differently, to act wisely on that conviction.

The plan of the book is quite simple. Part I is composed of eight articles relating events at two professional seminars held at Wheaton College's Honey Rock Camp in 1967 and 1968. These were first printed in *Action Magazine,* and later reprinted in a booklet by the National Association of Evangelicals. These chapters will serve to introduce the area of concern in this book, and provide insight into the whole pattern of our thought. My partners in planning and conducting the seminars, and my partners in concern for a revitalization of the life of the church, were my fellow Christian education teachers at Wheaton College, Drs. Lois and Mary LeBar.

Part II contains six chapters which examine the church as revealed in Scripture. As a conservative, sharing with other conservatives a firm belief in the full inspiration and authority of the Bible, I am convinced that any face of the church, old or new, must be in full harmony with relevant teachings of the Word of God. I also believe that these teachings have too long been neglected!

Part III highlights directions in which we can move to reconstruct local church life to fit biblical patterns. It includes several case histories of churches in the process of change, and suggests principles to guide church leadership in moving intelligently into a change process.

Part IV is completely speculative. That is, it looks from the known toward the unknown, to sketch a Christian church life for our culture which would be in harmony with the ideas developed earlier. This culminating section is the "new face," the new face I foresee for the church.

Earlier I noted three purposes I have in writing this book — to focus issues, to suggest directions, to motivate to action. There is a fourth; to cause reaction, even argument.

I say this for two reasons. (1) I honestly do not believe that I present definitive answers here, or have an authoritative viewpoint. I share my convictions with full awareness that I may be wrong at some, indeed, at many points, and I am eager to be instructed. (2) I also hope to stimulate many to debate — for in debating we conservatives are driven to Scripture to discover God's truth. Whoever seeks to discover by Scripture God's truth places himself under the authority of that truth, and thus he is bound to *act*. It seems to me that we who defend the Word of God so faithfully, must begin *as faithfully* to submit our total lives to it.

When we do, tomorrow is *sure* to hold a new face for the church.

LAWRENCE O. RICHARDS

Wheaton, Illinois

Part I

Introduction to the Church

1

Perspective

One of the most relevant passages in the Word of God for our day is Zechariah 7. The passage records how the men of Bethel, apparently disturbed by the lack of meaning in their 70-year-old habit of mourning and fasting in memory of Jerusalem's destruction, have come to ask a favor of the Lord — release from this tradition that has lost meaning for them. The Lord gives no specific answer, but He does ask a pointed question: "Was it for me you mourned and fasted these 70 years? Or was it for yourselves?" The passage then goes on to give God's view of the situation. "Jerusalem of old had my word. But they refused to respond. Therefore I brought the destruction on them. If you had identified yourselves with my purposes, you would never have initiated the fasting and mourning in the first place! Your form lacks meaning because it is not identified with my purpose. You do it for yourselves, not for me!"*

Today, as in Zechariah's day, many Christians question the meaning of our forms of worship and service. They dutifully attend services and meetings, yet are burdened by the meaninglessness of so much that is traditionally a part of our churches.

---

*Author's paraphrase.

Like worshipers of Zechariah's day, they sense the need for a new perspective, a new awareness of purpose.

My own awareness of need can be traced back over three years, beginning with a seminar held by the Wheaton College Christian Education Department staff. At that seminar we sat down with other evangelicals to evaluate trends in Christian education, and there, we were involved in a process that literally forced us to face the desperate need of our churches.

I invite you to share this experience with me — to take part in that first seminar, and a second the next year, and discover for yourselves why I am convinced today that we *must* have renewal.

So come, experience it with me.

The Process Begun

June 7, 1967, 11:00 a.m. Our first session is over. Today we started the process of tearing down. Dr. Mary LeBar introduced a 30-minute film, *Burlington, Vermont*. In it three members of a Burlington church debate the nature and mission of their church. Stimulated by their questioning, our group brainstormed to discover some of the basic issues we as evangelicals must face.

What do we mean by church? What is the mission of the church — to train believers? To be a vehicle for outreach? What is the place of organization and structure? Which is the key — the church gathered (to study and worship) or scattered (as individuals living in but not of the world)? What should membership entail? What is the place of children, youth? How do we change?

To deepen the awareness of weaknesses in today's church, Dr. Mary LeBar had assembled quotes from contemporary "main line" writers. These were passed out and the group released to read and to ask: How do these criticisms relate to evangelical churches? Do they portray us, too?

Here is a sampling of the quotes.

"In their organization, their theology, and their ways of relating to the world, our churches today are for the most part merely richer and shinier versions of their nineteenth century parents. Their organization (residential parishes) is based on the sociological patterns of about 1885. . . . Their Sunday-at-eleven culture is timed to fall between the two milking hours in the agricultural society. Sermons remain one of the last forms of public discourse where it is culturally forbidden to talk back . . . the church remains a patriarchal, agricultural, prescientific relic" (Harvey Cox, *The Secular City*).

"Religion as we know it today is something quite different from the Christianity of Galilee; it tends to attract a different kind of person from the kind who followed the original precepts; in its desperate effort to preserve its established entity, the Church has become fossilized" (Pierre Berton, *The Comfortable Pew*).

"If the Church were continuing in the power of the Holy Spirit . . . a social scientist who turned from his study of other social institutions to study the Church in the same terms could only be amazed and bewildered. Instead . . . confirm his judgment that the Church is simply one more social institution among the many others" (Joel Nederhoed, *The Church's Mission to the Educated American*).

"Made up, usually, of a small inner core of believers who assume the necessary posts of leadership with gratitude and devotion . . . and surrounded by a cloud of uninvolved and mildly approving witnesses" (Wesley Baker, *The Split-level Fellowship*).

"Basically, we do not want anything to happen on Sunday morning that will upset our daily routine. We want to be 'inspired,' to come away with a warm feeling, but we do not want to be disturbed, so subconsciously we structure the service in order to assure safe, predictable, comfortable results" (Clyde Reid, *The God-Evaders*).

"I would suggest that those of us who are called by the living God to belong to Him will be on mission in His world and we will take the shape appropriate to our calling. . . . I am not in any glib way writing off the whole church. But I am saying that, as I now see it and as I now understand the nature of the world, the structures in which the church is at present contained are irrelevant and simply do not allow the church to be on mission. They hinder the proclamation of the Gospel rather than further it" (Gordon Cosby, "Not Renewal, But Reformation" in *Who's Killing the Church?*).

After reading several pages of such excerpts, one of our group made a significant comment. "I want to say that these men are describing only the large denominations. But I can't help feeling that most of what they say is true of us."

Later I chatted with Bill Boyd, director of Christian education at a large Oregon church. He is thinking about the young people with whom he has worked who have come up through our churches and Sunday schools and yet are blankly ignorant of so many basic Christian truths. They, Bill feels, are not ready to face challenges the secular campus presents to their immature concepts. "Do you think a one-year college prep Bible school could be the answer?"

Like it or not, we have to agree that our churches are not doing the job. That somehow, through all our forms and organizations and agencies, vital Christian personalities are not being grown. And it makes us wonder.

The Stone Ax Effect

Wednesday, a.m. "A missionary ministering to an island tribe of headhunters ran into trouble. He had noted that they used stone axes for their rites. Reasoning that one way to help them out of the old way of life would be to introduce a cutting instrument without the old associations, he sent to the states for bright, shiny metal axes. The headhunters were delighted. They tossed aside the stone axes, and took to the metal ones at once; never had they had an ax so effective for cutting off heads!

"It wasn't until the missionary collected *all* axes and replaced them with machetes — a cutting instrument with an entirely different form — that he succeeded in helping them think of something that cut in a different way."

Today our churches in educational and other structures foster denial of basic Christian truths.

We say that our faith must be lived — that Christ invades us to transform every aspect of daily life. Yet we teach this faith in formalized classes or sermons far out of a life context. We know biblically and educationally that children and youth need daily guidance in living out Christian truths. Christ even taught adults this way. Yet by the forms church education has taken — the class, the sermon, the club — we promote the idea that parents can send (or bring) children to church to learn God's Word and thus fully discharge their responsibility.

We say that every believer is a priest, gifted and responsible for building up others in the Body of Christ. And we bring adults to church, set them down and tell them to listen — to a teacher or to the pastor. They have exercised no ministry, held no responsibility but to be quiet and orderly and have helped no one by their presence.

We say that parents are responsible for the Christian nurture of their children. Yet we develop more and more church programs to minister to them and thus promote the idea that parents can turn their children over to the church and the church will do the job of nurturing for them.

We say that each believer is to have an impact for Christ on the world in which he lives. Yet we encourage laymen to sit back and let the pastor evangelize. If the pastor gives an invitation most members are convinced their church has met its responsibility to confront the world with the claims of Jesus Christ.

It does not matter what we say. What we *do* talks most convincingly. And the fact is that our current church patterns and our educational programming intellectualize Christianity, promote parental irresponsibility, prevent believers from ministering to one another and permit Christians to feel comfortably evangelical without personally witnessing.

Some say the answer is, change the Sunday school, or improve the Sunday sermon. Revitalize the youth group, the weekday club, the visitation program, but remember the stone ax? As long as the new and better ax had the same form, the old pattern of thinking was necessarily associated with it.

"If the church is to fulfill God's purposes in our world, we must seek new forms of church life and ministry. We will be rid of the old patterns of individual irresponsibility only when we make a complete sweep of the church forms with which they are associated. We must abandon the Sunday school, the Sunday sermon, the youth group — and we must find *new* ways for the church to live intimately with God and impactfully in the world."

That was my part Wednesday morning, playing devil's advocate, demanding the extreme solution. The group did not agree, I didn't either — then, yet the problem we now faced was real.

How *do* we free ourselves from false concepts built into patterns of church life without changing the patterns? What changes must we make if we are to bring our actions as well as our words into conformity with the revealed purposes of God?

One thing Tertullian could say in defense of the church, writing in the second century after Christ, "though our numbers be so great as to constitute all but a majority in every city, we conduct ourselves with quietness." *All but a majority in every city!* We certainly cannot say that. Perhaps we *had* better attempt an honest job of evaluation. We had better be willing, if God should so lead, to drop any form, to try any form, that we may best fit His purposes.

On Friday, June 10, our session began with brainstorming on forms the church of the future might take. These forms included church services, agencies, programs and ministries. The result: 150 ideas with various degrees of likelihood. They ranged from the mild "replace V.B.S. with day camp" to the wild "eliminate all preaching and train laymen in groups of ten" — from "provide a church psychiatrist" to "require missionary service of every believer."

We felt listing these ideas on the board as the first step in our creative process had two advantages: it showed us the range of forms and variations possible and it gave us material for analysis.

It was exciting to realize that we are *not* limited to our present forms. The church can take on forms and functions that none of us had even considered.

Before the course began, Drs. Lois and Mary LeBar and I had projected four basic areas of concern, to which we felt any forms suggested could be related. The brainstorming confirmed our thinking, and one of these four areas was assigned for further study to each of four teams.

What were the four areas? First, *the relationship between the church and the individual.* The New Testament speaks much of God's purposes for the individual, both in terms of growth and of ministry. Certainly emergent forms must provide for maximum individual growth.

Second, *the relationship between the church and the family unit.* Nearly all Christians, at some time, are members of families. It is in the family, both Scripture and current research tell us, that the individual is shaped as a child and continues to grow as an adult. The church of the future must provide maximum support to the Christian home in its role as the unit that both shapes the values of its members and bears a witness to the world.

Third, *the relationship between the church and society.* The church of tomorrow must exist in forms that permit and promote maximum impact on the world. The lost are to be won for Christ and a testimony borne before all. The church tomorrow cannot be as ineffective as the church today.

Fourth, *the relationship between the church as an organization and its members.* Organism though it is, the church on earth exists also as an organization. As such it necessarily has structure, organization, lines of responsibility. As an organization it demands time, place, and involvement.

The question is, then: *what forms can the church take which will best enable the believer to function in each of these four relationships — as an individual, a family member, a member of society and as a responsible member of the church?*

Each team now adjourned to work Friday afternoon, Saturday and Monday morning on a projection of the forms which will best meet needs in its area. Our idea is to have each team come at the problem with its own bias — to spell out the necessary and best forms from its viewpoint. Then on Monday afternoon we planned to integrate the ideas and construct a picture of the church of the future — a church structured to face its challenge in each of the four basic areas.

Challenge of the Future

Monday afternoon we attempted an integration of the reports. Each team did its job well, and presented a strong case, with forms designed to reach its objectives. Here is a summary of the reports.

Relationship One:

Focus on the church and the individual

This team reported in the form of a skit with seven scenes, in which Werner strikes up a friendship with Fred, a widower who lost his wife in a recent fire. The scenes show Werner's interest in Fred; taking him fishing, introducing him to a home Bible class. In the class Fred (a sanitation worker) is accepted and welcomed, and invited to a group social. At the social he hears of an elective class on Job at church, designed to help those un-

dergoing suffering today. After going to the class Fred talks with
Werner about the secret of Job's peace and puts his trust in
Christ as Savior. The next scene shows Fred in a church membership class, where, because of his experience in Boy Scouts he is
channeled into the church boys' club ministry. Finally we see
Fred asking Werner to come with him as he takes one of his
friends fishing.

Through the skit the team has suggested certain *minimum
conditions that must exist for maximum spiritual growth and development of individuals.* Their triad of conditions:

1. Motivation for growth
2. Guided opportunities for growth
3. Outlets for expression

The accompanying chart shows a breakdown of these conditions in terms of principles and ideas for their implementation.
Note how these conditions were met both for Fred and Werner
in the relationship described, and through the ministries provided
by the church.

Of particular note to me — to truly meet conditions for individual growth — a close personal relationship with another individual seems necessary. We do not meet *these* needs in large,
impersonal services.

In terms of church forms the group stressed the following:

● The church must permit individual members time to minister to other individuals outside the formal agencies of the
church.

● The church must be structured to provide opportunities
for small-group Bible study-sharing experiences, into which
an individual like Fred (or Werner) can be integrated on
an intimate, personal level.

● The church must provide graded opportunities, with
grading thought of not only in terms of age, but also in
terms of interests, needs (Job study for suffering Fred) and
neighborhood (the group in the skit was a neighborhood,
not an in-church affair).

● The church must guide individuals into fruitful and
meaningful Christian service, both formal (Fred works in

boys' club) and informal (Werner takes Fred fishing). Both areas may well require training and support.

Figure 1. CONDITIONS FOR INDIVIDUAL GROWTH

I. Motivation

Principle	Implementation
1. Meet basic psychological needs (acceptance, love, security)	Spend time with people, show you care Be willing to listen Open home to individuals, groups Open church for study, recreation Accept people as they are
2. Provide recognition	Letters of appreciation, certificates Public and personal thanks News items in paper, church bulletin Dedication ceremonies Banquets for S.S. staff, etc.
3. Provide good examples	Paul-Timothy concept Involvement with Christian individuals Small group sharing, Bible study Informal situations — unstructured but planned — such as food, home coffee hour, fishing, etc.

II. Graded opportunities

1. Provide instruction	Age group classes Interest topics (Job) Special groups (single people, golden agers, etc.) Special needs (New Christians, etc.)
2. Permit decision making (with freedom to make mistakes)	Do not push people Respect rights, individuality Provide responsibility as individual is ready for it

III. Outlet for expression

1. Deepen relationship with God	Bible study (private, group) Prayer (private, group) Corporate worship
2. Deepen relationship to the church	Membership class Close relationships with members Working with members on projects Senses of identity and purpose
3. Direct relationship to the world	Boys' club (other outreach agencies) Contact individuals (Fred)

Relationship Two:

Focus on the church and the home

Team two stressed the need for each Christian family *as a unit* to be a spiritually growing, responsible fellowship.

This concept of the family-as-a-unit is a key one. Too often families are, in fact, loose associations of individuals whose basic needs are met outside the home. The biblical picture, and one stressed more and more by contemporary social scientists, is that the most basic needs — those dealing with personality development of both the adult and child — must be met within the family structure. Secular writers today note that a family unit will develop and mature much as an individual grows and matures.

Thus our study team is on firm ground when they see as part of the church's ministry, strengthening the family in its unit functions. What unit functions did they distinguish?

I. Procreation (Genesis 1:28; 2:18-24)

This role, the team felt, demands prayerful Christian planning. They foresaw the church providing guidance in seminars on family planning, elective classes on marriage and the Christian home, continuing counseling services with professional psychologists and sociologists as well as the pastor.

II. Growth and maturity (Deuteronomy 6:1-9)

The family unit is the context for growth of the husband and wife. It is clearly the context for the development of a child's personality. It is here that values and standards are inculcated, and guidance and discipline exercised.

The church, the team felt, should provide these minimum ministries: counseling, training for parenthood, re-organization of church meetings into a weekly "family night" program, and variety in the Sunday evening service with the meeting designed to minister to specific family needs (a demonstration of family worship, for instance).

III. Service (to both churched and unchurched)

In this regard the team viewed the family unit as the focus of outreach and service. To support such an emphasis the church might develop an "adopt-a-family" program, in which each family "adopts" a non-churched family, and builds contacts with them. The church might locate new families, promote the concept, train those who lack know-how, etc. The family unit could also take part in visitation, engage in family-to-family social projects, etc. Thus the Christian faith would become the positive core uniting families, and the family would become a living embodiment of that faith. With this kind of home context the next generation of Christians might be far stronger than our own. In terms of forms, this team envisions the following:

- The church must be structured to provide time for the family to develop a unit life.
- The church must *not* plan its ministries primarily for individuals torn out of the context of the family. It must begin to teach and train family units.
- The church must guide Christians in the area of their family life. Parents must be taught the importance of their role in Christian nurture and trained to fulfill it.
- The church must view the family as the focal point of its witness. In a family where both parents are witnessing as a normal part of life, the children will be more likely to grow up as fruitful witnesses.
- The church must conceive of education for Christian family unit life (both in its growth aspects and its outreach aspects) as the focal point of its ministries, and restructure its agencies accordingly.

Relationship Three:

Focus on the church and society

Our third team based its view on two scriptural concepts — the imperative of evangelism (Matthew 28:19, 20) and the cultural mandate to "hate evil and love good, and establish justice" (Amos 5:15). The team felt that the church should adopt forms which would provide the greatest impact on our society through both individual believers and ministries of the Church corporate. They suggested many points of contact, as illustrated in these possible forms.

Education — Support of campus evangelistic organizations, parent-teacher organizations, fellowships of Christian professors, etc.

Labor — Christians seeking and holding union positions, a Christian agency for collective bargaining, etc.

Industry — A Christian Businessmen's Committee to enlarge its ministry, attempt to exert a Christian influence in the business world on moral issues such as equal employment, etc.

The city — A "Christians Anonymous" club (to help anyone in any trouble), ministry to parolees, senior citizens, unwed mothers. Christian block clubs (like the political block clubs), coffee houses, a Christian pool room, etc.

Mass communications — Radio, T.V., telephone dial-a-message, spot announcements, etc.

Government — Christians to seek public office, a fellowship of Christian politicians, etc.

Fine arts — A Christian theater and movie studio, art school, etc.

Minority groups — Witness against social injustices, witness to individuals through live-ins (move into minority areas and live there), bus churches, etc.

The team then projected a church structured to implement ministries individuals cannot perform. The team also noted that many of these projects could not be carried out by a local church. It suggested that an organization, such as the National Association of Evangelicals, serve as coordinating agency, taking care to avoid any "super church" tones.

The implications of their recommendations for church forms seems to be:

● The church must adopt forms that are outward-oriented to reach those in society, rather than inward-oriented toward believers.

● The church must provide forms in which individual believers will find a point of contact with our 21st century world.

● The church must train and equip Christians for roles in such forms, expecting that as their lives are bent to Christ's purposes they will become more and more like Him.

● The church must be flexible in order to maintain meaningful contact with the world to which it is called to witness.

Conclusion: confusion

Team four (the church as an organization) reported and has projected organizational forms. We had hoped this would lead us naturally into an integration of the earlier reports. It did not. We adjourned until the next day.

The problem was simple, although the conclusion seems complex. The emphasis of each team seemed in important respects to exclude emphases and their corresponding forms envisioned by the others. Conflicts necessarily arose.

Let us look at Werner's home (we met him in the skit of team one). His church has wisely decided their old evening service does not meet their needs and plans to replace it with a more functional and helpful form. Werner, his wife and 18-year-old daughter, Sue, each hold a different concept of the strategy their church must adopt in this century of change. Werner (the individualist philosophy) sees Sunday evening as a time when the church can offer special interest classes to meet the needs of people like Fred. Werner's wife (the societal impact philosophy) wants to use the evening for development of a book club. Sue (the family-unit philosophy) sees this time as one freed for family use, to grow together or to invite in a non-Christian family which she and her parents can minister to together.

All three have a healthy view of their goals as Christians. All are evangelistically oriented. *Each views the strategy of the church for reaching their common goals differently,* and each expects the church to adopt forms suited to his or her own strategy.

When the Drs. LeBar and I structured this course we purposely planned a process which we felt would lead us to answers. We did *not* pre-plan the answers. At this point we simply did not have them.

2

Tomorrow's Church

Thinking Toward a Strategy

Tuesday, June 13. Monday evening was spent in informed discussion. At breakfast today the Drs. LeBar and I shared our thinking. By then some of the issues seemed clearer. At our morning session we followed these steps in building our portrait of the church of tomorrow, reformed to meet basic New Testament requirements in the world of the twenty-first century.

At first we had been surprised at the conflict between church forms focused on the individual, with those focused on the family or society. Now we noted interrelationships between our three areas of concern.

These interrelationships are summarized in figure 2. Here society (viewed in its scriptural light as cosmos) is formed primarily of the unbeliever, and while it often represents the good of which man is capable (Matthew 7:11), as a system it reflects values which are in conflict with God's. (See I John 2:15-17.) Society's influences will be detrimental to God's purposes. On the other hand the believer, by his witness to individuals and participation in civil life, is to have an impact for God in society. The same positive impact is true of the Christian family unit.

The Christian individual and the Christian family are, how-ever, tied together by strong bonds of mutual contribution. The person controlled by Christ brings into his family that quality of life necessary for the home to fulfill its scriptural functions. And abundant Scripture indicates that the family has ever been viewed by God as the context for development of the Christian personality. From God's evaluation of Abraham (Genesis 18:19) to Paul's comment on Timothy's home (II Timothy 3:15), from the pattern of child training given in Deuteronomy 6:6 f. and throughout the Bible, this emphasis on the home is striking.

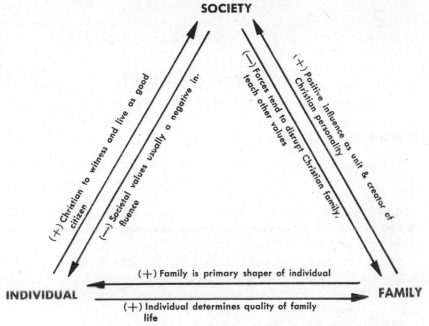

Figure 2. Interrelationships among areas of church concern

All this led to a crucial question. Is there a priority of one area over the others? Should one come first in our thinking? Since all three areas are of vital, biblical concern, it seemed clear that we should develop our strategy to focus on one area only if that focus produces results in the other two areas.

An Evaluation of Priority

The church's impact on the world through the gospel is consistently stressed in the New Testament. Yet it is clear that this impact depends on committed and witnessing believers, men and women whose overflowing lives bear testimony to the reality of their relationship with God in Christ. Thus the New Testament speaks primarily to believers about their relationship with God and with one another. Note too Paul's missionary strategy; when he sought to win a world to Christ he invested his time in a nucleus of believers. He moved among them as a father, exhorting each one, encouraging and "always pray(ing) for you, that our God may make you worthy of his call . . ." (II Thessalonians 1: 11-12 RSV). Through this ministry these people "became an example to all the believers in Macedonia and in Achaia" because from them "the word of the Lord sounded forth" (I Thessalonians 1:7-8).

Thus our group was driven to the conviction that the primary task of the church in this century is also the development of Christians who, strong in the faith, will turn to ". . . God from idols, to serve the living and true God" (I Thessalonians 1:9).

But how are we to build believers?

Again, it seemed clear from the New Testament that individual believers are not shaped in a vacuum. They are shaped within the framework of relationship with others in the Body of Christ. The Scripture clearly states that growth comes "from the whole body, joined and knit together by every joint with which it is supplied, when each part is working properly" (Ephesians 4:16 RSV). It is only as each believer ministers to others using his Spirit-given gift that the body grows and "upbuilds itself in love." Thus Paul's command not to forsake assembling together is seen, not as a demand for attendance at Sunday services, but as an invitation to involvement in a shared Life.

These thoughts led us back, away from forms focused on society and from forms focused on the individual to those focused on the family. Why?

The family is a focus of societal impact. Each member has relationships with others outside the family. These bring him into potentially fruitful contacts: the father at his work, the mother in her neighborhood, the children in school. As a unit the family also has contacts and can exert influences through agencies such as PTA or through a shared project of adopting a neighbor family as a special friendship and prayer concern.

There is another great advantage in seeing the family as the center of outreach. Husband and wife can support each other in daily prayer and sharing of experiences; the children can grow up in an atmosphere of expressed concern for the lost. We have seen it in our own church. Teens who responded to evangelism training to win others to Christ were in each case from homes where the parents are committed, witnessing Christians.

The family is the focus of personality development. We noted that a Christian personality develops in the framework of relationships with other believers. How significant then this added insight into the reason for God's institution of the family. There is no question that the family is the primary shaper of values; that the quality of family life is directly reflected in the character of the children. Not only this, but it is extremely significant (and normally overlooked) that in God's plan a person leaves one family relationship (to father and mother) only to institute another even more intimate one (husband and wife, Genesis 2:24). This relationship of two or more in families seems ever to be the context within which maximum personality and spiritual growth can take place.

Thus it seemed clear that the church of the future must provide ministries which will most encourage the development of strong family unit life and family outreach.

Has the Christian Family Failed?

If the criteria of success is the family as the focus of evangelical witness and the creator of growing, vital Christian personalities, we are forced to conclude that the average evangelical family is falling far short.

The reason for much of the failure can be attributed directly to our churches. Today most church ministries are focused almost exclusively on individuals. Family units are broken down into individuals in nearly all our agencies. Any sharing (and very little takes place in our pulpit-centered and teacher-centered services) is outside the family structure. I recently visited a church well known as a "family church." I asked Sunday school teachers who had children in other departments to tell me (1) what their children in other departments were taught the past Sunday and (2) how they had guided the children to relate the

Bible to experiences during the week. Not one person even knew what his child had studied.

Nor has the church concerned itself with the development of strong Christian family life. We in fact foster the idea that the church has taken on responsibility for Christian nurture. The very existence of agencies claiming to meet the need for instruction (Sunday school), for worship training (children's church), for training (weekday clubs), and for expression and fellowship (youth groups) promotes parental irresponsibility by suggesting that the church can, and is, doing their job. And what church today is even attempting to relate the ministry of its various agencies to the ministry of the home?

Structures	The Family Unit	The Growth Cell (Group)	The Congregation
Composition	All members of one family	All members of 5 family units (or 10 single adults)	All members of a maximum of 25 growth cells (approximately 250 adults)
Meetings	Total involvement in daily life, experiences	Once weekly of adults, teens, for in depth Bible study, sharing, prayer	Once weekly for a three-hour block of time on Sunday
Functions	Foster spiritual growth of each member	Provide a close fellowship relationship in which gifts can be used, maximum spiritual growth achieved	Train for and supervise life of the growth cells
	Support one another in propagating the gospel, individually and as a unit	Encourage personal Bible study and prayer	Provide graded Bible instruction for children during the three-hour Sunday block and relate this instruction to parental home ministry
		Plan cell activities and joint ministries	Permit corporate worship and congregational unity
		Provide context into which the newly saved can be introduced to share the life of the church	Guide the congregation in weekly Bible study, thus directing continual growth of the cells
			Plan special ministries of the congregation as a whole

Figure 3. The Re-formed Church

Finally, the church is doing little to provide the help needed by husbands and wives, fathers and mothers, to live distinctively in these relationships. Only infrequently by sermon or a special elective is training for these pivotal roles provided — and then usually in a shallow, superficial way.

What is required, then, if the church would re-form with the family unit as the focus of its ministry? We projected these basic elements:

- Responsibility for nurture and outreach must be shifted visibly from the church. There will be distinctive changes in church forms. Many of our present agencies and church services will be eliminated.

- Responsibility for outreach must be accepted by families. Evangelism will move out of the church. Revival meetings and evangelistic evening services will pass away. Each believer will bear the burden of evangelism — not just the pastor.

- Responsibility for nurture must be shouldered by the family. The home will accept responsibility for instruction, for leading in worship, for guiding in service and witness.

- Family units must be given support — as units. The church will be restructured to provide maximum support for families. This support will not be merely in the guise of classes and counseling. It will be organizational as well. It will provide conditions in which scriptural concepts of the use of spiritual gifts, can be taught and in the context of fellowship, realized.

The Church Re-formed: A Concrete Strategy

It is difficult at this point to express clearly the forms that emerged from our study. We each recognized difficulties in the pattern we envisioned. Yet we were all impressed by its many advantages. For it does seem to provide organizationally for scriptural functions which our present church patterns curtail.

Perhaps the best way to get an overview is to glance at the chart (figure 3) summarizing groupings of the re-formed church. The implications of this structure, which appears so simple, staggered us as they appeared. Some of the most striking should be noted here.

The pastor is freed for pastoral ministry. How many pastors today are worn out by round after round of organizational meetings which cut contacts with people in need and tear the pastor from the study of the Word of God? In this structure the pastor invests his time with people: training growth groups to function, counseling groups which seem to be breaking down, reproving and correcting. And he will be able to prepare fully for his one Sunday preaching/teaching responsibility.

The people are forced to assume responsibility. They cannot shift it to the pastor or a teacher or some church agency. This means, of course, that members of growth cells will be required to commit themselves to attend, to study the Word of God before sessions (since this is a time of group Bible study, not a "class"), and to meet other minimum requirements. No one can consider himself a disciple of Christ by merely dropping into a pew on Sunday. Many nominal church members of today may drop out, but membership in the church will once again mean dedication to Christ, not an easy conformity to a social custom.

Young people will be integrated into the life of the church. Older teens will be full and functioning members of the church and bear the same responsibilities as an adult. They will no longer be segregated into a "youth group" to be preached at and prayed for in isolation, but involved in the reality of Christian life and experience.

Every believer will minister to others in the free, sharing relationship of the growth groups. Here talents can be developed, recognized by the church, and each individual moved into leadership on the basis of spiritual maturity and gifts.

Perhaps most important, this form in a unique way creates conditions within which the scriptural concept of a committed fellowship, upbuilding itself in love, can be realized in spite of all the fragmenting influences of our century.

The Church Re-formed

The growth group. This structure meets a vital need. Maximum spiritual growth takes place in close fellowship with other believers. Yet in today's church most of our meetings are impersonal. We come to church only to sit and listen. Any conversation with others is usually on a superficial level — "Yes, it is hot." "Did you hear about Brother Brown?" Even in prayer meeting we do not share. We hear the same few pray the same prayers they have prayed for years.

The growth group takes on the functions now supposedly fulfilled by the adult Sunday school class and the prayer meeting. In the growth group God's Word is studied for spiritual growth. Each member shares how God has spoken to him through a common passage. There is no teacher. A growth-by-groups type study guide is used and each individual comes to the group meeting prepared. Prayer grows out of shared needs as well as requests sent by the pastor to the group representative. As the fellowship deepens, so does the level of sharing. Soon it is possible truly to "bear one another's burdens" for these are known, and we care.

The growth group meets in a home for one to two hours a week. The day and hours are selected for the convenience of the members. There are no refreshments. It meets for a spiritual purpose, and this is kept as the sole focus.

All members of a family unit of junior high age and above may be members of the growth group. Younger children are either left at home with baby-sitters or taken to the home of one member family. There they can be cared for by a mother or dad. This responsibility is rotated so no one misses more than one meeting in ten.

A growth group may be organized in one of three ways: (1) *By functional group* — Several families of similar profession or social strata may form a group in order to better reach outsiders of the same strata. New converts are inducted into the life of the group by the family which worked with them. After a group has grown to eight or nine families, it divides. (2) *By neighborhood* — Families living in the same area, band together. Such a group may sponsor a home Bible class in one of its homes, or use a Moody Science Film series for neighborhood evangelism. (3) *By age of children* — Families with children the same age have significantly similar clusters of problems. Sharing these can promote stronger Christian homes. Such a group might have a series of studies on their problems, either for the congregation or for themselves. This type organization also helps when children grow older. Teens are integrated into church life along with other teens at a time when peer support is so important to them.

Groups may also plan retreats and other activities together. Husbands may meet during the day in their job areas for prayer and mutual support in witnessing. Wives may meet over coffee. Each group thus becomes a context for deepened and extended sharing.

For growth groups to function effectively, several necessary prerequisites can be spelled out.

- *The group members must be trained to function in the group.* The pastor or Christian education director will have to work extensively with each newly established group. Purposes as well as principles of group dynamics and group roles must be understood by members. (A two-day retreat at the formation of a group could help provide such a start.)

- *Each family unit and individual must take responsibility for group life.* Each must covenant to prepare for the Bible study, to pray daily for each member in the group, to witness regularly and to work for the growth and witness of each person in his own family.

- *The group must be for believers.* This is a growth situation for believers, not an evangelistic meeting. Within this group believers meet; within the framework of the group and its responsibilities the church disciplines believers as enjoined in Scripture.

The congregation. Now we shall look at the congregation as a whole, meeting for worship and study on Sunday. The congregational meeting serves several distinct purposes, and the service is designed to attain them. These purposes? (1) To meet the need for a real and sensed unity of the body of Christ gathered. (2) To involve the community in worship, study and planning. (3) To plan for the impact of the church as a whole.

A single three-hour block of time is provided for each of three congregations using the same facilities. During this time adults and senior highs first gather to hear a message by the pastor. The message is related to the present life and growth of the people. Following the sermon the congregation reacts. Together or in small groups they explore the implications of the Word for individual, family and growth group life.

Some Sundays the congregation as a whole will lay plans for their response to the Word taught. On others the period will be used to survey what the children are learning and discuss how the truths can be related to their lives throughout the week. The key concepts, however, are (1) *the sermon is related to developing congregational needs,* and (2) *the people react to each message and discuss its implications for their lives.* The congregational meeting closes with worship.

During this time the children are taught in an extended session. Teachers are drawn from the membership, but no more than three from any one growth group, and no more than one member of any family. This way each teacher is still in close touch with the life of the church through both family and the growth group.

It is likely that the congregation as a whole will plan certain activities and ministries. A yearly missions conference, a day nursery for working mothers; such are valid expressions of congregational life, as are visiting Bible teachers who provide a week of special study on some book or topic, teen retreats, etc.

The church. Three congregations can use one building, thus consolidating the witness of the church in a given community and limiting building expense. A church of 750 adults, composed of three congregations, can use facilities designed for a third of that number, and the money saved could be better invested.

Advantages of the Re-formed Church

Clearly there are difficulties to work out in this new kind of organization. How long should a growth group stay together? Are our seminaries training men able to assume the roles envisioned? How do we discipline families that fail to meet growth group responsibilities? And many others.

Yet the advantages of this structure are striking. Look first at the pastor. Scripture portrays the pastor as a man who invests his life in people. He studies the Word and teaches it with care. He applies the Word to individuals, reproving and rebuking as well as encouraging and exhorting. This man has time to be in the Word, and to be with people.

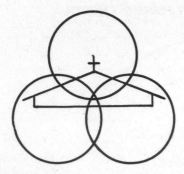

THE CHURCH

(3 congregations use the same facilities for different 3-hr. blocks on Sunday.)

THE CONGREGATION

(a maximum of 25 growth cells)

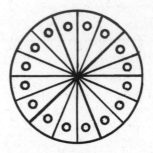

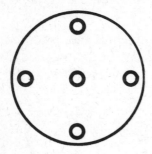

THE GROWTH CELL

(five families or ten single adults)

THE FAMILY UNIT

Figure 4.

ORGANIZATION OF THE RE-FORMED CHURCH

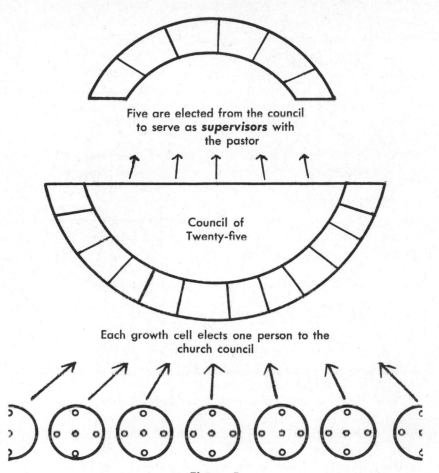

Five are elected from the council
to serve as *supervisors* with
the pastor

Council of
Twenty-five

Each growth cell elects one person to the
church council

Figure 5.

What of the pastor today? Overwhelmed with meetings, counseling rather than training men to teach others, he is frustrated by a myriad of tasks he was never called by God to perform. In the re-formed church he is reestablished in his biblical role. He ministers by training those in growth groups (he guides their establishment and moves in if they begin to fail) and by guiding the congregation through the Word on Sundays. The pastor is once again a pastor.

Second, look at the organization. In our churches today, democratic though a vote for officers may be, there is no direct line of responsibility from the governing board to the individual member. Many groups in our churches, particularly the younger couples, are unrepresented on the board. And they feel it. Communications are difficult and few feel an integral part of the church life. We hear many complaints that only about 20% of a church's membership are involved meaningfully. But when has this fact been traced back to poor organization?

How is the re-formed church governed? Each growth group elects one member to a Board of Counselors. Thus each group of five families is directly represented. The board members bring up needs felt by the groups and communicate back to the groups.

Five Counselors are elected to serve with the pastor as Supervisors. They work with him to plan the Sunday services, congregational ministries, and to carry on legal functions of the congregation as an organization.

In this simple way the pastor is guided and kept sensitive to the current needs of his people. There is a clear line of communication up from each member to the pastor and supervisors *with a minimum of intermediate steps.* And there is a clear line of communication down. Finally, through the study and interchange in the Sunday service, the whole congregation is intimately involved in shaping the total ministry of the congregation, and a fully integrated member of its life.

Third, look at the role of the layman. Biblically he has a responsibility to be a growing, vital Christian; to contribute to the growth of others in the church and his family; to be a creative witness to Christ in the world. In our churches today *these responsibilities are taken over by church agencies.* Agencies are developed to promote evangelism. Agencies are developed to spiritually develop teens and adults. Yet *scripturally such responsibility has never been vested in the organized church.* Luther proclaimed the priesthood of all believers: nearly 500 years later church forms still deny it.

The re-formed church returns responsibility to those on whom God has laid it.

3

Rediscovering Community

The major concerns which grew out of our 1967 studies at Honey Rock were that the churches today must rediscover the realities portrayed in the New Testament, but which are unrealized in their experience.

Whatever structures the church of tomorrow does develop, these structures must permit and support the biblical distinctives of Christian community which are being rediscovered today.

What distinctives? Primarily those related to the nature of the church. Today we are becoming more and more aware that "the church" cannot be identified with buildings and organizations and activities, but must be understood as *the people of God*. The basic question in church renewal is, "How are the people of God to live together and to live out Christ's life in the world?" This question is answered, clearly, in Scripture. The Word provides the pattern. Measured against the divinely ordained pattern, much of our church life today stands out starkly as irrelevant, misshapen and perverted.

What does Scripture demand that our present forms deny?

1. A body so living together that it edifies itself and thus grows. The church is a community in which believers mature

within the fellowship. In this community every believer must contribute, for growth is ". . . knit together by the joints with which it is provided, grows by the proper functioning of individual parts to its full maturity in love" (Ephesians 4:16). All are gifted; all minister; all contribute.

Today's church does not promote mutual ministry. In our churches the majority sit, silent, passive, listening to the Word. The concept on which our meetings seem structured is that spiritual growth occurs as biblical information is digested and regurgitated in a three-point, alliterative message by one so trained. (Why else are believers expected to *sit* and *listen* to three sermons and a Sunday school lesson each week?)

How different this is from Scripture, in which each man is seen as his own priest, each indwelt by the Holy Spirit, who is his teacher and enables him to share his personal experience with God with others, who also share with him! This and this alone is community. This and this alone will move the church toward dynamic spiritual growth for the whole body.

2. A ministry of reconciliation, which is not professional but a personal sharing of the good news of Jesus Christ with men outside of Him by every believer. The Word penetrated the Jewish world, spread into Samaria and spilled over into Gentile domains as simple believers "gossipped" their faith. Surely, men like Peter, Phillip and Paul were specially gifted to evangelize, and they did. But from the churches they founded the gospel was spread by laymen, not by leaders. From churches like that in Thessalonica, "the Word of the Lord sounded forth . . . everywhere" (I Thessalonians 1:8). Each believer, sharing the good news of Christ, was needed to reach the world.

Today we prod the professional staff to "preach the gospel" to the saints — who alone fill our churches — while a disinterested world passes by. Today we invent new methods to bring unbelievers *into* the churches. Unable to touch wary adults, we cast our nets for children, inventing agencies which never existed in biblical days — VBS, boys and girls clubs, yes, even Sunday school — to get them *into* the church where they can hear of Christ. And yet each day of our lives we brush against neighbors, against co-workers, against men and women alienated from God — and we refrain from speaking because they do not come to us on Sundays, where, within the safety of church walls, we find it convenient to talk about God.

The verdict first century men passed on the church was this: "These are they who turn the world upside down." These men went *out*, and in homes, in the marketplaces, on the street corners, shared God's redemptive Word with others who, like our neighbors today, were lost in sin's alienating hold.

Aggressive, personal, total, worldshaking witness alone, impelled by love and fired with confidence in Christ, must again mark the church if it is to be truly called "Christ's."

3. Families which will truly be the center of Christian nurture. Old and New Testaments agree. In the intimate relationships of family life, true faith in God is to be taught and learned. Faith cannot be taught as an intellectual assent to truth alone. It must be taught as a responsive life, lived in joyful sensitivity to the God who speaks the Word, and who leads us to apply it daily by His Spirit. Christianity as a life with God must be experienced to be understood; it must be seen in those we love, that we might be imitators, even as those we imitate imitate Christ.

Today church agencies attempt to nurture children. Parents are too quick to bring their young to learn, as information, truths which can become real only when learned through shared experience. The Sunday school, the children's church, the youth group, the clubs, the choirs: these are the means on which we depend to communicate a faith which must be lived, but of which we so often merely speak.

There were no agencies in the church of the New Testament. No shifting of responsibility from the home. And the church of tomorrow, to become again the *church*, must firmly return to the home responsibilities of Christian nurture that our programs today deny them.

There are other areas, other aspects distinctive to the church's life and work. The role of leaders, and how they lead. The calling of the church to glorify God in good works. The responsiveness of the whole body to its Head.

Rediscoveries like these tomorrow's church must make concrete by new forms; by a new organizational structure which will no longer hinder their realization, but encourage it.

Whatever organizational forms the church takes, these forms

must permit and promote a distinctive life for the people of God. Our structures must encourage sharing, that each believer in intimate relationship with other believers might use his spiritual gift in ministry to the body of Christ. Our structures must encourage witness; must train and support believers to carry the gospel out into the world, where the lost live.

Our 1967 seminar had pointed us in the direction we were now convinced that the church should move. But how? How do we make such radical changes? In 1968 we determined to explore the impact of change on our churches. And in the process we raised far more questions than we were prepared to answer!

Exploration the First Week

The first week at Honey Rock was structured to help our seminar participants experience the difficulty of change. Over the period of a year I developed a series of tape-recorded sessions on church change. Three churches used these tapes for a six week period, under the supervision of Drs. Lois and Mary LeBar, graduate students, and their own pastors. We discovered in the first church that many of the ideas we introduced (and many things in the *way* we introduced them) threatened church members, and hardened them in their resistance to change. We found in the second church an openness to the ideas, and a struggling toward any changes which would help the people become all that Christ had called them to be. In the third church also we found a receptiveness and a movement toward change. This tape series we now proposed to use with our study team.

In order to help our seminar participants understand how laymen might *feel* when presented with change ideas, our first morning was spent developing a "normal evangelical church." Each of our participants selected a typical church member whose role he could play. Thus our group "became," for the next two days, the board member, the eager new Christian, the rootless divorcee, the Sunday school superintendent, the housewife busy in nightly church activities, the older woman whose family is gone from home but who still demonstrates her dedication in Christian service. We had earlier discovered through research in business management and in sociology that any organization contains three types of personalities-in-relation-to-change.

There is the *innovator;* the person willing and ready to try any change that seems logically to offer progress. In most organizations about 10% of the members are innovators. There is the *conservative,* who is cautious about any change, and wants to be shown before he sets his foot on uncertain ground. Most organizations are composed of abut 80% conservatives. And there are the *inhibitors;* persons who fight change, who will not change, and who vocally resist. About 10% in most organizations fit into this group. So in our "typical church" we placed this proportion of innovators, of conservatives and of inhibitors. With the roles prepared, we led our church into the process of change.

What we learned. The next few days were uncomfortable for all of us. Men and women who would themselves have eagerly entered into our discussion of change, resisted. Each day we followed the tapes, listening and reacting individually to change ideas, then dividing into small discussion groups to discuss, in our roles, change for "our" church.

The "Sunday school superintendent" in my discussion group tried to manipulate the group members, and was quick to defend and praise his organization. The "young mother, a Christian only three years" was moved toward change by her sense of personal need — but she was troubled by possible threat to agencies her children enjoyed. The "Primary Department superintendent," sensitive about her unsaved husband and her heavy involvement in all sorts of church activities, alternately resisted and agreed. The "deacon" had an early clash with the superintendent and retreated to silent observation. He remained interested, but skeptical. A "young single girl" smilingly encouraged each new idea. Soon, because she *always* agreed, she was totally disregarded by the group. *The interplay of these personalities clearly affected the responses to ideas of change.*

After the taped study series was complete, we discussed the roles in our small group. What did each member feel? How could he or she have been helped to change? These significant insights were expressed by our group:

1. Change would have been accepted more readily if each member of the group had sensed a personal concern and support from the others. The group needed to feel unity and com-

munity before the ideas presented could be dealt with meaningfully.

2. The inhibitor, who strongly resists change, definitely affects others and increases their resistance to change. He seemed better able to sway the conservative majority, at least initially, than the innovator.

3. The group sensed a need for much authoritative material. They could more easily have accepted change ideas if these had been related directly to Scripture, with biblical bases for each change specified. This, the group felt, is to be expected of evangelicals who look to the Bible as God's authoritative word, as our source of values.

4. The tapes encouraged participants to look at *what* needs to be done in the church (such as making the home the center of nurture, focusing evangelism through the individual believer rather than through church agencies, etc.). In every case our group quickly shifted from a discussion of *what* they ought to do, to a consideration of *how* they might do it. They found it difficult to think in terms of goals apart from methods. Because they saw many difficulties in implementing the changes suggested (they could not clearly visualize the *how*), they tended to resist or reject suggested changes.

5. Each participant expressed a sense of need for concrete examples of churches actually making the changes proposed. This desire to "see it first" is a mark of the conservative, and thus a characteristic of most members of any organization. The expressed need in our group for proof — for examples, for certainty that changes could be successfully made — was acute. The group wanted the leader to show or tell them *how*.

6. Each felt threatened by the new way of life that change implied. All were aware that the changes called for new skills; skills they did not have. Our group would have been more open to change if they were sure that training would be provided to help them carry out their new roles.

The Second Week

Monday morning began with a brief survey of renewal movements in history. Two tendencies were pointed up: (1) a tendency of the renewed to form special "in" groups within the church, with resulting hostility between themselves and the majority, and (2) a tendency of the renewed to withdraw from the churches and to establish a new church or denomination. Anthropology professor Dr. Marvin Mayers suggests that in our day churches will again be split on similar lines; not on doctrinal deviation, but on openness to change against inability or unwillingness to change. This has been the experience of many "experimental" churches. A high percentage of the membership left the church as changes took place, or the group attempting change was forced out of the traditional church and forced to begin as a new work.

Neither of these alternatives is desirable. All in the churches, those ready for change, those threatened by it, those who resist it, *need* a closer walk with God and a fresh, growing experience with Him that is associated with church change.

Many might be concerned about this last statement: that a "fresh, growing experience" with God is *associated with change*. This statement is not lightly made. I personally find change in church structure and forms essential to fresh experience *for the majority*.

This is not to say that no individual or group can find fresh experience with God apart from changes in church structure. Obviously some can. But for the majority, *who depend on the church for guidance in growth*, new vitality is not an open option. Changes must be incorporated in the church to encourage vitality.

As we moved into our second week at Honey Rock, we found our focus necessarily divided. Some of our sessions emphasized the psychological and interpersonal impact of change. In these sessions our participants gained experience in working through the tensions created by "change" ideas. Since such sessions were experiential, they cannot be accurately reported here.

Other sessions were devoted to the development of a broader understanding of the kind of changes we contemplate. For this understanding, we addressed ourselves to three aspects of the problem of church change: (1) understanding the characteristics of today's church, (2) understanding the characteristics of tomorrow's church, and (3) understanding the methods by which movement from the one toward the other can be effected in *any* local church. (See Figure 1.)

In his paper, *Achieving Change in People: Some Applications of Group Dynamics Theory,* Dorwin Cartwright points out that "the behavior, attitudes, beliefs and values of the individual are all firmly grounded in the groups to which he belongs." For this reason, church change is not simply a matter of convincing individuals they ought to try new patterns of church life. The strategy which will achieve change must be a strategy of group change; a way to deal with the local church as a whole.

"To change the behavior of individuals," writes Cartwright, "it may be necessary to change the standards of the group, its style of leadership, its emotional atmosphere, or its stratification into cliques and hierarchies. Even though the goal may be to change the behavior of *individuals,* the target of change becomes the group."

It's necessary, then, to look at the church as a whole, as a social organization, and to understand it as an organization if we are to identify the sources of its problems and to visualize biblical patterns of life. Thus in our studies, we turned to an examination of the church that is, and the church that must come.

The Church That Is

Why is it so important that the church change? And in what areas must change take place? Is it enough to vary the format of the evening service? Or to eliminate non-essential educational agencies? (And if so, which are the non-essential?) Or are more basic changes required?

In order to see what kind of changes are needed, and why they are needed, it is necessary to look at the church that is.

Professed values. Nearly all evangelicals profess certain biblical values which define the Church's goals. The evangelical places stress, as does Scripture, on an initial conversion experience. In conversion the individual as a sinner comes to terms with God, and receives the forgiveness offered freely in Christ Jesus. From this point a new life begins, then comes the "growing in Christ." We might view this Christian growth as a process of socialization.[1] The values and motives and behavior of the world, which dominated our past life, are gradually replaced by values and behavior which find their source and validity in the

---

[1]The process by which norms and behavior patterns are learned and become part of an individual's personality.

nature of God, and which have been revealed by Him in Scripture.

The "mature" Christian, viewed by Scripture and defined by most evangelicals, might be characterized as a person who evaluates life from the divine viewpoint; whose character and behavior gives concrete expression to scriptural values. As God loves, this believer loves, ". . . not merely in theory or in words — let us love in sincerity and in practice" (I John 3:18). As God gives, this believer gives. As God involves Himself with man in need, this believer involves himself in the lives of those in the church, and shares himself with those outside it.

It is for this purpose, the evangelical believes, that the church exists: to help those won to Christ grow in Him. To help them grow until God's values are their values, until God's ways are their ways, until "Christ be formed within" them (Galatians 4: 19).

This, at least, is the purpose we profess.

Operationalized values. Strangely, an objective look at the church that is indicates that it actually guides members to develop other than its professed values. Not that any church member consciously denies the scriptural values. Evangelicals honestly hold these values and believe that they are working toward their realization. I do mean, however, that *when we reason back from the behavior we observe in our churches, the values exhibited are not those we profess!* Other values dominate our church life.

What are these other values? Values related to maintaining the church as an organization. At least three lines of evidence clearly indicate this fact.

(1) The major deliberations of church leaders focus on organizational problems. Where will we get that other Sunday school teacher? How can we keep our high schoolers from dropping out of Youth Group? What program will we plan when the district Women's Missionary Society meets next at *our* church?

Visit the official board, and listen to the problems they deal with. How much will it cost to get the air-conditioning turned on this summer? How about the drainage on the parking lot? Are we meeting the budget? Should we sell the old parsonage now, or will we get a better price later?

Now, this isn't criticism of church leaders. They desire to promote Christian growth, and give generously of their time to do it. But are they doing it? Is spiritual growth encouraged when the biblical values we profess are seldom actually discussed or considered? When what demands our time and effort is related to running an organization?

It's difficult to believe that what is ultimately important is that teachers be on time for classes, have lessons prepared, attend teachers' meetings and keep accurate records. That needed buildings be built, funds raised, workers recruited. That each believer play an assigned role in the organization — pastor, serve on a board, teach or work in an educational agency, attend regularly, or at least give generously.

Yet we not only give such matters priority, but these then become the criteria by which we evaluate success. Is the Sunday school growing? Is the budget up? Is attendance in the evening service steady? Do the regulars still come out to prayer meeting? Then the church is doing fine!

A moment's honest thought makes it clear. These do not necessarily indicate the success of spiritual transformation. Our biblical values say "success" when a love for Christ and others overflows in daily witness. When His love pervades the relationship of husbands and wives and children. When youth grow up and live out Christian values. (How significant that *two* recent surveys, one by Merton Strommen and one by Gene Getz and Roy Zuck, both indicate that the *values* of Christian youth are indistinguishable from the values of the general population!)

These, not numbers, not budget, not size, count . . . if we truly operate on our professed values.

(2) Status[2] in the church is ascribed on the basis of organizational performance.

We do "rate" church members by their organizational involvement. We tend to think of a "good Christian" as one who attends church Sunday morning and evening and on prayer meeting night, who teaches, or serves on a board. Dedication to Christ is measured by the number of nights a person is out involved in church activities!

As director of Christian education, I was at one time faced

---

[2]Status refers to the individual's position in the group, and in this paper is viewed almost as "rank" or "level of importance."

with a need to recruit workers to staff our many programs. I decided to telephone our whole membership; some 600 people. I recall one conversation particularly. The woman declined my invitation to become involved. Why? Because she and her husband gave their Sunday mornings to hospital visitation, and once a month held a special hospital chapel service.

Here was a couple who were not highly respected or well known in our church. They were not members of our appreciated, dedicated core. But it was clear that their ministry was potentially far more significant and selfless than teaching a dozen classes.

In a church we visited recently, I met a young man, newly converted, who was enthusiastically sharing his faith with his unsaved friends. The church members were concertedly pressuring him to take a job in their youth club program — so that he might have a ministry!

Status *is* ascribed on the basis of performance in the church organization.

(3) Christians *see themselves* in terms of their role in the organization.

Ask a layman in casual conversation about his church, and he's likely to respond, "Yes, I'm a Sunday school teacher there," or "head usher," or "I sing in the choir." Somehow many laymen feel it's necessary to identify themselves by the role they play in the organization.

This is significant, for it's vital that a Christian see himself primarily as a *Christian*. Too often laymen see themselves as a different order of Christian than the clergy. The clergy are to evangelize. The layman is to pay his salary, and perhaps bring in the unsaved for the pastor to preach to. The clergy, or specially designated laymen, are to teach. The rest are to sit passively and listen, but biblically every Christian is an evangelist; every believer a minister.

As long as Christians define themselves by their role in an organization rather than in their basic role as a *Christian*, they will not become what they are in Christ. Growth will remain stunted.

Goals versus Means

To this point I've suggested that, while the church professes to exist for the purpose of promoting spiritual growth, that goal has in fact been set aside. The machinery of running the church is so difficult to maintain that the church actually has to concentrate its energies on its own organization! The values and the behavior patterns that surface in this situation are *not* those it professes. And the church, rather than guiding believers to become growing Christians, finds itself guiding them to become churchmen.

Recently I spoke at a conference on the role of the layman in evangelism. One bubbly woman afterwards said, "You know, I've been a Christian for three years. And I just now realized. I don't know any non-Christians any more." Another young woman wistfully commented, after hearing of the enthusiastic young witness I mentioned earlier, "I was just like that when I was first saved."

What happens to so many zealous converts who also were once "just like that"? They become involved in the church, they "serve," but they trade away something *distinctively* Christian in the process of fitting in.

What causes the chasm between the professed goals of the church and its performance? Why can't believers seem to recognize the meaninglessness of much of their activity? Because those in the church honestly view its activities and agencies and meetings as *means* to the biblical ends, these means have become so closely associated with the ends that the means have unknowingly been *sanctified*.

Sociologist Robert K. Merton analyzed ways in which an individual might adapt to a social situation by clarification of the interplay between goal and means. An individual would conform if he accepted both the goals and the prescribed means. An individual would innovate if he accepted the goals, but sought new means to reach them. An individual fell into ritualism if he disregarded the goals but held to the means.

Christians today have largely reacted in one of these ways. They have given priority to *means*, and disregarded the goals.

The evidence? Look at the time and effort that's given to maintaining organizations and agencies. Look at status, ascribed to members on the basis of their performance in the organization, not on the basis of spiritual attainment. Look at believers, who identify themselves by their roles in the organized church, not in their basic role as Christians. Look at the fact that most church-goers today are somehow horrified when a change in the time or format of a traditional meeting is suggested. *They tend to resist any change in the organization, no matter how well that change may seem to promote the professed goals of the church.*

Somehow church activities have become "holy." A whole pattern of life has grown up centered on *church.* It doesn't matter whether or not church activities guide believers toward maturity. Week after week men and women come into services and go out unchanged — knowing that they have not been changed. And yet they return religiously, week after week, repeating behavior which seems unable to help them toward the spiritual reality they need. Sociologically speaking, an organization which guides members into patterns of behavior which support *means* without reference to success in reaching goals is a ritualistic organization.

And this *is* today's church.

The Church That Must Come

Gemeinschaft versus *Gesellschaft.* The German sociologist Tonnes developed two concepts which are helpful in understanding the church of today and of tomorrow.

One is *Gesellschaft* (society). In "society" individuals live peaceably with each other, but are separated by basic differences in spite of unifying factors. They are bound together by exchanged goods and services, not intimate personal relationships. The church today is a society. The pastor serves, and in turn receives his living. The members give, and in turn receive the services of the organization and of the pastor. The members exchange services in one agency ("I'll teach your child in Sunday school . . .) for service through another (. . . and you teach mine in Youth Group!"). Members are ranked by function in the organization.

In *Gemeinschaft* (community) the group is a family. This is a basic to the New Testament concept of the church (cf. 1 Timothy). The members identify themselves by their basic role as member of the community, not by status. In the church that must come, each believer sees himself and others primarily as "Christian," and accepts *all* the responsibilities and exercises all the privileges assigned this role in Scripture.

In "community" *unity* is found in a common life. A society bases its unity on organizational interdependence, but the New Testament church found its unity in a common life, identity and purpose. This is reflected both in Acts (cf. 4:32 f.) and many of the Epistles. Christians are to be of "the same mind, having the same love, being in full accord and of one mind . . . count others better than yourselves . . . each of you look not only to his own interests, but also to the interests of others (Philippians 2:3, 4)."

The New Testament pattern of the church as the body of Christ is basic. Here the idea that each member has a different function within the community is introduced (Romans 12; I Corinthians 12; Ephesians 4). But in no way does this idea involve the kind of interdependence that exists in *Gesellschaft*. The unity of the membership still rests on a common identity, and on their mutually binding ministry to one another. They may have different gifts, but each has the same obligation: to minister.

The church that must come, the New Testament church in tomorrow's world, must be such a *community*. Each member must see himself and others simply as Christians, and must accept a full share in the common life and purpose which unites them.

Priority of goals. The New Testament constantly focuses the attention of believers on the essential values of biblical Christianity, and does not even *develop* an organizational plan!

Our church must also constantly and consciously focus attention on these same scriptural values. If the biblical values are really given priority over the means, what will happen?

(1) Attention, time and effort will be given to the goals. Consultations in the church will not be primarily concerned with running the machinery. The church board will spend more time considering human need than the color to paint fellowship hall!

(2) Self, status and effectiveness will be evaluated by the professed values. The believer will not be satisfied that he is a "good Christian" if he attends church three times a week. The group will not rank its members on such activities. The church will not call itself successful merely if it has a growing Sunday school.

Instead individuals and the community will evaluate effectiveness in terms of the biblical values. Are we communicating

	The Church That Is	The Church That Must Come

Tendency of Group Life	Gesellschaft	Gemeinshaft
Effect on Group Life	1) highly organized	1) minimal organization
	2) ministries viewed as performed by agencies of the organization	2) ministries viewed as performed by each member of the community
	3) much effort given to maintaining the organization	3) little organizational maintenance required
	4) **means** (organization) tends to receive priority over values	4) values given priority consideration
	5) status assigned by position in the organization	5) status related to conformity to community values
	6) effectiveness evaluated in terms of organizational health (numbers, $, etc.)	6) effectiveness evaluated in terms of implementation of community goals
Results	Members are introduced into the organization, and guided to grow in "churchmanship"	Members are introduced into the community and are guided to grow in the values of the community.

Figure 6. Impact of "society" vs "community" type organization of the church

the good news to unbelievers? Is the love of Christ a controlling and practically expressed reality in our lives and in our fellowship? Spiritual maturity of individuals will be the criteria by which we measure.

(3) Because the biblical values are truly important to the group, the members will be free to try different means whenever these seem likely to help them reach their professed goals. This freedom to try new ways of communicating Christ or promoting Christian growth will protect against ritualization of behavior and, in turn, help keep the focus of the community on its goals.

Significance

Every organization tends toward *Gesellschaft* or *Gemeinschaft,* toward society or community. The church that is exists as society, is organized as society, and thus necessarily fails to develop characteristics of community which the New Testament church is seen to have in Scripture. When the church of today becomes *organizationally* a community, it will again be able to guide believers in spiritual growth. As long as it is organizationally a society, *it cannot effectively support the biblical values which demand community for their actualization.*

Thus the church as an organization must change. It cannot remain what it is and guide its members into the spiritual growth and the fullness of experience portrayed in the biblical record. The church must move toward Gemeinschaft.

Toward Gemeinschaft. How is it possible to develop that community which the church once was and which it must become again? To develop community, *a basic requirement is a certain order of interaction of community members.* That is, people do not develop a sense of community apart from frequent, regular social interaction with one another. They have to spend time together. They have to get to know one another — well. They have to *share,* to dig deep into their own lives with God and openly seek together His answers to their problems and needs, and His direction and power for their lives.

If interaction is to produce a shared identity and purpose, it requires a strong desire on the part of members to involve themselves in each other's lives. And, finally, the interaction must *focus on the values which the community professes to hold in common,* and which it seeks to make real in the lives of its members. They must share deeply of the Word and of the Spirit of God.

Only by this kind of interaction can the church become a community, where members will be guided in spiritual growth.

In the church today, social interaction is infrequent. Believers come together for only an hour or two a week. When they are together, their role is primarily that of listeners together, giving attention to a sermon or lesson. Most churchgoers leave church without significantly interacting with *anyone* concerning the value of ideas expressed by the speakers. In those meetings where people do talk and discuss, the topics under consideration tend to be related to maintaining the organization — not to the biblical values.

Without deeply personal interaction, without discussion and sharing focused on biblical values, a sense of *community* cannot develop, and people will learn to "fit in" the organization without even necessarily learning to "fit in" with Christ! Sadly, the very forms of church activity we struggle so today to maintain actually *inhibit* social interaction, or focus on means rather than goals. Our meetings and agencies are not structured to promote sharing or to promote the mutual implementation of scriptural values. And thus the church today does in fact fail to guide the majority of its members into meaningful growth in Christ.

So it's true. For the majority, a fresh, growing experience with God *is* necessarily associated with change in church forms. Until the church becomes *community*, basic biblical values will neither be promoted nor permitted.

Somehow a pathway must be found for the church as a whole; a way in which a total local church can move from society toward community.

The easy way out today is for the renewed to withdraw from the churches. To start all over again, with others who have felt Christ's second touch, and found community in small groups outside the structures of the church. But what is really needed is for those who have a vision of what Christ's church can again become — a community of the committed — to seek God's wisdom for the ways in which change can be guided.

4

Problems, and Progress

The changes envisioned to transform the "church that is" into "the church that must come" are drastic ones. Drastic in that they require the restructuring of our present church forms and organizational structures, and drastic in that they involve changing a total pattern of group behavior and norms. Yet even as we struggled in 1968 to see directions and guidelines, there were indications of ways open to us, and some evangelicals were already stepping out on them.

Scores of books and articles today call for church renewal and criticize the church as an institution. Some say that the institutionalization of religion *always* leads to spiritual deadness. Others suggest new organizational patterns. One writer calls for "abandonment" of all church buildings and publishing houses and other physical properties as basic to renewal. Many demand that we leave *all* present forms and begin again.

The problem here is that, when we accept this call *in a surface way,* we identify "the Church" with its organizational expression — the very tendency renewal writers (including myself) criticize in the contemporary church! "The church" is people in relationship — not their meetings, or agencies, or programs. Eliminate all present forms and activities; group all believers in intimate circles for discussion; provide materials and guidelines for "at home" Christian nurture — and you still have not changed "the Church." *The church has not changed until the perceptions and values of the church members have changed.*

Thus, in thinking of church change, we have to put stress on the subjective state of church members. How they feel and think and respond. Rules, norms and values are far more significant in understanding and changing behavior than such objective considerations as the location, date, time, length and seating arrangement of meetings.

The crucial question, then, is: How can norms and values be changed? How can the norms of the church that is, the *Gesellschaft*, be transformed to the norms and values of the church that must come, the *Gemeinschaft?* And how can such community be maintained? It is a tragic oversimplification to suggest that by changing organizational forms alone "the Church" can be revitalized.

Certainly it is true that the form of church meetings has an impact on the values and norms church members develop. The kind of meetings planned for the re-formed church have to be those which support community. But it is important to realize that extant values and norms and our contemporary organizational structures are so tightly interwoven that it is not *safe* to attempt to change forms without giving careful attention to the feelings and expectations of churchgoers. For instance, one pastor attempted to institute change by placing the pulpit in the center of the sanctuary, and rearranging the pews in a rough circle around it, in order to invite dialog. The unusual arrangement so disturbed his congregation that many left the church! He dealt with objective obstacles to meaningful interaction, but failed to consider subjective obstacles — the norms, feelings and expectations of his people.

Change, then, cannot be intelligently guided except by careful attention to both subjective and objective factors; to both the way church members feel and perceive, and to forms that encourage or inhibit meaningful social interaction.

Changing Norms

What are the component parts of normative (or socially expected and approved) behavior patterns? We might state them like this:

An individual (the actor) views himself as in a certain role on any given occasion, and thus in a given situation feels constrained to respond in a socially expected way, the consequences of his response being predictable and being evaluated by himself and others.

Break down this rather complicated statement, and the crucial elements of normative patterns are seen to involve:

(A) The actor: and how he views himself in a given situation.

(O) The occasion: and the demands of that situation on one with the actor's view of himself.

(R) The response: which is expected of (that which "should" be done by) such an actor in the given situation.

(C) The consequences: that is, the *evaluation of the response* by the individual and others concerned.

Let's take an example. Two men (A) walk into a church at the same time. Thus, entering the church is the occasion (O). One of them responds (R) by finding a seat toward the back of the sanctuary and settling down into it for the duration. The other responds (R) by going to the front of the church and climbing on a platform. There he prays, makes announcements, vigorously leads singing, preaches, etc. These different responses are in each case evaluated as "right" by all those present, including the two men involved. (These evaluations are the perceived consequences (C).)

How do we explain different behavior from the two men in the same situation? And the different evaluation by others of their responses? Simply. One saw himself as "layman." As such he knew that his role in church was to be passive while the other, the "pastor," performed. The *actor designations* (pastor, layman) differed, and so the behavior of the two men on this occasion differed.

Put the same two men in a different situation, such as a meeting of the church board at which the layman is "chairman" and the pastor "employee," and the behavior of each changes significantly!

It appears, then, that *varying one or more elements of the*

A-O-R-C equation changes the behavior patterns in social inter-action.

It is by varying the *A-O-R-C* pattern in contemporary church life that church change, *change in the people who make up the church*, can be achieved.

Changing actor-designation. People will usually act in the way they think it is appropriate for them to act. Appropriateness depends, to a great extent, on the self-image, the picture a person has of himself. It is this dimension of the self-image, this "who I am" concept, to which "actor designation" refers.

I noted earlier that the contemporary church promotes a far different actor-designation for the layman than does the Bible. In the church today it is appropriate for the pastor to preach, to teach, to evangelize, to counsel, to minister. It is appropriate for the layman to listen, to bring people to church to be evangelized, to give money, to be counseled and ministered to. Biblically these are distorted actor-designations.

Admittedly there are today certain intermediate roles, such as elder or Sunday school teacher, in which the layman is supposed to minister. But even these laymen do not see themselves in an *overall* minister's role. Their ministries too often are restricted as to time and place and specific function. Yet the biblical picture is one of every believer a minister, with a spiritual gift and with ability to contribute to the welfare of the body. Every believer is to evangelize. Every believer is to train up his own child.

When, during the first week at Honey Rock, we attempted to live through the introduction of change ideas in an average church, we felt a great need of scriptural orientation. We wanted passages which clearly *required* the changes suggested. These could not be found! For the Bible does not give an organizational pattern. The Bible, however, does spell out who the Christian is, it does provide a clear designation.

In an earlier chapter I mentioned the tape-recorded set of six sessions designed to introduce local congregations to change ideas, which we used at Honey Rock. I had developed these and used them with three churches in the Chicago area before our seminar at Honey Rock. In one of these churches, Riverdale Baptist, pastored by the Rev. Earl Phillips, the change ideas were accepted with apparent readiness. Why? For over a year Pastor Phillips' preaching and teaching geared toward change. One of his primary emphases was this: the Christian layman is to evangelize in his daily life, he is to witness to co-workers, to neighbors, etc.

When the tapes suggested ways this kind of witness might be implemented, the people were ready to accept the change ideas. One woman commented, "We ought to know we're supposed to witness. Pastor Phillips has been telling us that for a year now."

Because the people saw themselves as "witnesses-in-daily-life," changes which would help them in this role were acceptable and even welcome. In another church the people saw themselves as "witnesses-in-church-agencies." When the same changes were suggested in this church, the people were not able to accept them. The changes did not fit their actor designations!

Understanding the significance of the actor designation provides a vital key to bringing about change. A young pastor friend of mine took an old church in a rural Michigan town. When he arrived, he discovered what he had inherited. The two previous pastors had both absconded, one with funds and the other with one of the local ladies. The people were completely demoralized. Their church was looked down on by all, they were at all-time lows in attendance and were sure their only hope was the Second Coming. For six months my friend's preaching focused on one theme: "In Christ we're just as good as anyone else." The second six months his emphasis was, "God can use us." This thrust, designed to change the people's view of themselves and their usability by God, combined with a new approach to reaching families in that community, led, within a year and a half, to the first new addition the church had had in 80 years. And within two years the people and the community had a totally revised picture of the church, and several new families had been won to Christ and added to the membership.

The pastor is clearly in the best position to lead in modifications of the actor designation. The Word of God defines who we Christians are. His messages from the Word can highlight portions which clarify our privileges and responsibility. He can explain the nature and function of spiritual gifts, the calling of believers to spiritual priesthood, the responsibility of all his people in the ministry of reconciliation. And he can challenge the patterns of life into which we have settled.

Means other than sermons can, of course, be used. Relevant

topics can be covered in adult Sunday school classes or home study groups. Books and articles which call for new involvement by the layman can be distributed, and all can be thoroughly discussed by the church boards.

Yet to change the church it will not be enough to change only the actor designation. It is important to introduce change in all elements of the *A-O-R-C* equation.

Varying the occasion. The pastor of a church in Elmhurst, Ill. announces that next Sunday evening after the usual service a discussion of the sermon will be held in fellowship hall. The pastor of Chicago's Elm-LaSalle Bible Church moves his morning service to 10, and at 11 features guest speakers who make brief presentations on controversial subjects and then enter into sharp dialog with the congregation. Chicago's Circle Campus Church disbands the evening service entirely to sponsor various activities in the homes of members — or urges members to simply invite non-Christian neighbors in for supper and the evening. In Phoenix, Camelback Bible Church during the summer replaces the Sunday evening service with 6:30 study groups and 30-minute vespers service.

All these approaches, and others, move in the direction of involving the church members in meaningful interaction. All introduce this element by changing the format and, often, the time and place of traditional church services. Such mild modifications of normal church patterns can be extremely helpful.

In the last chapter I pointed out that one of the difficulties church members sense when change ideas are introduced relates to their inability to see *how* the suggested changes will work out. An insight into the value of modifying stated meetings comes from Riverdale Baptist. Pastor Phillips, prior to our retreat with his laymen, had for six weeks changed the prayer meeting format. He divided his people into small groups of 12-15, and provided written guidelines for group Bible study. A passage was suggested, key questions were provided, and the individuals asked to study the Scripture separately, jot down ideas, and then share together *without* a professional leader. Then, lest the new situation become too threatening, the normal format was resumed.

In our tape series on change we suggested such group Bible study as a basic structural element in the new church. Because people in this church had some experience with this kind of group, they could visualize more clearly *how* such a form could be worked out. And they were better able to evaluate the advantages and difficulties of this form of Bible study. As a result, the people at Riverdale were more open to forms which demanded the layman take personal responsibility for Bible study and sharing than those in the other churches, to whom this approach was merely "theology."

Variation *in easy stages* is important in moving toward change. Pastor Phillips' approach, of setting a time limit for the initial "experiment" and then reverting to the regular pattern, seems especially wise. The change thus did not overly threaten inhibitors, yet gave conservatives an opportunity to become convinced by experience — the one way such people can be convinced. And it gave members a basis in experience on which to evaluate more permanent changes which might be later suggested.

Modifying response. The third element of the *A-O-R-C* pattern is often conceived of as "just happening." When an individual is in a certain situation, he "just naturally" responds a certain way. Put a layman in a small group, the theory goes, and he automatically begins to share. But our responses are *learned.* A visitor to a liturgical church finds it difficult to know just when to stand and when to recite. But one brought up in the church finds the responses almost automatic — because he has learned them.

It is a tragic mistake to think that a change in church forms will lead people to automatically respond in appropriate ways — that asking for discussion after a sermon will lead to meaningful dialog, or that dropping some educational agencies will lead families to actually train their children. All responses — whether these or techniques of sharing Bible study, naturalness in personal witness, or spontaneity in prayer — have to be learned. And until an individual has some experience in responding, any new situation will be threatening.

This is another value in Pastor Phillips' approach in temporarily varying the prayer meeting structure. He gave his people an opportunity to use skills other than sitting and listening to him! Certainly, this six-week experience did not train them for effective group Bible study, far more training is needed for that. But with this experience behind them, his people had at least a taste of the kind of experience change ideas encourage, and of the kinds of skills they might later be called on to develop and refine.

I think we evangelicals tend to underestimate the importance of response training in Christian education. Some of the cults take great pains in training new members to witness. A new member is assigned to an effective worker, and goes with him from door-to-door. He observes, discusses the experience with his trainer, takes the lead himself, is evaluated, and in this one-to-one apprentice relationship is led to become effective.

In the re-formed church we are challenging believers to become witnesses. We are challenging believers to train their children in the home, rather than to rely on the church and its agencies. We are insisting that each take his place as a minister in the body of Christ. We require that each become actively responsible for studying and sharing the Word of God. *Unless we can promise, and provide, meaningful training that will teach our people HOW to fulfill these roles, they simply are not going to be able to change.*

How can such training take place? It may be done partly in shared small group experiences. It will certainly require time spent together by Christian parents, discussing their problems and seeking guidance from books, from Scripture and from each other's experiences. It may require that new believers be assigned to "imitate" Christian families or individuals who have developed needed skills and attitudes. It may require week-end retreats of the whole church, during which the principles and skills required for one aspect of Biblical ministry can be developed. It may require that the pastor start with one man: to train him to witness, to guide his family, to study the Word and to share.

Whatever methods we adopt, this is certain: change in the church demands careful attention to equipping God's people with the skills needed for responses which are appropriate to the demands of life in tomorrow's re-formed and renewed church.

Evaluating consequences. A church had 1,500 members, was considered elite in the denomination, it was confident, relaxed, satisfied, and then the leadership began to evaluate. Yes, it was the largest in the conference. But it was 100 members *smaller* than it had been ten years ago, and during that same ten years, the size of the community had tripled! Suddenly the picture changed, and the church was no longer confident, no longer relaxed and no longer satisfied. The people now saw the need for change.

This is the thing to note about the final factor in the A-O-R-C equation. It does not concern the actual consequences, but the *perceived consequences.*

A Chicago-area church is sure that it is an evangelistic church, reaching out effectively into its community to win the lost to Christ. The basis for this confidence? Some growth, plus a club program that involves some 400 boys and girls. And the fact that 35 of these children during the past year raised their hand in profession of faith in Christ.

What is the *real* situation? Is this a program actually reaching the community? One fact: most of the growth has been by transfer. Another: the 35 boys and girls were not followed up and personally counseled in a continuing program. The homes of the 35 were not visited or their profession discussed with their parents. And, during the year, not one *parent* from any of the many non-Christian homes represented in the clubs made a profession of faith.

To me this is *not* effective evangelism. This is *not* reaching the community. But as long as the members of the church view their club program as they do, no call for "evangelism" is likely to be heeded.

How do we help churchgoers evaluate their group and their individual Christian experience? How do we move them to set their own goals (thus mobilizing one of the major forces which can successfully initiate change)? Elmo Warkentin, dynamic elder statesman of the Evangelical Mennonite Church, has gone into dozens of churches to help them evaluate the effectiveness of their own programs. His evaluation guide demands that the people look at their church *objectively* and draw their own conclusions. The resulting reevaluation of the consequences of present patterns of church life has proven a strong impetus to change.

Guiding Change

In summary, then, I have suggested that churches, as complex interactional systems, can be changed, and that the people in the churches can be changed. How? (1) By changing the way the average believer views himself (actor designation). (2) By changing the normal patterns of meetings to require new responses from participants (changing occasion). (3) By equipping members for new responses which will enable them to carry out their responsibilities. (4) By changing the people's evaluation of the consequences of present church activities, and of the new forms which we seek to establish.

It should be clear that the pastor and other leaders of a church are in the best position to introduce variations in these four areas. It should also be clear that the guiding and effecting of such changes as are envisioned *must involve the responsible participation of all members of the church.* Believers in Christ are not pawns to be manipulated by one "in power." The end in view, that each might express his full priesthood and responsibility, requires that *in the process* each individual also be involved as a free and responsible person.

How can a person best be involved in the change process? At what stage should the long-range goal of change, a total restructuring of the church, be shared with the congregation? In what ways should the board be involved, take part in guiding change and working with other members of the congregation? None of these questions has an easy answer, and seemingly there is no single formula to fit every situation.

Yet changes are taking place.

In Chicago

"Change? We have to change," smiles the Rev. Bill Leslie, for seven years pastor of Chicago's Elm-LaSalle Bible Church. "Our backs are against the wall."

Elm-LaSalle was established 32 years ago as a mission of the famous Moody Church. It continued as a mission church, with its emphasis on children and its staff largely Moody Bible Institute students. Through waves of population change, the area shifted from Italian to Japanese to Puerto Rican to poverty level whites and blacks. Today Elm-LaSalle is surrounded by four different communities; poor whites to the east, poor blacks to the west, and highrises like Carl Sandburg Village bringing in young adults and older couples. At present 90 percent of Pastor Leslie's interracial congregation is between 20 and 30 years old, and the church has a 70 percent turnover of its 250 adherents each year. No wonder Rev. Leslie comments, "Our backs are against the wall!"

When other LaSalle Street churches left the people of the inner city and retreated to the suburbs, Pastor Leslie and his leaders determined to stay and to minister. But staying meant basic changes must be made in the church's life.

"We were convinced that, to minister in our neighborhood," the pastor says, "three basic changes were necessary.

"First, our church could no longer be a children's mission. We must reach the adult population.

"Second, we needed to get out of the four walls. We would have to train our people to be the church out in their daily lives. Thus we had to emphasize training them for ministry in their homes and personal evangelism of friends and co-workers.

"Finally, we were convinced that we had to develop the gifts of the Spirit which God has given to every Christian. In the past our people had ministered only to children; now we felt we had to help them minister as adults to adults."

It has not been easy at Elm-LaSalle to implement the ministry thus laid out. Changes are hard to sell. At first there was conflict between the older men in the church, who composed the board, and the younger adults.

Young people today, as Anthropologist Marvin Mayers suggests, are either going to find a ministry meaningful or they will not take part. The "church loyalty" which holds so many older people to a church which is not meeting their needs simply is not a part of the makeup of today's youth.

So the younger generation at Elm-LaSalle pushed hard for change. The conflict was resolved there when the board voted to invite the officers of the young adult group to serve with them as full members of the official board. This Acts 6 gesture was one key to the far-reaching changes made in Elm-LaSalle's ministry.

What does the church look like today? Programs and activities are being restructured to get participants personally into the Word, to permit maximum ministry of layman to layman, and to reach meaningfully into the community.

Sunday school at 9 Sunday morning precedes a 10 a.m. worship-centered service. Elective classes have doubled the adult Sunday school attendance. At 11 a fellowship hour features dialog, as outside speakers with challenging ideas are brought in, or as panels discuss issues related to the life and ministry of the church.

The traditional evening service is being replaced with discussion of questions that trouble church members, such as: Why does God permit suffering? What is the role of the social in the gospel? Why was Jesus' death necessary? Can a believer be a segregationist? What's the Bible's position on pacifism, etc.? A hand mike and roving pastor allow all to take part in this open exploration of issues, and the group is constantly challenged to relate their thinking and ideas to the Word.

The church has a decentralized prayer meeting, with four cell groups currently meeting in homes, and 12-15 showing up at church for a study conducted by the pastor. These cell groups, Rev. Leslie says, are vitally exciting, and in them adults *are* beginning to minister to each other.

The church also has a Sunday afternoon tutoring program, in which 50 children from the neighborhood are helped in reading and math on a one to one basis. "We discovered," says Bill, "that some Junior High kids who came to our church couldn't read even the simplest Bible portions. We began the tutoring program to minister to the whole person. We were convinced that kids wouldn't grow up to be good citizens or good Christians without basic educational skills."

In addition the church has worked with teens through science and radio clubs, and has a weekend coffeehouse ministry to youth in Chicago's Old Town.

How does a church move from the traditional to the varied approach of Elm-LaSalle, with its *one* preaching service a week and multiple service, outreach and growth activities?

"Change," says Pastor Leslie, "is a constant struggle. But we're determined to keep flexible, and to minister only in ways which prove effective. We've lost a few people over change, but very few. We have tried to bring everyone along with us."

Pastor Leslie's prescription for bringing people along is one he's worked out in years of experience. The basics, he feels, are these:

1. Keep people abreast of what's going on elsewhere. Elm-LaSalle brings in people who can share what's happening with the whole Church.

2. Xerox new ideas and feed them to the board. Pastor Leslie is constantly alert for new ideas, articles and books, which he

passes on to board members and key leaders, and discusses in board meetings.

3. Have a committee evaluate constantly. Elm-LaSalle doesn't leave change to chance. A group of men are charged with constantly evaluating the effectiveness of every ministry of the church, and recommending changes to meet needs discovered.

4. Bring new ideas to the congregation at least six months before the change should be instituted. The pastor notes that it usually takes leaders some time to decide to make a change. He feels it is unreasonable to expect the church members to accept the changes right away. So he uses the pulpit and guest speakers to discuss and prepare for planned changes.

5. Do everything on a trial basis. Changes that are made, are made with the understanding that after six months the church will meet and the congregation vote on whether or not to continue the ministry. With this "try it and see" attitude, it's easier for people to adjust to new experiences and new ideas.

At Elm-LaSalle, the church with its back against the wall, change is becoming an exciting way of life.

In Phoenix

It wasn't back-against-the-wall pressure that brought Pastor Bob Girard and his associate, Carl Jackson, to the place of change. It was an evaluation of the spiritual tone of the young Our Heritage Wesleyan Methodist Church, in Arizona's fast-expanding Scottsdale. A surprising evaluation, since the growing suburban church seemed — by the test most of us apply — a vital work.

In just three years the church had grown to well over 100 members, with 250 in Sunday school. Services were well attended, and a full "every night" program was being carried on. There was something for everyone: graded children's choirs, clubs, youth activities, teaching and committee opportunities for laymen who wanted to serve. The church was struggling somewhat financially under the burden of new buildings, yet obligations were being met. And, most important, people were being saved. Quietly, by ones and twos, people were responding to the Word of God and finding Christ as their personal Savior.

But less than one year ago, when Pastors Bob and Carl sat

down to evaluate, they were deeply burdened. With all the programs, with all the evangelism, with all the running and running of pastors, the people seemed spiritually stagnant. "The program," says Bob Girard, "simply wasn't doing the job. There wasn't the kind of openness and honesty there had to be if we were to share Christ's life together, and to mature. I had to ask myself," he says, "if God really had called me just to win people to Christ, and then to take care of baby Christians till He comes."

Two things happened at that critical juncture of Bob and Carl's life. They found a new reality in their own relationship with Christ through Watchman Nee's exposition of the faith-rest life, and they read the *ACTION* Magazine articles on the reformed church.

In both cases, the reading pointed the way toward solutions that have been proven valid this last year in the life of Our Heritage.

Pastors Bob and Carl found a new thrill in their own life as they rested in Christ and discovered He would live out His life in them. And the church has found a new vitality as it has *reorganized* its life in just one short year! From a traditionally organized church, Our Heritage is quickly becoming a pattern renewal church, with its life centered in a participating, sharing, growing lay membership.

The key to change has been the stripping away from the life of the church all activities that are not clearly and definitely contributing to spiritual growth, and the introduction of growth cells, called at Our Heritage CHUM (Christian Home Unit Meeting) groups. To move toward this structure, suggested in *ACTION*, the pastors tied on to the ministry of Campus Crusade for Christ. Crusade was invited to the church to train the laymen in personal evangelism. Immediately afterward two CHUM groups were set up with the stated purpose of giving opportunity to share witnessing experiences, and work out problems together.

"The groups," says Pastor Carl Jackson, "have two major goals. One is to get our people into the Word of God firsthand. The second is to honestly share our life in Christ with each other."

From the original two, the groups have expanded. Today there are 85 members of the church meeting in CHUM groups of 8 to 10 people each, with one group grown to 16 and ready to divide. The junior and senior high-school kids each have their own CHUM groups too, as this sharing time has replaced the normal "youth program" approach to ministry.

"We've found," says Carl, "that a flexible pattern works best. We've let the groups grow in their own way, without trying to direct them or make them fit a mold. We've found it's best not even to prescribe a given passage of Scripture or a study for the groups. They're free, under the leading of the Holy Spirit."

The CHUM approach caught on fastest at Our Heritage with the new converts, who had no traditional ideas to bind them. Older Christians there were introduced to sharing a pastor-led class. But all groups, as they dig into the Word and into the excitement and difficulties of living for Christ, are learning to share.

"Our Thursday morning women's group is a good example of what's happened," both pastors say. "The class started in a home with three women who were Christians and about eight others. Today all these women have come to know the reality of Christ, and one has become a Christian. The great thing is, this is largely without us. God has taken these women, and He is teaching them through each other."

What's happened to the "program" at Our Heritage? It has almost disappeared. There's still a Sunday morning service and Sunday school, as in most churches. In place of the midweek service the CHUM groups meet, including now about half the members of the church. In just one short year Our Heritage is down to only *one business meeting or committee of any kind!* The church board meets for two consecutive months, and the third month there is a congregational meeting.

Has this unstructured approach hurt the church? What's happened to the "spiritually stagnant" people?

"I've never been so excited in my nine years as a pastor," says Bob Girard. "There is actual, measurable, evident spiritual growth in every one of our CHUM group members. What's more, people are beginning to depend on each other spiritually. In the past they called the pastor with every problem, now they're calling each other. The Ephesians four pattern of ministry of adults to each other is happening here!

"And our people are witnessing. In our time here we've seen some 180 people come to know Christ. Today these people are being won by our laymen, and they have no trouble at all talking openly and freely about Jesus Christ."

There are still challenges facing Our Heritage. One is getting *all* members into the group life. "The people who are growing are in our CHUM groups," the pastors agree.

Another is how to build the CHUM groups into the organizational structure of the church. "Sunday morning used to be seen as the center of church life," says Bob Girard. "I now believe that the CHUM groups are, actually, the life of the church. These groups are 'the church!'" How to make this an organizational as well as experimental reality is a challenge.

Another is helping families become the center of Christian growth, as outlined in *ACTION*. This has burdened Our Heritage leaders, who are now planning ways to help adults build their at-home ministries around the teaching of the Sunday school.

With all its problems, Our Heritage has undergone an amazing transformation in less than a single year. It has moved away from programs and from spiritual stagnation to a growing, vital, witnessing laity that is simply exciting to see. While some members have been lost because of change, the majority have remained, sharing the life of Christ in small groups which has led rapidly to the kind of reality many of us dream of, but few have experienced.

Can we change, too?

The experience of Elm-LaSalle and Our Heritage suggests that the answer is, "Yes." It's easy to object, "We're different. We're not like either of these churches." Of course not. No church is really like another. But each church — whether the struggling inner-city work, the expanding suburban ministry, or the stabilized rural establishment — has within it the capacity to change. The Spirit of the Lord indwells those who have trusted Christ; and where the Spirit is, there is freedom.

Too long we've been bound by our traditions and our habits. Too long we've been content to try to do God's work in our old ways, unwilling to step out in faith and try His new ways. Too long we've denied our freedom and said, "We cannot change."

I remember what Bill Leslie said when I asked him if he felt that churches today are ready for change. His answer was short: "We have no alternative."

In a way, the rest of this book grows out of the conviction that Bill Leslie expressed: that we have no alternative but to seek renewal. In the next few chapters I believe you will find that the Bible leaves us no alternative but to change. And in subsequent chapters that we need no other alternative. Change is possible, for us, today.

We stand before an open door.

Part II

The Church in Scripture

5

The Nature of the Church

Contemporary Christianity tends to see the church and her role in a variety of lights. To some the church is the servant community, called to serve the world in which she finds herself. To others the church has a prophetic calling, to speak out to the world and to call men and society back to righteous paths. Whatever the church may be to you, the church has a relationship to the world, a mission to unredeemed humanity individually, and/ or in society.

This whole approach to the church is one which jolts me; it seems to tear the concept of "church" brutally from the framework of Scripture, and to cast us adrift in unresolvable uncertainty about the nature and function of the Christian church. For whatever we can say about "the Church" it is clear that we can find no such named scriptural entity which dealt with governments, or which, as an organization, developed programs to collect its quota of neighborhood children and unwary adults. Peculiarly, the church of Scripture seems quite nebulous organizationally and while its members were given responsibilities toward their world, the church itself (whatever that may be) was given no similar charges.

Yet, when we strip away centuries of societal accretions and view "the Church" *within* the framework of Scripture, the simplicity of her nature and her function mark out clearly the directions we must take if what we call "our churches" are to be churches indeed.

This scriptural framework of the Church can be sketched adequately (though not exhaustively) by looking at four elements: (1) the relationship of the people of God to Christ; (2) the relationship of the people of God to one another; (3) the function of the church as a transforming community; and (4) the relationship of the church to the world.

The Relationship of the People of God to Christ

In a culture as individualistic as ours, it's not surprising that evangelicals have stressed the relationship of the *individual* to God, even to the extent that we have been criticized by others. Of course, we have had our reasons. Salvation is an individual affair: a personal relationship between the individual and his God. There's an awesome *aloneness* attached to the Gospel, for the Gospel brings each of us to a precipice of decision on which he stands alone. There, face to face with God, each must choose to reject his wasted powers and tarnished virtue and rest his hope only in Christ. Or, unwilling to trust, he must turn back toward foolish self-reliance. Whichever way he turns he will find much company, but at the moment of choice he stands alone. At the moment of choice he knows that the full responsibility for the decision is his alone.

Stepping into the salvation-relationship God offers, we retain our identity as individuals. And as individuals each one struggles to live his faith; to be a channel through which God's love can flow out to wash over men who have lost all contact with Him. In this too we often feel alone, and as each new responsibility is recognized we feel its weight. "As children copy their fathers you, as God's children, are to copy Him. Live your lives in love — the same sort of love which Christ gives us and which he perfectly expressed when he gave himself up for us in sacrifice to God" (Ephesians 5:1).* Here is something no one can do *for*

---

*Except as designated, quotes from this point are from the Phillips revised translation of the New Testament.

me. In this responsibility, in this pattern of daily choices, again I alone can be responsible.

But then for the Christian the *aloneness* of the Gospel is transformed. And the secret, Paul writes, "is simply this: Christ *in you!* Yes, Christ *in you* bringing with him the hope of all the glorious things to come" (Colossians 1:27). For in coming to know God the believer steps into the most intimate of all possible relationships with Jesus Christ — with God Himself. The One who created and who fills the universe comes to share his life, to negate his aloneness, and to express His love through the believer. No wonder Paul writes triumphantly that "my present life is not that of the old 'I'; but the living Christ within me. The bodily life I now live, I live believing in the Son of God, who loved me and sacrificed himself for me" (Galatians 2:20).

It is not surprising in view of realities like these that evangelicals have focused on the individual: the individual confronting Christ in salvation, and the individual experiencing Christ as a living Presence in his daily life. It is tragic, however, that our emphasis on an individual relationship with Christ has led us to neglect the corporate relationship of the people of God to Christ.

One of the basic truths about this relationship (one essential to an understanding of the nature and function of the church), is that "we are not separate units but intimately related to one another in Christ" (Ephesians 4:25). And that it is all of us together which Scripture calls "the Church." Viewed from one perspective we are individuals, each with his personal relationship to Christ and his personal responsibilities. Viewed from another perspective we blend together to form a spiritual entity which also has a relationship with Christ, and which has corporate responsibilities.

Often this relationship between Christ and the church is spoken of as a relationship between a head and its body. "Now," the Bible says, Christ is "the head of the body which is the Church" (Colossians 1:18). Just as the individual believer is indwelt by Christ, so is the church. "God has placed everything under the power of Christ and has set him up as head of everything for the Church. For the Church is his body, and in that body lives fully the one who fills the whole wide universe" (Ephesians 1:21, 22).

This concept of a corporate reality is a hard one for us to grasp. I can easily see myself as an individual, responsible for my choices, living my own life for God or for whatever values I may choose. But how do I live as a part of the body of Christ? It is clear that being partners with other Christians in a body which, as a body, is to be responsive to its head, fully explains Paul's concern for the church at Corinth. "Now I beg of you, my brothers," he writes, "by all that our Lord Jesus Christ means to you, to speak with one voice, and not allow yourselves to be split up into parties. All together you should be achieving a unity of thought and judgment" (I Corinthians 1:10, 11). For as a part of the church, *corporately* related to Christ, I must be in harmony with other partners in Christ to be in harmony with Him.

All of this gives us some preliminary insight into the nature of the church. The church of Scripture is *people*: people in relationship with Christ, and thus in relationship with one another. "As the human body, which has many parts, is a unity," the Bible says, "and these parts, despite their multiplicity, constitute one single body, so it is with Christ. For we were all baptized by the Spirit into one body, whether we were Jews, Greeks, slaves or free men, and we have all had experience of the same Spirit" (I Corinthians 12:12, 13). If a person comes to know Christ, that Spirit which effected his salvation joined him to all other believers in a corporate unity know as "the Church" — the body of Christ.

The Relationship of the People of God to One Another

It is a happy peculiarity that the most difficult and mystical elements of our faith are *incarnated*. God Himself must have seemed hazy and far off to the Old Testament saint. Like Moses, many must have been eager to see Him. And then Christ came, "and we beheld His glory." Scripture indicates that God's design is that "the Church" be incarnated also, that its nature be made visible in the relationship between Christians.

"Make it your aim to be at one in the Spirit," says Paul to the Ephesians, "and you will inevitably be at peace with one another. You all belong to one body, of which there is one Spirit, just as you experienced one calling to one hope" (4:2, 3). In every locality the biblical evangelists drew the believers together into a local church; an *assembly* of those who were part of the "Church which is His body." These men and women were to work out the reality of that mystical relationship in their corporate experience.

We all know something of the world into which the Gospel came. Great social gaps existed — between Jew and Gentile, between slave and free. Yet the cross "made a unity of the conflicting elements of Jew and Gentile by breaking down the barrier which lay between . . ." Relationship to Christ made "utterly irrelevant" antagonism between them, and joined all together as "fellow citizens with every other Christian" (Ephesians 2).

These diverse elements were to "achieve a unity in thought and judgment." They were to bear one another's burdens. They were to love one another. Relationship between believers is so significant that it is pointed to in Scripture as an accurate gauge for judging relationship with God. "Anyone who claims to be 'in the light' and hates his brother is, in fact, still in complete darkness" (I John 2:9). "If a man says, 'I love God,' and hates his brother, he is a liar. For if he does not love the brother before his eyes how can he love the one beyond his sight? And in any case it is his explicit command that the one who loves God must love his brother also" (I John 4:20, 21). No wonder Paul looks at the squabbling and partisanship in Corinth and says, "While one of you says, 'I am of Paul,' and another says, 'I am one of Apollos' are you not plainly unspiritual?" (I Corinthians 3:4). To be out of harmony with one another is to be out of harmony with God.

A local incarnation of the unity which exists in the mystical body of Christ, and a relationship of love between those who share in Christ, is basic to the Gospel. As the Gentiles began to enter the New Testament church, and as a primarily Gentile church was formed at Antioch, a visiting Peter shared fully in its life and worship. Then some Jewish Christians came down from Jerusalem and Peter withdrew from the Gentiles and ate apart from them. Paul reports in Galatians that "the force of their bad example was so great that even Barnabas was affected by it. But when I saw that this behavior was *a contradiction to the truth of the Gospel*, I spoke up to Peter so everyone could hear" (Galatians 2:13, 14). Not even reverence for the Old Testament law must be allowed to cloud the fact that a salvation offered freely to all, apart from law, brings all who accept it into a relationship of mutual union, no matter what their habits of life and worship might be.

At this point we can see more clearly the nature of the church. As a mystical body it is all believers in union with Christ. As a manifested reality, it is a local assembly of believers in a relationship of union with each other.

A local church is to *incarnate* this union; to incarnate the love that is to mark it. As the Scripture says, "To us, the greatest demonstration of God's love for us has been his sending his only Son into the world to give us life through him. We see real love, not in the fact that we loved God, but that he loved us and sent his Son to make personal atonement for our sins. If God loves us as much as that, surely we, in our turn, should love one another" (I John 4:8-10). Thus the church is a community of believers in which we see, and experience, real love.

The Function of the Church as a Transforming Community

To understand the church it is necessary to do more than see it as a company of people united to Christ and to one another, and the local church as an assembly of believers charged with incarnating the mystical reality of that union. We need to ask about its function. For what purpose did God create the church? Why doesn't He simply deal with us as individuals? Why does He insist on dealing with us in community?

And insist He does. It is His intention "that all the angelic powers should now see the complex wisdom of God's plan being worked out through the Church, in conformity with that timeless purpose which he centered in Jesus Christ, our Lord" (Ephesians 3:10). His purpose is being worked out through the church — not simply through isolated individuals.

The function of the church, this community of believers, is clarified when we note the association of the concept of "spiritual gifts" with the concept of the Body. A body, the Scriptural analogy goes, has many parts, with different functions. So the Body of Christ has many members. And each member has been given a special ability enabling him to contribute to the well-being of the whole. "Naturally there are different gifts and functions; individually grace is given to us in different ways out of the rich diversity of Christ's giving" (Ephesians 4:7). This diversity of individual spiritual abilities was carefully planned. And gifted individuals were given to the church "that Christians might be properly equipped for their service, and that the whole body might be built up" (Ephesians 4:12). Thus believers are placed in an *interdependent relationship* with each other. Each Christian has a service; a unique contribution to make, and each needs the contribution of others. "God has harmonized the whole body," the Bible says, "by giving importance of function to the parts which lack apparent importance, that the body should work together as a whole with all the members in sympathetic relationship with one another. So it happens that if one member suffers all other members suffer with it, and if one member is honored all the members share a common joy" (I Corinthians 12:24-26).

Again, this interdependence is a *functional* one. The body is to work "together as a whole with all the members in sympathetic relationship with one another" for a purpose. Ephesians specifies that that purpose is one relating *to itself* and to *its members*. "The whole body, as a harmonious structure knit together by that which every joint supplies, *grows by the proper functioning of individual parts to its full maturity in love*" (4:16, italics mine). The function of the church is a nurturing one. It is to facilitate the growth of its members and itself as a community into "full maturity in love." Within the womb of interpersonal relationships, individuals and the community are to be transformed.

No one should be surprised at this postulation of a personality transformation role for interpersonal relationships. When Adam could find no one to meet his needs as a person within animal creation, God made Eve as "a help suited to him." She was necessary for his personality growth and development. When God instructed Israel on the pattern for bringing up children, His first command (Deuteronomy 6) was that His word should be "in the hearts" of the parents, and then that as they lived life they should daily share His words with their children. The reality of the words, expressed in the common life of the parents, could be communicated best in the framework of family relationships. Thus human relationships were understood as vital to communication of their relationship with God. And even after a child grows up, it is the normal course that he "leave his mother and

father and cleave unto his wife." Man lives and grows in relationship.

It is particularly significant that the modern behavioral sciences have located the key to transmission of values and behavior patterns in social interaction rather than in concepts. This
is not to deny the power of an idea, but it is to suggest that
ideas must become incarnate in life for their effective communication. Values must be lived to be shared. As far as the Christian faith is concerned, one introduced to Jesus Christ as Savior
must then step into a community of those who love and who live
His truths if that person is to grow to his full maturity in Christ.
The function of the church is one of personality transformation.

It seems strange, in view of all the teaching of Scripture, that
we have lost awareness of the urgency of such transformation.
"Wherever the Gospel goes," Paul wrote to the Colossians, "it
produces Christian character, and develops it, as it has done in
your own case from the time you first heard and realized the
truth of God's grace" (1:6). To Timothy he wrote, "the ultimate
aim of the Christian ministry, after all, is to produce the love
which springs from a pure heart, a good conscience, and a genuine faith. Some seem to have forgotten this and to have lost
themselves in endless words" (I Timothy 1:5, 6).

Personality transformation is so significant scripturally that
believers are told: "don't associate with the brother whose life is
undisciplined, and who despises the teaching we gave you. You
know well that we ourselves are your examples here, and that
our lives among you were not undisciplined" (II Thessalonians
3:6, 7). The Christian is simply to become a new and different
person. As a Christian the believer is to "reach out for the
highest gifts of heaven" . . . to give his "heart to the heavenly
things, not to the passing things of earth." This means a rejection of the whole pattern of life and values of sinful human
society. In its place the Christian "as God's picked representatives of the new humanity, purified and beloved of God Himself" is to "be merciful in action, kindly in heart, humble in
mind." Christians are to "accept life, and be most patient and
tolerant with one another, always ready to forgive if you have a
difference with anyone. Forgive as freely as the Lord has for-
given you. And, above everything else, be truly loving, for love
is the golden chain of all the virtues. Let the peace of Christ

rule in your hearts, remembering that as members of one body you are called to live in harmony, and never forget to be thankful for what God has done for you." The passage concludes, "teach and help one another along the right road" (Ephesians 3).

This is the kind of transformation, the kind of character, that is appropriate to the Gospel, and that is *expected of every believer*. And to facilitate this kind of personality transformation — this reorientation of life and values — God has provided a community of men and women who are to "teach and help" us along the right road, and whom we in turn are to teach and help. As members of this community, this Body, each of us is equipped with a special ability, or gift, to help others in the body grow *when we are involved in their lives* — when we love one another, and minister to one another as we are able.

The function of the church as a community of believers, then, is focused on itself and on its members. The local church is to incarnate the unity and love of the church which is His body because *within such a community* Christian individuals grow, and Christian character is formed. The function of the church is foremost and essentially the personality transformation of its members, and of itself as a community.

The Relationship of the Church and the World

In several places in Scripture the church and the world are thrown into contrast. In each of these places (such as in Colossians 3 f. and Ephesians 5 f.) the contrast drawn is between patterns of life. Men immersed in the pattern of life of the world are said to "live blindfolded in a world of illusion, and are cut off from the life of God through ignorance and insensitiveness." They are said to have "stifled their consciences and then surrendered themselves to sensuality, practicing any form of impurity which lust can suggest." The Christian is to be "mentally and spiritually remade, to put on the clean fresh clothes of the new life which was made by God's design for righteousness and the holiness which is no illusion" (Ephesians 4:17 f.).

Seen as a pattern of life, *the world* is in a sense contradictory to the church: it is an interpersonal system expressing values and behavior energized by Satan. Men living in and by this system are said to "drift along on the stream of this world's ideas of living," and to obey "its unseen ruler (who is still operating in those who do not respond to the truth of God)" (Ephesians 2: 1-2). Thus biblically "the world" is a socializing agency, just as is the church. The world, as an interpersonal system with its own values and ideas of living develops the capacities for sin which exist in unredeemed mankind: the church as an interpersonal system with its own values and ideas of living develops the capacities for response to God which exist in redeemed men. These systems overlap in our experience, but they do not touch each other.

Now, I realize that this rather specialized concept of "world" does not exhaust the biblical meanings of the term. And that normally when a contemporary writer speaks of the "church and the world" he is not thinking of either in this sense. Rather he is thinking of human individuals and human institutions, and he has a worthy desire to bring individuals and institutions into harmony with God's righteous ways of life.

The problem I have with this is that at no point, biblically, does the church (which we have seen is to function as a system of interpersonal relationships) touch society. If we take seriously the biblical picture of the church as people in relationship, and if we take seriously the biblical function of the church as a transforming community, its forms can never be relevant to society or to societal institutions. The forms of the church, if the church is true to herself, can be relevant only to her scripturally assigned task — the personality transformation of believers. The church, as a community of believers, *exists only for its members*.

This is not, though it may seem to be, an isolationist position. I am not advocating withdrawal from non-Christians, or from society. In fact, I am personally convinced that we believers must involve ourselves more deeply in the lives of the unsaved than we do; that we must struggle within our society to shape its institutions. This involvement, however, and this struggle is that of the Christian man, and not of the Christian church. For the Christian church does not even *exist* except as believers in relationship with one another! The church cannot exist as an organization in organizational relationship with the unsaved, or as an institution in relationship with societal institutions. Whatever such an organization or institution may be, and whatever we may call it, it is not and cannot be "the Church."

All of this serves to further limit and clarify what I am talking about as I try to describe "a new face for the church." To me, renewal first of all demands a sharp and simplified understanding of what the church is, is to be, and must become. If the church *is* believers in relationship with Christ and one another, our concern must be to reshape a believers' church. If the church is ordained by God for the purpose of providing a context of human relationships in which His Spirit can work to transform our characters and our personalities, then our concern must be to develop personal relationships with one another. Our church structures and experiences must encourage us to minister to each other, to love each other, and to teach and help each other along His way.

If we confuse the church with an organization or an institution, and lose sight of it as believers-in-intimate-relationship, we will find no guidelines on which to pattern renewal. But if we keep the scriptural concept in clear focus, the guidelines are many. And the characteristics of Christ's church stand out distinctly and unmistakably.

6

The Role of the Church in Christian Experience

It seems to me that the term "Christian" is one much misused by its friends. On the one hand some of us have squeezed it into so narrow a scope that it includes only those who agree with us in every doctrinal detail. Others of us have broadened it to include anyone who wishes in any way to nod toward the Palestinian Carpenter. Either way the original impact of "Christian" — little Christs — has been diffused, and a dimension of discipleship too often disregarded.

As I am necessarily dealing with the idea of "Christian" in this chapter, it seems only fair that I state what I mean when I use the word.

In drawing my definition I do not intend to exclude anyone who wants to be counted in. It is God's business to separate the wheat and tares in His kingdom — not mine. I set down these thoughts only that I might be understood, and that the role I am suggesting for the church in Christian experience might be more sharply seen against the background of our cultural confusion about what is and is not "Christian."

For this we simply have to dip into the nature of man as drawn in Scripture and held by our orthodox Christian faith.

The Christian Man

No one is all bad. All of us have qualities that, looked at in any normal light, would be called "good." As the old cliché has it, "anyone who likes dogs can't be all bad!"

Even Christ seems to have recognized this kind of good in some of the worst men of His time. "If you then, being evil, know how to give good gifts to your children . . . ," He once prefaced some remarks. And the publicans and sinners of that day acted decently toward each other too: they loved those who loved them, and exchanged greetings with their own circles (Matthew 5). So when the biblical portrait of man tends to be the blackest, and when I sketch the pattern of life of the unredeemed, neither the Bible nor I are asserting that all men are as bad as they could be. Or that being a "sinner" means the complete absence of what we might call "common decency."

Even so, the biblical picture of mankind is starkly pessimistic. The society of the unsaved is seen as one of men who are "blindfolded" in that "world of illusion" mentioned in the last chapter. And they are seen as "slaves of various desires and pleasant feelings," with "lives . . . spent in malice and jealousy." Even with all the decent things they do, the Bible suggests that we must realize that underneath it all men are (for example, as the newspaper headlines, or the last misunderstanding you had with your wife, and your last unguarded thought all testify) "hateful, and we hate one another" (Titus 3:1 f.). In short, men are warped, our personalities are out of phase with God, and with good. We are so far out of phase that the Bible calls man a "spiritually dead" being. It says that we "drift along on the stream of this world's ideas of living," and "follow the impulses and imaginations of our evil nature" (Ephesians 2:1 f.). Our intellectual grasp of life and its meaning, and our non-rational emotions and desires, are both affected. Thus in the Bible the whole *pattern* of unredeemed human life is called evil, and we individually are called sinners.

This black portrayal is a difficult one for us to accept. It is hard to resist focusing on the many individually "good" acts all of us may (more or less regularly) perform. It is hard to look instead at the *pattern*: the pattern of thought, desire, and behavior that characterizes human personality. But we must realize that in viewing man pessimistically, we are in accord with what the Bible does. It looks at the pattern of our lives, and puts us under condemnation. If we do reject this evaluation of ourselves and our society, we deny our nature. Then the Bible says we "live in a world of illusion and truth becomes a stranger to us" (I John 1:8). Whether we see it or not, "the whole world system, based as it is on men's primitive desires, their greedy ambitions and the glamour of all that they think splendid, is not derived from the Father at all, but from the world itself" (I John 3:15). Mankind truly is caught up in a *pattern* of sin.

It is within this framework that the most stark and brutal of all scriptural evaluations of humanity must be understood — and accepted. That . . .

> There is none righteous, no, not one.
> There in none that understandeth,
> There is none that seeketh after God;
> They have all turned aside; they are together become unprofitable;
> There is none that doeth good, no, not so much as one.
>
> (Romans 3:10-12, AV)

With this in mind, it should be easy to see why the Bible labels a person not by what doctrines he says he believes, or by his appreciation for the teachings of Jesus, but by whether or not his sinful personality has been redeemed.

In the same biblical passage in which Paul talks of the unredeemed as men who "live blindfolded" and who are "cut off from the life of God through ignorance and insensitiveness," he speaks of a "new humanity." This humanity is one "mentally and spiritually remade," with a "new life which was made by God's design for righteousness" (Ephesians 4:17 f.). In the passage where the Bible calls men "dead in trespasses and sins" it postulates a new humanity to whom "Christ has given life." "Even though we were dead in our sins, God, who is rich in mercy, because of the great love he had for us, gave us life together with Christ" (Ephesians 2:1 f.). Here then is a contrasting group: one not marked out by a pattern of sin, which means death, but by a pattern of righteousness, which springs from life. This is truly a new humanity, and it is members of *this new humanity* to whom I refer as "Christians."

In defining a Christian as one who has this new life from God,

I am not criticizing other definitions. Someone might say that a Christian is a person who has come into personal relationship with God through faith in Jesus Christ as Savior. Fine. A Christian has done that. Another might speak of one who has come to trust the finished work of Christ on Calvary as full payment for his sin. So would I. A Christian only becomes a Christian through the merits of the cross of Christ.

But a Christian *is* a person with God's new life implanted within. In the words of Peter, "the live, permanent Word of the living God has given you his own indestructible heredity" (I Peter 1:24). A person who does not have this life, this heredity, whatever ideas he professes to hold, and no matter how highly he may regard Jesus, is not a Christian.

Now, the unique thing about the new life possessed by the Christian is that it is in full and inherent harmony with God. It is *His* life. And participating in His life, we are able to share in God's ways of thinking and living. "It is for you now to demonstrate the goodness of him who has called you out of darkness into his amazing light," the Bible says (I Peter 2:9). The *pattern* of this life is, and is to be, as fully in harmony with the nature of God as the *pattern* of unredeemed human life is strange to Him.

Having God's new life brings with it a new set of perceptions concerning the meaning of life, and a new set of desires and motivations. It means that we have the potential to share that which God Himself sees and experiences as "good." Thus the Bible asserts that the man living out his new life "has an insight into the meaning of everything, though his insight may baffle the man of the world. This is because the former is sharing in God's wisdom" (I Corinthians 2:15, 16).

The Good News of Christ then is the message that a new kind of life is held out to all men as a free gift: that God loves, and in the fullness of His love He gave His Son that we might live. Coming bodily into the fouled stream of humanity God Himself shared our human predicament, and in His culminating act of redemption took the full burden of our sin upon Himself, and washed it away on His cross. Who can wonder that a life which springs from that sacrificial act is given solely "by grace, and not by (human) achievement?" Who can wonder that we are saved only by being "lifted right out of the old life to take our place

with him in Christ Jesus in the heavens" (Ephesians 2:8, 9)?
And who can wonder that only those who have in fact received
new life from Christ's nail-pierced hands have the right to claim
the name Christian?

Faith and Works

It is characteristic of life that it expresses itself. Even the
amoeba, without any selfawareness, expresses its life by moving,
probing, engulfing, feeding, growing. Why then should we be
surprised if the Bible insists that the new life from God must
express itself as well? Why should we be surprised to find an
urgent insistence that when one claims the Christian faith (carrying as it does an intrinsic assertion of a share in God's life and
nature), it requires an appropriate change in character and behavior?

"What use is it," James asks his brothers, "for a man to say
that he 'has faith' if his actions do not correspond with it? Could
that sort of faith save anyone's soul?" (James 2:14). In raising
the question James is not attacking the idea that faith, as full
confidence in Christ's finished work, is in fact that stretching out
of our hands by which we receive God's gift of life. He is attacking the idea that any "faith" which is not staked out and
clearly marked by a changed life is Christian faith. It is counter-
feit. True faith brings new life, and new life expresses itself.
New life *works*.

It is to works, to the development of that new life from a
struggling *capacity* to a mature *ability*, that the Christian is to
devote himself.

"Let us have no imitation Christian love," Paul insists. "Let us
have a genuine break with evil, and a real devotion to good.
Let us have real affection for one another as between brothers,
and a willingness to let the other man have the credit. Let us
not allow slackness to spoil our work and let us keep the fires of
the spirit burning, as we do our work for the Lord" (Romans 12:
9-12). For the life of God must be nourished; it must be developed; it must be *lived*.

The kind of life the Bible describes is not an easy one. The
view of reality this life is based on and its pattern of willing
submission of (as the world might view them) personal "rights"

seems foolish judged by the philosophies of men. "When trials come," one passage says, "endure them patiently; steadfastly maintain the habit of prayer. Give freely to fellow Christians in want, never grudging a meal or a bed to those who need them. And as for those who try to make your life a misery, bless them. Don't curse, bless. Share the happiness of those who are happy, and the sorrow of those who are sad. Live in harmony with one another. Don't become snobbish but take real interest in ordinary people. Don't become set in your own opinions. Don't pay back a bad turn by a bad turn, to *anyone*" (Romans 12:12 f.). All this, and far more, is the expression of the new life which God plants in those who come to know Him, through His Son.

While we may recognize the person who never lets brotherly love fail (or who never refuses to extend hospitality, or who thinks of all who suffer as if he shares their pain — Hebrews 13: 1 f.) as one of "nature's noblemen," few envy such individuals. And of those who do, how many see in the pattern of selfless love (left as a legacy by Christ to be re-lived constantly by the church) the only *meaningful* life? And even more importantly, who has resources within himself to live genuine love with real devotion, and no imitation intruding? But the Gospel comes bringing just this kind of new life, and God works in His child, guiding, disciplining, and "when it is all over we can see that it has quietly produced the fruit of real goodness in the characters of those who have accepted it (the disciplining) in the right spirit" (Hebrews 12).

Bluntly, then, the Bible insists that a new *way of life* is essential for those who have inherited a new *kind of life* from Christ.

"No more evil temper or furious rage; no more evil thoughts or words about others, no more evil thoughts or words about God and no more filthy conversation. Don't tell one another lies any more, for you have finished with the old man and all he did and have begun life as the new man, who is out to learn what he ought to be, according to the plan of God" (Colossians 3:8-10).

"If you have really heard his voice and understood the truth that Jesus has taught you," the Bible says, "what you learned was to fling off the dirty clothes of the old way of living, which were rotten through and through with lust's illusions, and, with yourselves mentally and spiritually remade, to put on the clean fresh clothes of the new life" (Ephesians 4:21-24). The sort of character that follows from this learning, that "springs from sound teaching," is this: "the old men should be temperate, serious, wise — spiritually healthy through their faith and love and patience. Similarly the old women should be reverent in their behavior, should not make unfounded complaints and should not be overfond of wine. They should be examples of the good life, so that the younger women may learn to love their husbands and their children, to be sensible and chaste, home lovers, kindhearted and willing to adapt themselves to their husbands — good advertisements for the Christian faith. The young men too, you should urge to take life seriously, letting your own life stand as a pattern of good living." In short, the believer is to learn "to have no more to do with godlessness or the desires of this world, but live, here and now, responsible, honorable, and God-fearing lives" (Titus 2 and 3). The "life" that a Christian has received from God is to be fully developed.

The Christian Community

"Life expresses itself" seems a simple equation, but the higher the form of life, the more necessary *training* seems to be for full expression. Some living things spawn or drop eggs and die; the young do all they need to do by nature. A mother fox or bear may train her young till they develop hunting skills, and then leave them, but a human being must live for years with his parents. He must receive specialized training in schools and universities. Throughout his life he is constantly learning in his associations with others the attitudes and behaviors he needs to grow, to change, and to become.

It is significant that when the Bible talks of the Christian's new life, it speaks in terms of *growth*. Continue, we are told, "to learn more and more of the life that pleases God, the sort of life we told you about before" (I Thessalonians 4:1). None of this negates the fact that the Christian is to "live (his) your whole life in the Spirit," and that such a relationship frees the whole power of God's Holy Spirit to energize the life God has planted within (Galatians 5:16 f.). But the concept of growth in Christian experience parallels the important concept of right relationship. For Christians do grow and. learn and mature in their new life; they do develop it over the whole of their lifespan. Such development, according to Scripture, is something upon which we must "concentrate" (Titus 3:8).

I suggested in the last chapter that the church is to be a "transforming community." That within the supportive framework of loving Christian relationships the believer's new life is to grow and to develop. In a sense, the church is a womb which nourishes the individual — a womb which we never cease to need and from which we are never to separate ourselves.

Now we can see why such a womb is necessary. It is necessary because the Christian's life-long experience is one of growth, "till Christ be formed in you" — and it is also necessary because of the *otherness* of the new life the Christian has.

What I mean is this. A child learns his values, attitudes, and ways of life from his parents. His character is molded in a form which is set by theirs. When he moves out into a broader society he again is acted upon — and he responds. He experiences, he selects and rejects, both consciously and unconsciously. And so a human being grows and changes, so his character is formed. On the one hand what he selects is based on what he is: on his nature — but on the other hand he can only select, only be shaped and changed, in accord with *what is there*. He cannot learn a pattern of life for which he has no pattern, with which he has no experience!

If as a Christian a person is thrust into a society of men whose whole pattern of living is out of harmony with God's way of life, he *must* be influenced by *what is there*.

This difficulty is compounded by the fact that a Christian's new life does not *replace* his old life, his old ways of seeing things, and his old appetites. It comes in alongside. God provides a capacity for insight, a capacity for a totally new way of living. But God does not remove the capacity to look at life in the old, crooked ways. He does not remove the capacity to sin. Tragically, the dominant personality developmental forces (being the social, interpersonal influences all around us) do in fact incarnate the ideas of living of the world.

It is essential, then, for the Christian's new life to develop fully, that he have close personal relationships within which the *otherness* of God's way of life can find concrete expression. It is essential that there be a community in which God's life is in fact incarnated.

Moving into such a community a new Christian can experience, he can learn, he can grow and change. He can be molded by what is *there*. The life of God within can be encouraged, strengthened, trained, disciplined, motivated, by sharing the reality of that life with others.

I find it interesting now to look at the book of Romans and see what I missed before. To see the first eleven doctrinal chapters fulfilled and completed by the last four, once almost dismissed as "merely practical." For now these chapters seem to me as significant doctrinally (and thus as vitally practical) as the rest.

In the first chapters of Romans Paul deals with man's universal need for righteousness (1-3), concluding that "there is none righteous, no not one." He then explains God's provision of righteousness in Jesus Christ, demonstrating clearly that a God-kind-of-righteousness that hinges on faith is freely extended to all (3: 24-5). He next explores the provision made for the believing individual to live a righteous life (6-8). Again, the keystone of daily life is seen to be faith, with faith freeing God to energize His life within and live it out through us. All of this raises questions about God's promises and purposes as revealed in the Old Testament, so in chapters 9-11 Paul integrates his new revelation with the old, demonstrating the righteousness of God's seeming departure from His prophesied course. Finally he moves (in the section I once thought of as only "practical") to discuss *the community which God has provided as a context for our growth in righteousness.*

Any careful study of these chapters should lead the reader to an appreciation for the place the church must have in developing Christian experience.

Briefly, Romans 12 begins with an appeal for total dedication of the believer to Christ. All are urged to "let God remold your minds from within" and to move by obedience "toward the goal of true maturity."

Immediately Paul focuses our attention on the community within which this remolding is to take place. He speaks of the many individuals who make up the body of Christ, and urges each to full involvement and use of the special gift he has received to minister to others. In verses 9 f. he describes the interpersonal relationships which are to mark the community — that genuine love and "real warm affection" we read of earlier.

In chapter 13 Paul touches on the relationship of Christians to the civil community. As one living in the world, the believer is to be obedient to the laws of the state. However, the ultimate code of conduct is not wrapped up in obedience to civil authority; it is epitomized in love. "Thou shalt love thy neighbor as thyself," as "love hurts nobody: therefore love is the answer to the Law's commands."

After an exhortation that we "be Christ's men from head to foot, and give no chance to the flesh to have· its fling," we focus again on relationships in the community of believers. In particular, chapter 14 shows how believers are to live together harmoniously in spite of individual differences and different evaluations of various non-essentials. Rather than being critical of others, we are to watch ourselves and our conduct, to be sure that we "concentrate on the things which make for harmony, and on the growth of one another's character."

The passage then sharply draws the helping role of the community. "We who have strong faith ought to shoulder the burden of the doubts and qualms of others and not just go our own sweet way. Our actions should mean the good of others – should help them to build up their characters. For even Christ did not choose his own pleasure. . . . May the God who inspires men to endure, and gives them a Father's care, give you a mind united toward one another because of your common loyalty to Jesus Christ. . . . So open your hearts to one another as Christ has opened his heart to you, and God will be glorified."

In a final expression of confidence, Paul again alludes to the helping role of the community when he says, "I feel certain that you, my brothers, have real Christian character and experience, and that you are capable of keeping one another on the right road."

The Functions of the Community

It is possible (though not necessary in this quick sketch) to multiply examples. The fact of the helping role of the community in the development of Christian character (that is, in the growth and nurture of the life of God in believing men and women) stands out again and again in the New Testament, if we but look for it. This help takes many forms. What are a few of the ways in which we are to guide the development of character within the community?

One is simply that of encouragement. "Let us think of one another and how we can encourage one another to love and do good deeds," the Bible says (Hebrews 10:23). It is easy to become discouraged: to set high standards as a Christian, and to fail. And then, if we are alone, or unable to share our discouragement, it is so easy to give up. Or to work hard on appearances, so no one will know how badly we feel we have failed. Knowing how greatly each of us needs encouragement, it is no wonder that the Bible tells us to "give your positive attention to goodness, faith, love, and peace, *in company with* all those who approach God in sincerity" (II Timothy 2:22, italics mine). We need such company. We need to "help one another to stand firm in the faith every day," being wary that none of us "become deaf and blind to God through the delusive glamor of sin" (Hebrews 3:13).

Another way we help each other is in giving and receiving love. "This is how all men will know that you are my disciples," Christ said, "because you have such love for one another" (John 13:33). I know a girl whose father and mother always fought; who lived out her childhood in such fear that as a young woman she "forgot" her past life. I have a pastor friend whose father beat his mother, and tried to kill him. Neither of these people learned how to love or to be loved. Each desperately needs to learn; by loving, and by being loved. When we love "our love for him grows more and more, filling us with complete confidence for the day when he shall judge all men — for we realize that our life in this world is actually his life lived in us. Love contains no fear — indeed fully developed love expels every particle of fear" (I John 4:14 f.). We learn to love by loving and being loved. No wonder we are told over and over again to become a member in a Christian community that loves, genuinely.

Another way we help is by disciplining each other. "If your brother wrongs you," Christ said, "go have it out with him at once — just between the two of you." Ultimately, "if he still won't pay any attention, tell the matter to the church. And if he won't even listen to the church, then he must be to you just like a pagan — or a tax collector" (Matthew 18:17). If we see a brother sin, we are to pray for him (I John 5:16 f.). Or if a member of the community acts consciously in sin, we are to judge him, that he might be restored. If he will not repent we are to expel him from the fellowship (I Corinthians 5), for the church is to faithfully incarnate the life of God. Thus by setting and insisting on Christian standards of life and character we are to channel and guide the development of the life of God within one another.

There are many other ways we help, but all of them merely serve to amplify the main theme of this chapter, that growth in the Christian life *requires* a community of Christians. This does not necessarily mean a "church," as we call our religious organizations today. But it does mean a church as marked out in Scripture: an association of believers gathered together, and involved in the lives of one another, to encourage, to love, to discipline, to strengthen, and to sustain the budding life of God and character of God within each Christian.

7

The Mutuality of the Ministry

Imagine yourself taking part in the formation of a new church. As several families gather together and talk of the new congregation, one of the first concerns is sure to be, "Whom will we get to be the minister?" Whom can we invite to come and serve our church, to help us grow as Christians, to teach us, to exhort us, and to comfort us in time of sorrow? Feeling a need for help (and we all feel such a need), a church today looks outside itself to some one person who will come and minister.

Now, I am not about to attack the way our churches do business. Nor am I questioning the "pastor" role in the contemporary church. Churches do need leadership (a topic we'll look at in the next chapter). And Scripture seems to leave quite open the title we assign to our recognized leaders. So have a pastor if you will.

At the same time, please note the inherent contradiction to God's revealed way of doing things in His church in looking for help to any one person. When the New Testament speaks of ministry in a local church, it is a ministry of all believers to each other. "Teach and help one another along the right road," the Bible has it. We are not to look to any one person for the kind of help we need to grow in Christ, or to suppose that grace and guidance for the church will flow through the pastor alone.

Again, forgive me if I seem to attack our present church organization. My only desire here is to point up a concept: a concept utterly basic in understanding the functioning of the church, and utterly basic in guiding us to renewal. The concept is this: *the ministry is to be mutual.* The ministry is the function of the whole people of God.

The Ability to Contribute

In passages quoted early about the church as a body, the idea of "spiritual gift" was mentioned. Little was made of this concept then. But now, as we speak of the "ministry" of the church, we have to return to it. For ministry *is* to "serve one another with the particular gifts God has given each of you."

If I wanted to labor the point of this chapter, I might go back and underline "serve one another," and "gifts God has given each of you," before finishing the quotation. It goes on, ". . . as faithful dispensers of the magnificently varied grace of God. If any of you is a preacher [one of the gifts] then he should preach his message as from God. And in whatever way a man serves the Church he should do it recognizing the fact that God gives him his ability" (I Peter 4:9 f.).

This short passage sketches sharply the key features of ministry in Christ's Church; features which are developed in the "Body" passages of the Word of God. Briefly these features are that: (1) Each believer has a gift, a special ability from God. (2) The abilities and ministries differ. God's grace is said to be "magnificently varied." (3) The abilities are to be used in service in the church. These are the helping ministries each of us needs for the full development of the life of Christ within us. The ministry of each member in the whole community is essential, for we grow "by that which every joint supplies."

Each with a gift. As Paul thought of a planned journey to Rome he made a statement that at first is hard to understand. He gave a backward glance at the churches he had established in his long ministry, and expressed a sense of freedom to leave them "since my work in these places no longer needs my presence" (Romans 15:22). How could Paul abandon the churches he had founded? How could he have left each after so short a time, making only infrequent follow-up visits, and writing short letters of advice? It was because Paul understood the nature of the church, and he understood that God supplies all that we need to grow as Christians through each other.

He writes of God's plan for the nurture of the church in several places. Perhaps the most familiar of these is I Corinthians 12-14. "Men have different gifts," Paul wrote, "but it is the same Spirit who gives them. There are different ways of serving God, but it is the same Lord who is served. God works through different men in different ways, but it is the same God who achieves His purposes through them all. *Each man is given his gift by the Spirit that he may use it for the common good.*"

He repeats this truth in Romans. "Through the grace of God we [all] have different gifts."

"Just as you have many members in one physical body and these members differ in their functions, so we, though many in number, compose one body in Christ and are all members one of another. Through the grace of God we have different gifts. If your gift is preaching, let us preach to the limit of our vision. If it is serving others let us concentrate on our service; if it is teaching let us give all we have to our teaching; and if our gift be the stimulation of the faith of others let us set ourselves to it. Let the man who is called to give, give freely; let the man who wields authority think of his responsibilities; and let the man who feels sympathetic for his fellows act cheerfully" (Romans 12:4-8).

"The ministry" is thus divided among *all* the members of the body of Christ. Each is given an ability to contribute, and each is to use it fully.

The gifts differ. In the passage above we see what I take to be a representative (and not in any way an exhaustive) listing of the kind of abilities that make up the *ministry* of the church. Just a glance at them shows why it is reasonable to understand the "gifts" (as does I Peter) as abilities to contribute. Each ability listed here is one which is used interpersonally, socially. Our ability may be preaching, or stimulating the faith of others, or giving, or exercising authority, or simply feeling (and expressing) sympathy. Each of these abilities, and a myriad of others, are required to meet the complexity of human needs. Each will be needed by believers-in-relationship if the life of Christ in us, and our common life in Him, is to be nurtured and one which flourishes.

"God has arranged all the parts in the one body, according to his design. . . . The fact is that there are many parts, but only one body. So that the eye cannot say to the hand, 'I don't need you!' nor, again, can the head say to the feet, 'I don't need you!' On the contrary, these parts of the body which have no obvious function are the more essential to health; and to those parts of the body which seem to us to be less deserving of notice we have to allow the highest honor of function" (I Corinthians 12:18-23).

I suppose it is only normal that we focus attention on those in our churches with obvious functions. But we have failed to realize (and the spiritual level of American Christianity demonstrates the seriousness of this failure) that others, with *no obvious function,* "are the more essential to health."

This is a hard saying. It means that in our search for renewal we must resist looking to better theological education for our ministers, or to multiple staffs, or to better training for laymen in organizational positions. It means we must focus attention on those with "no obvious function," on the average layman, who, as a member of Christ's body, has been given an ability which in the nature of the church he *must* be permitted to use.

The abilities are "for the church." I say that the nature of the church demands that the layman use his gift "for the church." Scripture makes it quite clear that members of the church itself, other believers, are the recipients of the ministries.

In Corinthians Paul says each of us are given gifts "for the common good." These gifts are a family affair. They are for the "benefit of the Church" (1 Corinthians 14:5).

What we see then when we look at the teaching on spiritual gifts is the church, as people, involved in one another's lives — involved in sharing with others what they themselves have received from Christ. It is the members of Christ's body *being* with each other, and in their shared love and shared life discovering that the Spirit within each flows out. That the Spirit within taps the special ability He has given each to contribute, and so nurtures the life of God and forms the character of God in each believing individual.

This *is* the church. And this *is* the way God planned the ministry. Each of us is needed, and each has ability to contribute. So whatever forms we find for our church gatherings, and whatever our organizational structures, to bear the name "church" they must promote the mutual ministry that is God's ministry in His church.

An Aside

Shortly I intend to look at the question of church meetings and what was done in them. But before I do, two questions about gifts which are often raised should be answered.

The first has to do with such gifts as that of accomplishing physical healings and speaking in tongues. Are these included in my list of special abilities, or aren't they?

I don't intend to go into a thorough discussion of spiritual gifts here. This whole section is designed only to survey a part of ecclesiology, not to be an exhaustive text in theology. Nor do I care to try to convince anyone of my ideas about "should we" or "shouldn't we" expect to speak in tongues. My opinion on this shouldn't be too important to anyone.

What should be important is that, whether such gifts are given by the Spirit today or not, everyone understands that *every* believer has some special ability from God. And that this ability is given to enable him to minister to others (I Corinthians 12:7). Possession of an ability to "speak in tongues" is *not* the one sign of the Spirit's presence. The Bible says that God distributes to each of His children a special ability, "sovereignly, as he wills" (KJV). The particular gift or gifts we receive is dependent on His place for us in the body, but each believer has a gift.

It is also important to keep central the truth that gifts are given to enable us to contribute to the growth of other Christians. Thus in I Corinthians 14 the exercise of tongues in church is regulated, and the congregation is instructed to "set your hearts on preaching the Word of God, while not forbidding the use of 'tongues'" (14:39). As Paul says of tongues, "you may be thanking God splendidly, but it doesn't help the other man at all. I thank God that I have a greater gift of 'tongues' than any of you, yet when I am in church I would rather speak five words with my mind (which might teach something to other people) than ten thousand words in a 'tongue' which nobody understands."

Let's all then resist becoming "excitable children," and keep the biblical perspective on gifts. For gifts are God's granting of special abilities to each of us to contribute to the common good;

to take our place as *ministers* of the manifold grace of God to one another.

One other aspect of the biblical concept of gifts raises questions. In Ephesians 4 God's gifts to the church seem to be *men*, not special abilities to all individuals to minister. Thus a "special class" of ministers seem to be introduced: apostles, preachers of the Gospel, etc. Certainly the gifts given to different individuals equip them for different roles in the church. And some (if not all) of these men seem to function outside the framework of the local church as itinerant ministers to the whole church. But even here there is no *conflict* with the idea of mutual ministry. In fact, the Scripture says that these gifted men are given to the church "that Christians might be properly equipped for *their* service [e.g., ministry]." For it is only with every believer ministering that "the whole body might be built up until the time comes when, in the unity of common faith and common knowledge of the Son of God, we arrive at real maturity — that measure of development which is meant by 'the fullness of Christ.'"

Ministering in the Church

Every believer ministering sounds exciting and fulfilling, but it also sounds confusing. How practical is it to expect a mutual ministry to be implemented in our churches? How might such a ministry be carried out?

Several insights from Scripture suggest directions for us. At the same time, it seems to me that the particular style of our meetings is left quite open. No "scriptural order of service" can be found. No biblical prescription regulates fully the actions of the church as it gathers. However, there are principles, and within the framework of these principles God has given us (as He has every culture) the freedom to develop our own forms. He demands only that what emerges truly be the church, and function as the church.

The principles that seem to me both suggestive and limiting concern such issues as (1) what constitutes a local church, (2) when are mutual ministries normally exercised, and (3) what is to happen in a *meeting* of the church?

What is a local church? When twelve adult Jewish males lived in a community they were to form a synagogue. We have no such limits set for the church. Writing to Philemon Paul spoke of "the church that meets in your house" (verse 2). He sent his love in the letter to the Romans to "the little church that meets" in the house of Priscilla and Aquila (16:5). "A church" seems here to be equivalent to our "small group"!

Yet most of Paul's letters are addressed to larger communities of believers; one encompassing all believers within a large area, such as "the church of God at Corinth" (I Corinthians 1:2). The church at Jerusalem included thousands by actual count: on the day of Pentecost alone "about three thousand souls were added to the number of the disciples." This church continued to function throughout Acts as "a church," or as "the church at Jerusalem." The Bible records that the believers there "continued steadily learning the teaching of the apostles, and joined in their fellowship, in the breaking of bread, and in prayer." The unity of this large group was maintained, even though size dictated many smaller fellowship groups as well as great assemblies. "All the believers shared everything in common; they sold their possessions and goods and divided the proceeds among the fellowship according to individual need. Day after day they met by common consent in the Temple; they broke bread together in their homes, sharing meals with simple joy. They praised God continually and all the people respected them" (Acts 2:41-47).

It seems hard to fit this broad biblical usage of "church" into the meanings of today. To us "a church" means a particular group of people who worship in this building in contrast to that building ("the church at 2nd and Main"). Or perhaps it means Christians with this particular doctrinal slant which differs slightly from the slant of that group over there ("the Baptists and the Presbyterians each have a church on Fourth Avenue"). All this is foreign to the New Testament. There "the Church" refers always to the people of God, whether to all believers in a locality, or to a small group gathered in a home. The distinguishing feature of *a church* is simply this: *people who have the life of Christ within gather to share that life with one another.*

It is interesting to note that no factor other than this was allowed to distinguish groups of believers in the New Testament. The Corinthian church was, at the time of Paul's letter, divided into factions, each loyal to a different person or to doctrines associated with a leader. In writing of the meetings of the church to hold communion Paul criticizes the believers because "when you meet for worship I hear that you split up into small groups, and I think there must be truth in what I hear. For there must be cliques among you or your favorite leaders would not be so conspicuous" (11:17 f.). The church failed to recognize the unity that was essentially theirs in Christ, and opened themselves to censure. They had lost the very genius of relationship which could constitute them as a church.

Whenever a church is gathered (and whatever the size of the gathering — home-size, or city-wide), it is essential that the nature of the church be recognized. The church is one: the church is the body of Christ in which all who share His life are full members.

What all this means to me is simply this: *a church* is constituted wherever and whenever believers meet together. "When two or three are gathered in my name," Christ said, "there am I in the midst." And when two or three believers are gathered to share the life of Christ, *there* is a church.

Thus a church may meet in a home; it may meet in a hall. It may meet as two or three families for prayer and praise. It may meet as thousands at an Easter sunrise service. It is only and always the coming together of believers which constitutes a church.

When are mutual ministries exercised? The ministry of believers is not dependent on the coming together of the church. Much of our ministry to other Christians is performed informally, in the context of normal daily life. In their daily lives Paul says older women are "to be examples of the good life, so that the younger women may learn to love their husbands and their children." Families, the Bible says, are to be hospitable. Even talking with one another is seen as an occasion for ministry. "The keynote of your conversation should not be nastiness or silliness or flippancy, but a sense of all that we owe to God" (Ephesians 5:4). In all our relationships, a genuine love for others is to be expressed, and thus we constantly minister.

The New Testament over and over again focuses on the importance of genuine love in our living together as Christians. When Paul wrote to the Corinthians they were uncertain about meat sacrificed to idols — should we, or shouldn't we, eat it? Paul points out that *knowledge* forces us to conclude that "no idol has any real existence." Thus we are free to eat. At the same time he encouraged the believers to make their decisions on a different basis. "Remember," he writes, "that while knowledge may make a man look big, it is only love that can make him grow to his full stature. For whatever a man may know, he still has a lot to learn: but if he loves God, he is opening his whole life to the Spirit of God." Thus we are to live with one another in love. "Surely you would not want your superior knowledge to bring spiritual disaster to a weaker brother for whom Christ died? When you sin like this and damage the weak conscience of your brethren you really sin against Christ. This makes me determined that, if there is any possibility of meat injuring my brother, I will have none of it as long as I live, for fear I might do him harm" (I Corinthians 8:1 f.).

Our total lives with others are an occasion for ministry, and all we are, all we do, has the potential of helping. Through our daily relationships with other believers God works to build up His church.

The meetings of the church. While ministering to one another is clearly not limited to the official gatherings of the church, one of the major concerns in the renewal movement today is, rightly, *What should happen in a church meeting?* Is the principle of mutual ministry operative here or, as today, are our gatherings merely sessions in which the silent majority come to sit rather than to share?

It is clear that the New Testament church had meetings. James is disturbed because sometimes the world's way of viewing men carried over into church meetings. "Suppose one man comes into your meeting well dressed and with a gold ring on his finger, and another man, obviously poor, arrives in shabby clothes?" Are we to pay more attention to the rich man? Never! For if we do we "are making class distinctions in (y)our mind . . . a very bad thing" (James 2:1 f.). For in the church of Christ all are equally important, all equal participants in the life of God. But, *what happens in these meetings?*

We can suppose that different procedures were fitting then as now for different situations — that when three thousand gathered as the church they did not conduct themselves the same way as thirty. Yet all we have in Scripture to give us insight into church meetings is found in a few snatches from Acts and the epistles. We know from Acts that the church often gathered to pray

(Acts 12, etc.). We can surmise that "psalms and hymns and Christian songs, singing God's praises with joyful hearts" (Colossians 3:16) also played a part in church life. We know that the brethren came together to worship and take communion (I Corinthians 11), and thus show Christ's death, till He comes. But we still have to ask, What else happened?

The two passages which give us clear indication that the principle of *mutuality* did dominate the meetings of the church, and that the special abilities given each believer made each a potential participant and contributor in the gathered church, are found in Hebrews 10 and I Corinthians 14. The first passage is strongly suggestive; the second invites us into a church gathered for ministry. This last phrase, gathered for ministry, is important. Other passages do show the church gathered for decision making. For, if you will, a "spiritual business meeting." But there is no other that shows us the inner workings of a church gathered as the church to minister to the body.

In Hebrews 10:24, 25, the writer exhorts the believers, "let us not hold aloof from our church meetings, as some do." The context provides the reason for this charge. "Let us think how we can encourage one another to love and do good deeds . . . Let us do all we can to help another's faith, and this the more earnestly as we see the final day drawing near." Why not hold aloof from church meetings? Because in the meetings of the gathered church we can encourage one another to love and do good deeds; because there we can help one another's faith; because the meeting *gives us an opportunity to minister!*

This suggestion that the meetings of the church are to be occasions for mutual ministry, in which all have opportunity to participate, is confirmed in Paul's portrait of a Corinthian church meeting.

In chapter 14 of his first letter Paul is expressing regulations to correct excesses in the use of tongues. In one paragraph of his instructions he sketches a meeting of the church, showing us how other spiritual gifts are used in a mutual ministry. The paragraph follows, with particularly significant portions in italics.

"If the question of speaking with a 'tongue' arises, confine the speaking to two or three at the most and have someone to interpret what is said. If you have no interpreter, then let the speaker with a 'tongue' keep silent in the church and speak only to himself and God. *Don't have more than two or three preachers, either, while the others think over what has been said. But should a message of truth come to one who is seated, then the original speaker should stop talking. For in this way you can all have opportunity to give a message, one after the other, and everyone will learn something and everyone will have his faith stimulated. The spirit of a true preacher is under that preacher's control, for God is not God of disorder but of harmony, as is plain in all the churches"* (I Corinthians 14:26-34).

It is clear that meetings of the church were open ones — not open in the sense that they lacked discipline, but open in the sense that "all have opportunity to give a message, one after the other." Each person was potentially a minister, as well as one who was to listen and think over what had been said. Each was potentially a stimulator of the faith of others, as well as a learner. While several men may have been designated "speakers," all were free, and expected, to take part as God led.

Now, I don't intend from this passage to set up any "biblical pattern" for church meetings today. I doubt very much that this was intended by God. I truly do believe the biblical principles permit extremely flexible application from culture to culture, and time to time. But I am convinced that the whole line of argument through this book thus far, the entire New Testament concept of the church, demands that the meetings of a church be structured for mutual ministry. That there must be openness in all our meetings to permit the participation of any and every member. This is a principle which is basic, significant, and crucial in the renewal of the church.

Each believer does have a special ability from God to contribute to the common good. The life, and the meetings, of the church *must* recognize the existence of these gifts, and make provision for their exercise.

8

Leadership in the Church

Recently I talked with a pastor who is very disturbed by some of the things I have written and said. He deeply fears the apparent loss of individuality to the group, and he is particularly concerned about "undermining the leadership" of the churches. After all, in a fellowship of believers in which *all* are ministers, what role is left for leaders? If laymen in our churches today take this teaching seriously, what will happen to the pastor in the local church?

I will have more to say on this last question later in the book. Right now it is more important that we look at principles which must undergird all of our developed practices. Certainly his fears do raise questions of principle. Are all believers, who *are* equally ministers, equal in other ways? Does the mutual ministry principle negate all need for spiritual leaders?

A glance through the New Testament shows that these two concepts cannot be contradictory. That the call of all believers to minister, and the appointment of some believers to leadership, are both features of the life of the New Testament church.

As Paul and his fellow missionaries won converts throughout the Hellenized world they established churches. And, the Bible tells us, "they appointed elders for them in each church, and with prayer and fasting commended these men to the Lord in whom they had believed" (Acts 14:19 f.). Writing to Timothy, Paul gave instructions on the kind of men to be chosen for local church leadership. He addressed his letter to Philippi, not to the usual "church of God at . . .", but "to the bishops, deacons, and all true Christians at Philippi" (Philippians 1:1). Apparently this local church not only had recognized leadership, but there were several leaders and at least two offices: bishop (or elder) and deacon.

So we certainly cannot suggest that granting ability to minister to each believer obviates the need for leadership. Nor did the presence of leaders alter the need for all to minister. Even Paul (who surely had more to give than the greatest among us today) guarded against the impression that he was just a dispenser of the grace of God to others, and not a recipient of that grace from them. "I want to bring you some spiritual strength," Paul wrote the Romans, and then hastened to add, "and that will mean that I shall be strengthened by you, each of us helped by the other's faith" (Romans 1:12). The principles of mutual ministry and spiritual leadership stand side by side.

At this point perhaps, I ought to make clear what I want to do in this chapter — and what I do not want to do. Most simply stated, I want to keep the focus of our thinking on the basic issues, and to avoid endless arguments about what officers we ought to have in our churches today, and whether today's "pastor" role is valid scripturally, and whether or not our ministers should be paid, etc. There are several reasons for avoiding such questions. One has been stated before: Scriptural principles allow us a broad range of applications. Dr. Gene Getz suggests a concept that I feel is very helpful here. It is the concept of *functional equivalency*. The issue which we should be concerned with is not, "Have we reproduced the New Testament church and its offices," but, "Does our church leadership today function in the same way as did the leadership of the New Testament church?" Call a man what you will — pastor, teaching elder, preaching elder, brother, deacon, president, etc. Equivalence of function is the issue, and nothing else.

And so I feel that the issue we should stick with is this: What is the biblical concept of leadership? And, how does leadership in the church function?

This does not mean that I have no opinions on the other kind of questions — I have. But I don't believe these areas are vital to our understanding of church leadership. For instance, I believe it is perfectly all right for a leader in the local church, or several leaders, to be supported by the church so full time can be given to the ministry. As the Bible says, "elders with a gift of leadership should be considered worthy of respect, and of adequate salary, particularly if they work hard at their preaching and teaching" (II Timothy 5:17). But this doesn't mean that a church *has* to have salaried men in its membership. In most instances where the New Testament mentions financial help it seems to refer to the temporary support of itinerant ministers (those men who were gifts to the church, which we mentioned last chapter). So "to pay or not to pay" isn't really a relevant question.

Other questions may be more significant — such as whether there is to be one leader in a local church or several. Here I can find no case in which local leadership was limited to one person. All New Testament references are to elders (plural), none to "the elder" (e.g., leader) of the church at such-and-such. But even this question is less significant than the points at issue in this chapter. If we understand what leadership is, and how church leaders function, the details can be worked out locally. Whatever is decided it *must* have a functional relationship to the leadership of the New Testament church. Only when the leadership of the church is patterned on New Testament principles will our churches find the renewal we all seek.

The Biblical Concept of Leadership

I suggested in earlier chapters that God's way of looking at things is different from man's. How clearly this is illustrated in the New Testament concept of leadership!

Two major passages in the gospels introduce us to the kind of leadership appropriate to Christ's church. In one passage Christian leadership is contrasted with the spiritual leadership of the scribes and Pharisees in Israel. In the other Christian leadership is contrasted with that of civil rulers. In each, a sharp contrast is drawn between the implication of *superiority* in the normal way of thinking about leadership, and the implication of *servanthood* inherent in Christ's.

Then Jesus addressed the crowds and his disciples. "The scribes and the Pharisees speak with the authority of Moses," he told them, "so you must do what they tell you and follow their instructions. But you must not imitate their lives! For they preach what they do not practice. They pile up back-breaking burdens and lay them on other men's shoulders — yet they themselves will not raise a finger to move them. Their whole lives are planned with an eye to effect. They increase the size of their phylacteries and lengthen the tassels of their robes; they love seats of honor at dinner parties and front places in the synagogues. They love to be greeted with respect in public places and to have men call them 'rabbi'! Don't you ever be called 'rabbi' — you have only one teacher, and all of you are brothers. And don't call any human being 'father' — for you have one Father and he is in Heaven. And you must not let people call you 'leader' — for you have only one leader, Christ! The only 'superior' among you is the one who serves the others. For every man who promotes himself will be humbled, and every man who learns to be humble will find promotion" (Matthew 23: 1-12).

The spiritual leadership in the Israel of Christ's day exercised authority, but were neither examples nor servants of God's people. And thus they stood condemned.

The theme of power and servanthood also is foremost in this bit of private instruction to the disciples.

You know that the rulers of the heathen lord it over them and that their great ones have absolute power? But it must not be so among you. No, whoever among you wants to be great must become the servant of you all, and if he wants to be first among you he must become your slave — just as the Son of Man has not come to be served but to serve, and to give his life to set many others free (Matthew 20:25-28).

When we think of *leadership* in Christ's terms, the normal connotations must be put behind us. Leadership in the church is not related to authority: Christ only is our "leader." Christ only is the Head of His church. Leadership in the church is not related to self-aggrandizement: the leader is to be, like Christ, the servant of all. In this context Paul's instructions concerning the selection of church leaders can be easily understood. For a man to wear the mantle of leadership humbly, and to lose himself in service to others, his *character* will be far more important than his accomplishments. What he *is* is crucial. For the office of bishop, Paul advises Timothy:

> . . . a man must be of blameless reputation, he must be married to one wife only, and be a man of self-control and discretion. He must be a man of disciplined life; he must be hospitable and have the gift of teaching. He must be neither intemperate nor violent, but gentle. He must not be a controversialist nor must he be fond of money-grabbing. He must have proper authority in his own household, and be able to control and command the respect of his children. (For if a man cannot rule in his own house how can he look after the Church of God?) He must not be a beginner in the faith, for fear of his becoming conceited and sharing the devil's downfall. He should, in addition to the above qualifications, have a good reputation with the outside world, in case his good name is attacked and he is caught by the devil that way.
>
> Deacons, similarly, should be men of serious outlook and sincere convictions. They too should be temperate and not greedy for money. They should hold the mystery of the faith with complete sincerity.
>
> Let them serve a period of probation first, and only serve as deacons if they prove satisfactory. Their wives should share their serious outlook, and must be women of discretion and self-control — women who can be trusted. Deacons should be men with only one wife, able to control their children and manage their own households properly. Those who do well as deacons earn for themselves a certain legitimate standing, as well as gaining confidence and freedom in the Christian faith (1 Timothy 3:1-13).

The church, then, is to select as leaders those who have made distinct progress in the Christian life, and whose characters show definite evidence of a transformation wrought by God's Spirit.

But far more is implied in the concept of *servant-leader* than this. One of the features of the contemporary church which disturbs me is the insidious sense of *distance* which exists in most churches between our pastors and our people. In saying this I am charging neither side with sin. I am merely observing that a distinction is often made between a pastor and people which strikes at the heart of the servant-leader concept, and which makes the exercise of a truly scriptural leadership most difficult.

Somehow most of us insist on locating the pastor somewhere "above" us, and in viewing him as somehow *different from* us. Aware of this, a pastor often feels forced to maintain a facade of perfection, lest he "destroy the confidence" of the people in him. And he is often told to resist developing close personal friendships within his church lest he be thought to "play favorites." And thus a real and deadly distance develops.

This is tragic, because scriptural leadership requires that the leader be completely open in his relationships with others, and that he become deeply involved in their lives.

The Apostle Paul stands here as a model of Christian leadership. His life and ministry were marked by both openness and involvement. He often threw open his life to those in the churches, even when his critics might use the things he revealed against him. Never did he hide his own spiritual struggles for fear others "might lose confidence" in him!

"Our dear friends in Corinth," he wrote in one letter, "we are hiding nothing from you and our hearts are absolutely open to you" (II Corinthians 6:11). He demonstrated this throughout his letter, but especially in an early paragraph, in which he made a confession few of us would dare make today. "We should like you, our brothers, to know something of what we went through in Asia. At that time we were completely overwhelmed; the burden was more than we could bear; in fact we told ourselves that this was the end. Yet we believe now that we had this experience of coming to the end of our tether that we might learn to trust, not in ourselves, but in God who can raise the dead" (II Corinthians 1:8, 9).

The ability of a leader to help and guide others *never* rests on his own accomplishments or perfection. Only as he has discovered the grace of God in the extremities of his experience can he share that which will help others in theirs. And only as he shares those personal needs which led him to discover the sufficiency of God; only as he reveals his humanness, can he be a channel of blessing to others. There is no room here for the distant professional. There is no room in the leadership of the church of Christ for the man who must pretend he has arrived! The servant-leader must share himself, and give himself in his ministry to the church.

Nor is there room for *impersonal* leadership, that withdraws from depth-relationships with others in the body. Paul again serves as our model. He reminds the Thessalonians:

> We made no attempt to win honor from men, either from you or anybody else. Our attitude among you was one of tenderness, rather like that of a devoted nurse among her babies. Because we loved you, it was a joy to us to give you not only the gospel of God but our very hearts — so dear did you become to us. Our struggles and hard work, my brothers, must be still fresh in your minds. Day and night we worked so that our preaching of the gospel to you might not cost you a penny. You are witnesses, as is God himself, that our life among you believers was honest, straightforward and above criticism. *You will remember how we dealt with each of you personally* (italics mine), like a father with his own children, stimulating your faith and courage and giving you instruction. Our only object was to help you live lives worthy of the God who has called you to share the splendor of his own kingdom (II Thessalonians 2:1-13).

Thus, in the full investment of the servant-leader in the lives of individual believers, as well as in group ministries, the task of the leadership in the church is fulfilled.

Now, none of this defines the function of leadership in the church, and this we must do. However, it does clear away some of the chaff in our thinking about leadership. It does help us realize that leadership in the church must depend, not on training or degrees, but on growth in Christ. That leadership in the church is not to be approached from the standpoint of "What is the authority of the leader?" but "How does the leader serve." It must take the view that leaders are not *different from* others in the church, but like them in all respects, and are to be deeply involved in the lives and experiences of individuals.

The Role of Leaders in the Church

Apparently some theologians enjoy and set great store by paradoxes. They spend a great deal of time developing opposite and apparently contradictory truths. I confess that I don't enjoy this kind of theologizing. I feel much more comfortable attempting to harmonize truths than attempting to develop apparent inconsistencies.

Yet at this point, having said some critical things about "authority," I want to take the other side and assert the authority of church leadership. I want to assert it because it definitely is a biblical concept. Paul mentions — and at times used — his authority as an Apostle in dealing with church problems and with self-assertive individuals. And the writer to the Hebrews charges believers to "obey your rulers and recognize their authority. They are like men standing guard over your spiritual good, and they have great responsibility. Try to make their work a pleasure and not a burden — by so doing you will help not only them but yourselves" (Hebrews 12:16, 17).

Paul told the elders of the church at Ephesus to "be on your guard for yourselves and for every flock of which the Holy Spirit has made you guardians — you are to be shepherds to the Church of God, which he won at the cost of his own blood" (Acts 20:28). Surely God who has given the leadership of His church such responsibilities has also equipped them with authority necessary to carry them out!

Actually, a reading of the New Testament impresses us with the fact that authority is not, in itself, bad. God expects men to function within the framework of life-as-it-is. And this demands adjustment to authority in many of our human relationships. Parents have authority over their children. And the children are to obey. Masters had authority over their servants. The book of I Peter develops the theme of submission-within-authority patterns quite completely, and shows that willing submission to those over us is pleasing to God, as a recognition of His sovereignty. And submission is possible for us because God does exercise control over our circumstances for His glory and for our good. So certainly there is nothing intrinsically wrong with postulating authority for the leaders of the church. There is nothing inherently contradictory to authority in the servant-leader concept of church leadership.

It seems to me that our problem in understanding any apparent conflict lies in the unfortunate connotations of "authority" based on its exercise in the world. Authority exercised in the church of God is distinctively different. And the difference lies in *the way the leader exercises authority*, not in the fact of his authority.

I suggest, then, that when we understand the way a leader

in the church is to lead (that is, when we see his roles in the fellowship of believers), our problems in this area will be lessened.

In writing to Timothy (a man who served as a missionary and troubleshooter, rather than as an elder or leader in a local congregation), Paul gave instructions which help us see the two primary roles of the Christian leader; the two primary ways in which the leader exercises the authority he has received from God. "Keep a critical eye both on your own life and on the teaching you give," Timothy was warned. It is these two issues which are crucial in the exercise of leadership in the church.

Your own life. I suggested earlier that Paul might well stand as a model of Christian leadership. I want to suggest now that *this* is one of the two major roles of the Christian leader: to model. To be an example. To be a concrete expression of the life the believer is to lead.

This theme often appears when leadership is discussed in the Bible. To Titus Paul said, "Let your own life stand as a pattern of good living. In all your teaching show the strictest regard for truth, and show that you appreciate the seriousness of the matters you are dealing with" (Titus 2:7, 8). To Timothy he said, "You will be doing your duty as Christ's minister if you will remind your church members of these things, and you will show yourselves as one who owes his strength to the truth of the faith he has absorbed and the sound teaching he has followed" (I Timothy 4:6).

Peter, writing to fellow leaders, also focused on their roles as examples:

> Now may I who am myself an elder say a word to you, my fellow elders? I speak as one who actually saw Christ suffer, and as one who will share with you the glories that are to be unfolded to us. I urge you then to see that your "flock of God" is properly fed and cared for. Accept the responsibility of looking after them willingly and not because you feel you can't get out of it, doing work not for what you can make, but because you are really concerned for their well-being. You should aim not at being "little tin gods," but as examples of Christian living in the eyes of the flock committed to your charge. And then, when the chief shepherd reveals himself, you will receive that crown of glory which cannot fade (I Peter 5:1-4).

This is leadership that leads, not pushes. Which demonstrates, not demands. No wonder Hebrews can say of such men, "Remember how they lived, and imitate their faith" (Hebrews 13:7).

The teaching you give. This is the other primary responsibility of leadership. To teach. Paul wrote Titus that an elder, to be charged with spiritual responsibility for the church, must be "a man who takes his stand on the orthodox faith, so that he can by sound teaching both stimulate faith and confute opposition" (Titus 1:5). And it is in this context, that of teaching, that his *authority* is specifically referred to.

A quick look through Paul's letters to Timothy is instructive here. In I Timothy 1:18 Timothy is told to set out "to battle for the right, armed only with your faith and a clear conscience." The Word of God and a transformed life are sufficient equipment. Thus equipped, the leader is to "concentrate on your reading and on your preaching and teaching," fully using "the gift that was given to you in the proclaiming of God's Word" (I Timothy 4:12-14). A critical eye is to be kept both "upon your own life and on the teaching you give."

In a second letter Timothy is told that "everything you have heard me teach in public you should in turn entrust to reliable men, who will be able to pass it on to others" (II Timothy 2:2). Not only the content of the teaching is important, however. The attitude, too, is crucial. "The Lord's servant must not be a man of strife: he must be kind to all, ready and able to teach: he must have patience and the ability to gently correct those who oppose his message. He must always bear in mind the possibility that God will give them a different outlook, and that they may come to know the truth" (II Timothy 2:24, 25).

The authority of the teacher need not be asserted — the message authenticates itself as God's Spirit applies it in power. The teacher's authority rests in his ordination by God and in the faithfulness with which he lives and teaches His message. The authority is intrinsic. Thus the Christian leader has no need to demand or to scheme, to politic or to plot. He is free to trust his only resources: the faith, and a clear conscience.

Thus Timothy is "solemnly charged" to "preach the Word of God. Never lose your sense of urgency, in season or out of season. Prove, correct and encourage, using the utmost patience in your teaching." As a leader he is to remain, and "to stand fast in all that you are doing, meeting whatever suffering this may involve. Go on steadily preaching the gospel, and carry out to the full the commission that God gave you" (II Timothy 4:1-5).

This is the dual role of leadership in the church, and it carries with it its own unique stamp of God's approval, thus bearing its own authority.

This concept of the *self-authenticating nature of leadership in the church* solves, for me, questions raised by juxtaposition of the concepts of servant-leaders and authority. The Holy Spirit lives in Christ's church, and that Spirit is fully able to bring harmony to the church, to bring all into obedience to their Head, as leaders in the church pattern their ministries on His Word.

This seems to me to be confirmed in warnings to leaders. They are to trust nothing but the power of example and the teaching of the truth. "Don't reprimand a senior member of your church; appeal to him as a father," Timothy is told. "Treat the young men as brothers, and the older women as mothers. Treat the younger women as sisters, and no more" (I Timothy 5:1, 2). Being a leader means being a servant, and no servant commands.

Paul himself serves as a beautiful example of this leadership style in his little letter to Philemon. Concerning Philemon's runaway slave, Onesimus, Paul says in his deeply loving note, "although I could rely on my authority in Christ and dare to *order* you to do what I consider right, I am not doing that. No, I am appealing to that love of yours, a simple personal appeal from Paul the old man, in prison for Jesus Christ's sake. I am appealing for my child, Onesimus!

"Oh, I know you have found him pretty useless in the past but he is going to be useful now, to both of us. I am sending him back to you: *will you receive him as my son, part of me* (italics mine)? I should have dearly loved to have kept him with me: he could have done what you would have done — looked after me here in prison for the Gospel's sake. But I would do nothing without consulting you first, for if you have a favor to give me, let it be spontaneous and not forced from you by circumstances" (7-14).

In the life of the church, authority which *can order*, is to appeal. And in the life of the church the man who leads by example and gentle instruction is the man who will successfully fulfill his responsibilities.

So it is with our leaders today. We can call it what we will, but men gifted by God to lead our renewed congregations will lead by example and by teaching. *And they will not take to themselves other roles which are not theirs to take.*

9

The Structure of the Church

When I sketched the roles of leadership in the church in the previous chapter, I failed (purposely) to raise one important issue: decision-making. It is time to raise that issue now.

In most human organizations decision-making is a function of leadership, of "top management." Others in an organization may make certain decisions that relate to their jobs, sections, departments, or divisions. But these decisions are normally limited to the implementation of the broader policy, decisions which are made at the top level.

This way of doing business has tended to carry over into church government, with the added attraction in congregational churches of confirmation of such decisions by majority vote. So our church boards and our pastors have become, at times, decision-makers *for* the church, rather than men charged with carrying out the decisions *of* the church.

I don't wish to suggest that a congregational meeting should be held for every expenditure of $10.00 on Sunday school supplies. I do question our general approach to making decisions, and I must. For decision-making is integrally related to the nature, and thus the structure, of the church. To understand the structure of the church, we have to understand how the decision making process operates in the Body of Christ.

When this feature of the life of the church is marked out, all that we have seen before can be fitted together, and the basic biblical features of church organization viewed as a whole. On this framework we can rebuild the contemporary church.

Decision-making in the Church

Earlier in this section we noted that the Headship of the church is reserved to Christ. "God has placed everything under the power of Christ and has set him up as head of everything for the Church," says Ephesians. "For the Church is his body, and in that body lives fully the one who fills the whole wide universe" (1:22, 23). If Christ truly is the Head, the direction of the church is for Him. *He* is our "top management." If He truly is the Head, the experience of the early church ("the Holy Spirit spoke to them, saying, 'Set Barnabas and Saul apart for me for the task to which I have called them'" [Acts 13:2]) should be our experience too. Christ should make the decisions for His church, and we, His body, should carry them out.

Thus the question of decision-making resolves itself into another. It is not a problem of "Who makes the decisions in the church?" It is a problem of *communication*. "How does Christ communicate *His* decision to the church?" What is the method, and what are the marks, of true communication?

At this point the theological and actual *unity* of the church seems to me especially significant. At this point, *the church is one.* Let's remember here that there is within the church much room for individual freedom, for individual responsibility to Christ. "One man believes that he may eat anything; another man, without this strong conviction, is a vegetarian. The meateater should not despise the vegetarian, nor should the vegetarian condemn the meateater — they should reflect that God has accepted them both. After all, who are you to criticize the servant of somebody else, especially when that somebody else is God?" In many matters believers *are* to make individual decisions. As the Bible says, "Christ is the Head of every man." Christ is not only Head of the *church*. Thus "every man [is to] be definite in his own convictions" (cf. Romans 14:1 f.).

Individual freedom is not in question here. In fact, I assert it, and insist that it is not the function of the church to limit freedom, short of sin. The function of the church is to develop strong individuals, believers who will be mature in Christ, strong men and women in their own right — not to force individuals into conformity with all, or create a dependency which hinders them from relating to God apart from the others.

While there are, then, many decisions each of us *should* make for ourselves, there are other decisions which do affect the Body. And decisions which affect the church are to be made by all the church together, acting as the *one* they truly are in Christ. The issues they face may range from doctrinal disputes (Acts 15) to problems of discipline (I Corinthians 6); from judging a dispute between believers (I Corinthians 6) to giving an offering to meet the needs of others (II Corinthians 8, 9). Whatever the issue, *if it affects the whole church* it is a concern of the Body. And then it is the concern of the whole (or local) body affected to discern together the will of God, and to do it.

Clearly then we see the reason for the biblical insistence on church unity. How, if "all the time there is jealousy and squabbling among you," and the church is thus "living just like men of the world," can Christ's will for the church be discovered? The church *must* "make it your aim to be at one in the Spirit." As members of one body, with "one God, one Father of us all, who is the one over all, the one working through all and the one living in all" we are to be all, *as one*, responsive to Him (Ephesians 4).

This principle of *joint decision-making* in matters having to do with the church, in which all believers (as they are equally members of the body) are to take part, can be demonstrated in a number of ways.

The basic principle is clearly defined in Philippians chapter 2, along with practical guidelines for its implementaton in the church. The passage begins with an exhortation to the church. As they have experienced Christ, they are to "live together in harmony, live together in love, as though you had only one mind and one spirit between you."

The *attitude* of believers toward each other is crucial in attaining this unity. All are to reproduce the attitude of Christ, seen in His self-emptying when He came among us to live and to die. "Never act from motives of rivalry or personal vanity, but in humility think more of one another than you do of yourselves.

None of you should think only of his own affairs, but each should learn to see things from other people's point of view."

In this context of "one mind and one spirit" the church is urged to "work out your own deliverance with a proper sense of awe and responsibility" for "it is God who is at work within you, to will and to do His good purpose."*

It is clear that in this context, as in Philippians 1, "deliverance" is a better rendering of the thought than "salvation." The eternal state of Paul or the Philippians is not in question. What is at stake is the solution to difficulties in which each finds himself, the deliverance from uncertainty to full knowledge and the accomplishment of God's will. This deliverance the Philippians are to work out together, knowing that God is at work among them, to communicate His will and accomplish His purpose.

Such assurance is open to every church. As we discover in renewal the unity which is ours as assemblies of believers, we will rediscover the exciting reality of Christ's personal direction. We will work out, together, the opportunities and the problems facing each congregation. Facing new situations, the early church utilized this problem-solving method.

Soon after the ascension, Peter sensed a need for a man to be chosen to take the place of Judas and fill out the number of the Apostles (Acts 1:15 f.). He brought this to the brothers — "there were about a hundred and twenty present at the time" — and the company put forward two candidates. At this time the believers cast lots to discover the one God had chosen (the last recorded time this method was used in the church). The main point to note is that even here, before the church was constituted as a Body, *leaders did not act on their own* in making decisions. They brought the question to the brothers, and apparently after some discussion, it was the whole company that put forward the two qualified candidates.

Soon the Jewish council became concerned about the Christian movement (Acts 4:13 f.). They put pressure on Peter and John not to speak any more of Jesus. These leaders "went back to their friends and reported to them what the chief priests and elders had said to them. When they heard of it they raised their

---

*At this point I depart from Phillips, and resort to the ASV, which gives a better rendering of the original.

voices to God in united prayer. . . ." Again need had brought the church *together,* to turn to God and seek His will. And "when they had prayed their meeting-place was shaken; they were all filled with the Holy Spirit and spoke the Word of God fearlessly."

In this same context we are told that the church met and acted "by common consent" (5:12b). The unified church met to face their problems, to discover and to do God's will in the strength He provided.

When a dispute arose about the division of the resources of the church, the twelve Apostles "summoned the whole body of the disciples together" (Acts 6:1-4). Peter suggested the appointment of men with good reputation to be in charge of the daily distribution of food, and said to the community, "you, our brothers, must look round and pick out from your number seven men of good reputation who are both practical and spiritually-minded and we will put them in charge of this matter. This brief speech met with unanimous approval, and they [the church] chose. . . ."

In this situation, too, the leadership (endowed with an Apostolic authority few today would claim!) did not attempt to solve the problem *for* the church. They involved the whole church in working through a suggested solution which had been received with "unanimous approval."

When Peter broke tradition by entering the house of Cornelius while winning this Gentile and his household to Christ (Acts 11), many in the church were upset. "You actually went in and shared a meal with uncircumcised men!" Peter explained what had happened, and how God had given the Gentiles faith in Christ and the gifts of the Spirit which had marked the formation of the Body on Pentecost (Acts 2). When the church heard this "they had no further objections to raise. And they praised God, saying, 'Then obviously God has given to the Gentiles as well the gift of repentance which leads to life!'" Here again the leader accepted the right of the church to challenge his actions, and the church recognized God's will and rejoiced in it, *even though it was contradictory to their whole way of thinking!*

When the Antioch church was warned of a famine coming, "the disciples determined to send relief to the brothers in Judaea, each contributing as he was able. This they did, sending their contributions to the elders there personally through Barnabas and Saul" (Acts 11:27-30). Again it was the "disciples" who *decided*.

A crucial period in the life of the young church saw it divided into parties. One, the "Pharisee party," held that Gentile converts to Christ must be circumcised and place themselves under the authority of Mosaic law. Men of this persuasion from the Jerusalem church went to Antioch and taught. The Antioch fellowship was troubled, and sent a delegation back to Jerusalem to confer "with the apostles and elders about the whole question." This conference is reported in Acts 15. In the report we can discern the method by which a group of believers normally arrives at a knowledge of the will of God. First, the issues were thoroughly and openly discussed. James finally expressed an opinion with which all the members of the council could agree. "I am firmly of the opinion that we should not put any additional obstacles before any Gentiles who are turning toward God. Instead, I think we should write them telling them to avoid [in order not to offend the sensibilities of Jewish brethren] anything polluted by idols, fornication [which I take here to indicate marriage in a degree prohibited in Jewish culture but not in Gentile — such as our restrictions concerning marriage of first cousins], eating the meat of strangled animals, or tasting blood. For after all, for many generations now Moses has had his preachers in every city and has been read aloud in the synagogues every Sabbath day."

At first glance this chapter would seem to indicate the decision here was reached by an aristocracy of leaders and the church was not involved. Certainly it would have been hard for the thousands who made up the church at Jerusalem to meet together for such an extended discussion. Yet we do have indication that the sense of the discussion was conveyed to the church, and that the church as a whole felt involved. For the passage continues, "then the Apostles, the elders *and the whole Church* agreed to choose representatives and send them to Antioch with Paul and Barnabas." The representatives carried a message from "the apostles and elders who are your brothers," reassuring the Gentiles that "since we have heard that some of our number have caused you deep distress and have unsettled your minds by giving you a message that certainly did not originate with us" those in Jerusalem had "unanimously agreed" to correct their teaching; a decision which "seemed right to the Holy Spirit and to us."

This passage then does introduce the possibility that the leadership of the larger church (the church at Jerusalem, or the church at Chicago) might reach decisions affecting it. But it also leaves room for communication with and participation of the church at large. We have no way of telling how long the discussion at Jerusalem took, or how deeply each small unit of the church was involved in seeking God's will.

More important, however, is the indication of the place of "unanimous agreement" (mentioned several times in this passage) as significant in church decision-making. It focuses our attention on the key role of *consensus*.

In summary, then, the experience of the early church agrees with the principle drawn from Philippians 2. And this principle is inherent in the very nature of the church as one body. Coming together in the unity of the Spirit, in discussion and reliance on the Spirit of God, with full reference to the Word of God (cf. Acts 1, 15), the church perceives the will of God and arrives at a consensus.

To this point I've resisted referring to church history, but not because I have no sense of connection with it. In church history there *should* be groups who have attempted to build their common life on New Testament principles. There should be many men today who sound much alike — if what they say is truly reflective of the teaching of the Word of God.

But I have tried to avoid identification with any of them. One reason for this is an idea I have about the way the human mind works. We like to pigeonhole. We are all prone to struggle with an idea until we can classify it — and then forget it. Somehow a classified idea is easier to dismiss. "Oh, she's just a little paranoid," someone may remark about a friend. With this classification made, we feel much more free to dismiss her and her needs from our concern! I'm afraid that this same thing might happen with what I am saying. "Oh, he sounds like an Anabaptist." Or, "Guess he's been reading Watchman Nee." So identified, all the ideas I suggest can be dismissed with a shrug. There's nothing compelling about human schools of thought.

This is my concern. That you as a reader might look at the issues raised here from one perspective only, and ask only one

question — "Are these teachings in harmony with Scripture?" but
How are they true (or untrue) to the Word? I am concerned
about this, because the teachings of Scripture cannot be pigeon-
holed and dismissed. The truths are compelling for those who
know and who trust the God of the Word.

Even so, I want to share a passage from Franklin H. Littell's
chapter, "The Radical Reformation," found in *The Layman in
Christian History.* For this passage gives insight into consensus
decision-making as I see it; a process which involves the church
in discerning the will of God.

Littell comments on the quality of the laymen in churches
which believed the ordinary member shared the priesthood and
responsibility for the witness of the church, and continues . . .

> Such a view of the role of the member produced a quite dif-
> ferent personality-type from the docile subject of an earlier
> period. The extraordinary qualities of the laity in the early Free
> Churches was a matter of constant comment (and contempt)
> on the part of those who believed that commoners should keep
> their appointed silent stations in society *and* in the Church.
> And indeed some of the activities of radical Reformers and the
> Churches of the establishments were unusual and embarrassing.
> They appeared to be always appealing decisions, as it were,
> from the duly constituted authorities to a "higher court." They
> denied that decision rested exclusively with the ordained or
> theologically schooled, and claimed *Sitzerrecht,* i.e., their own
> right to sit in judgment on the meaning of Scripture under the
> guidance of the Spirit (I Corinthians 2:13, 15 f.). They openly
> challenged the decisions rendered by "duly constituted" church
> authorities. Anabaptists, Independents and Quakers were trying
> to prove this principle by such odd behavior, even though it
> often resulted in ejection or incarceration.
>
> One of the first recorded instances of such appeal to another
> level occurred during the debate between Ulrich Zwingli and
> the Anabaptist leaders at Zurich. During the Second Disputa-
> tion it became clear that Zwingli intended to refer the pro-
> gramme of reformation back to the Town Council, while the
> representative of the Catholic party wanted the university facul-
> ties circularized for opinions (*Gutachten*). Simon Stumpf took
> the floor to argue that the decision had already been taken, in
> the meetings for Bible study and prayer where earnest Chris-
> tians had considered and reached a mind on these matters, "The
> Spirit of God decides. And, if my Lords intend to recognize

and maintain a position which is against the judgment of God, then I will pray Christ for his Spirit and teach and act against it." This incident has been used repeatedly by state-churchmen to demonstrate that the Swiss Brethren were "enthusiasts" and individualists like the Zaickau prophets, and that such behavior denies the reality of the Church. But that was not the direction of Stumpf's plea. He was arguing that decisions on such matters are made by brethren who follow the pattern of apostolic decision-making, that is, by the Holy Spirit in the midst of his people. Such decisions cannot be referred outside the congregation, outside the setting of full participation by all those who live in the Church under the guidance of God the Holy Spirit. What the Anabaptist was trying to say was that the decision had been properly reached in the Church, with Bible study and common prayer and discussion on the part of all duly concerned. The Holy Spirit had decided, and the proper report would be, "it seemed good to the Holy Spirit and to us" (Acts 15:28).

In decision-making, as in ministry, the *whole* body is to be involved. For making decisions is not the prerogative of church leadership; it is the prerogative of Christ. As the Body is in fact one, the Church is to function as one and come to know in full consensus the will of God for the body.

Derived Structure

At this point it is possible to discern the structural skeleton of the church; the major beams which support development of its common life. Blending biblical "Body" concepts of mutual ministry, servant-leadership, and consensus decision-making seems to indicate that the church meets and acts in these general patterns.

(1) The smallest churches (or units of the church, if you prefer) are neighborhood gatherings, no larger than can comfortably fit in a home. In these meetings all the functions of the church take place, and this is the prime location for mutual ministry. Home meetings may be held at any time, with any frequency. As Christian character and graces are developed by the Holy Spirit, ministering to each through the others, the gifts of the Spirit emerge and are recognized by the community. As gifts emerge and are recognized, church leaders are selected.

(2) The church at times will assemble as a larger group, for a

variety of purposes. One of these is the Sunday meeting, in which several men serve as ministers of the Word of God, and in which great freedom to participate is extended to all. A general meeting may be for the purpose of community worship, or joint communion. Or the church may gather to consider some problem facing it as a whole. In open discussion of the problem, and in the full participation of each member in its solution, a consensus reflecting the mind of God will be reached. This process may well involve extended prayer and study, with the issue investigated in each home-church, and several meetings of the church at large.

(3) The leaders of the church meet together and with their own home-church groups. These leaders, one or more of whom may be supported by the believers to free them for full-time ministry, are equally recognized by the congregation. There is no one preeminent man in the local fellowship: no single pastor to whom all look.

Leadership as exercised by these men is within the biblical framework. In their own lives and dealings with others they exemplify that Christian character which Christ's church is designed to produce. In their teaching they involve themselves deeply in the lives of others. Yet in every respect they are like their brothers; at most first among equals. If they excel, it is in giving themselves to serve the church of God, which He purchased at the price of His own blood.

This portrait of the local church is not the whole picture, of course. There is still the universal church (about which I am not primarily concerned in this book). At times a member of a local assembly will be separated by God to minister to the church at large — to establish new churches or to serve as itinerant teachers. These men will travel, not to extend denominational influence or to build a movement, but to establish colonies of believers. These colonies — new churches — will be as the Body of Christ fully under His direction, not under human ecclesiastical rule. Because Christ is fully able to direct the life of His Body, the organizational safeguards we find so necessary — the centralization of control — will be forever absent. As each church lives in fellowship with God, Christ Himself will coordinate its life with that of every other unit in the Body. And thus the church will grow, and carry out its task of nourishing and transforming the life of the believer, freeing each individual to fulfill his potential in Christ.

It is to a church structured in this manner that we must look for renewal.

10

The Commitment of the Church

I am aware that this sketch of the church leaves much unsaid. There are many practical questions of implementation, many questions of transition. There are many unknowns. What will happen to the Sunday school? What about the other agencies of today's church? What about the pastor? How can he leave his (often unasked for) role as *the* teacher, leader and guide and shift to one more in harmony with the multiple leadership and servant-leadership concept of Scripture? How is the church to shift its pattern of decision-making from the "democratic" procedure of majority vote to the biblical pattern of Spirit-led consensus?

All these questions plague us. While I hope to suggest some practical guidelines to transition in the next section of this book, and to project an idealized "final solution" in part IV, I sense with others the uncertainties. And I realize that we all fear the unknown. That no matter how we may be drawn to an ideal, tremendous pressures are on all of us (especially church leaders) to maintain the status quo. We may be free to dream, but we are not free to *do*.

Yet I am optimistic about change. There is a spirit of daring and of trust abroad. There is a new awareness that our old patterns have failed, and are failing much more obviously in to-day's neo-pagan world. I am optimistic about change in *any* church, providing that its leadership and its people recognize a need to become a community in which the life of Christ in each of us can be nurtured, and that together they fully commit them-selves to the Lordship of Christ and the authority of His Word.

Christ and His Word

Tradition has tremendous power. "The way we do things" seems, in any organization, to take on a certain sanctity. Break-ing out of the patterns of the past are difficult and painful. But often human traditions are built, as is a pearl, to insulate against irritation — to block out anything that attacks our comfort, or constantly pricks our consciences. Or something that demands attention.

It was that way in the Judaism of Christ's day. Tradition had built up great walls insulating God's people from His Word. Un-der the guise of religion, thick trappings had been thrown over the clean and powerful — and demanding — Word.

Jesus' reaction to criticism based on tradition was quick and to the point. One passage particularly is instructive.

> Jesus was approached by the Pharisees and some of the scribes who had come from Jerusalem. They had noticed that his dis-ciples ate their meals with "common" hands, — meaning that they had not gone through a ceremonial washing. . . . So the Pharisees and the scribes put this question to Jesus.
> "Why do your disciples refuse to follow the ancient tradition, and eat their bread with 'common' hands?"
> Jesus replied,
> "You hypocrites, Isaiah described you beautifully when he wrote —
>
> > This people honoreth me with their lips,
> > But their heart is far from me,
> > But in vain do they worship me,
> > Teaching as doctrines the precepts of men.
>
> You are so busy holding on to the traditions of men that you let go the commandments of God" (Mark 7:1 f.).

I am not quoting this passage to demean any who may dis-agree with me and hold a more "traditional" view of the church.

I do it to point out that all of us can become "so busy holding on to the traditions of men" that we can "let go the commandments of God." And that if we in fact do this, it can only be because we have lost confidence in God: lost that complete willingness to abandon ourselves to Christ and to His Word.

The church is to exist as a company of those who are committed — committed to Jesus Christ and to His Word. And this gives me confidence that renewal in evangelicalism can become a reality. Christ lives, and His Word is powerful enough to break through *our* traditions, and bring us to experience His full reality, individually and in our church communities.

I have no hesitation here in associating Christ with the Word. In my personal commitment I accept the teaching of I Corinthians 3. God has *revealed* in trustworthy written form, in "words taught by the Spirit," that which is not open to discovery through human experience. Thus the Scripture is authoritative and trustworthy, fully the Word of our Lord, Christ.* It is as basic to the life of the church, as it is to the life of the Christian.

Not long ago a pastor expressed great concern that I was promoting a pure subjectivism — that the concept of consensus decision making makes the group the authority, and dethrones God. Not at all. As I view the church, full commitment of each member to God and to His Word is inherent in our participation in Christ. Thus the Word provides an objective rudder for the church. The Word of God is God's communication to us, which the Holy Spirit in each situation will interpret and apply as we, individually and in community, seek His will.

At the same time I do not hold that Scripture was given us simply to master. It was given us to *live*. And this is the role it must have in guiding us in our renewed and re-formed churches. Without this dimension of personal submission and disciplined obedience to the Word of God, the church can never be herself.

The words of the letter to the Hebrews stand as a warning to all of us as we handle the Word, as it links obedience to Scripture to trust in God. "Who was it that heard the Word of God and yet provoked his indignation? Was it not all who were res-

---

*For full development of this position, with an extended application to the teaching of the Word to all age-levels, see my book *Creative Bible Teaching*, published by Moody Press.

cued from slavery in Egypt under the leadership of Moses? And
who was it with whom God was displeased for forty long years?
Was it not those who, after all their hearing of God's word, fell
into sin, and left their bones in the desert? And to whom did
God swear that they should never enter into his rest? Was it not
these very men who refused to trust Him?" Thus while we may
hear the Word of God, its productiveness is dependent on our
trust — on our willingness to do what God' has said. "The message proclaimed to them did them no good, because they only
heard and did not believe as well" (Hebrews 3:7 f.).

On the other hand, look what responsiveness to the Word does
in our lives and our fellowships. It is by "obeying the truth" that
we make ourselves "clean enough for a genuine love of (y)our
fellows" (I Peter 1:22 f.). Christian character springs from sound
teaching (Titus 2:1 f.), and God intends to "make you holy by
the work of His Spirit and your own belief in the truth." So we
are to "stand firm, and hold on! Be loyal to the teachings we
passed on to you, whether by word of mouth or in our writings"
(II Thessalonians 2). Since the message of Scripture is "solid
truth" we can speak it and live it "with absolute certainty, so
that those who have believed in God may concentrate upon a
life of goodness" (Titus 3).

In the Scripture, then, church and Christian have an objective,
trustworthy standard for their life. Because Scripture is God's
truth, in full harmony with reality as He knows it, we are to un-
hesitatingly "keep my words in your mind as the pattern of
sound teaching, given to you in the faith and love of Christ Jesus"
(II Timothy 1).

The commitment that Christian faith demands to Christ and
the Word has a double impact as we consider renewal. On the
one hand it challenges us to take the risks involved; to dare to
trust God in committing our lives and our fortunes in introducing
change. "The man who claims to know God but does not obey
his laws is not only a liar but lives in self-delusions," says the
Bible. "Obedience is the test of whether we really live 'in God'
or not" (I John 2:1 f.). If this section on the church in Scripture
has accurately portrayed the teaching of the Word, and if a
reader is convinced by God of its truth, he *must* begin to act.
Others have "stumble(d) at the Word of God, for in their hearts
they were unwilling to obey it — which makes stumbling a fore-

gone conclusion" (I Peter 2:8). We dare not hold on to our traditions if God is calling us back to full obedience to His Word.

The second impact of commitment to the Word is one which frees us. How do we dare move out in directions of which we are unsure? How do we dare institute processes of change, not knowing where they lead? We dare because we can act on God's Word without hesitation — for He is utterly dependable. If we obey the Word of God, and look to His Spirit for guidance, we can *know* that God will transform us and our churches; that God's Word will "produce Christian character, and develop it, just as the Gospel has always done" as the Word has been heard and obeyed.

The Overflow of a Life

My understanding of the church, bound as it is by Scripture, is that it must be different. The church described in the Word, and realized at various times in history, does exist for itself. The church, the community of those who believe, ministers *as a community* only to believers. It is no "church" which organizes itself to minister to the broader society beyond itself.

At the same time, I insist that this view of the church is not a selfish one. It does not constitute a withdrawal from or abandonment of the world. In fact, letting the church be herself, a transforming community, is the only way we can effectively communicate God's love to the men around us.

Paul's teaching was apparently misunderstood by some to indicate withdrawal (a kind of "non-involvement" which has plagued much of evangelicalism, by the way). He wrote to correct the impression, "In my previous letter I said 'Don't mix with the immoral.' I didn't mean, of course, that you were to have no contact at all with the immoral of this world, nor with any cheats or thieves or idolators — for that would mean going out of the world altogether! But in this letter I tell you not to associate with any professing *Christian* who is known to be an impure man . . ." (I Corinthians 5:9-11). The Christian, called to live Christ's life *in the world* (John 17), *must* be involved.

What does involvement mean?

Jesus was once approached by a leper, "who appealed to him, 'If you want to, you can make me clean.' Jesus was filled with pity for him, and stretched out his hand and placed it on the leper, saying, 'Of course I want to — *be clean!*'" (Matthew 8: 2, 3). Can you imagine a man in whom this Christ lives, untouched by human need? Unwilling to stretch out *his* hand? Unwilling to say, "Of course I want to help"?

Often we evangelicals have been unwilling to admit that a compassionate view of men in the world is valid in itself. We have "justified" social concern by making it the means of evangelism. We tutor a child, not because it is wrong for him to grow up defrauded of opportunity, but because it will give us an opportunity to witness. We deliver Thanksgiving and Christmas baskets, and excuse our charity by telling how we slipped in a half dozen colorful tracts! Then we settle back till the next holiday, feeling no responsibility to share the real burden of the needy, or to root out the cause of injustice in our society. How tragic in a day when the ugly blemishes of social and racial injustice stand out in stark contrast to our national prosperity that the churches seem so unwilling to become involved. We seem to care only at long distance, and at best to support only activities which have some direct evangelistic goal.

It is interesting to me that Christ did not "use" His compassionate works to convert. Of course they did authenticate His position as one who spoke in the Name of God, but they didn't really produce faith. Look through the New Testament, and over and over you find that only a superficial response to Christ was gained by the miracles. Men "believed" — but as He taught many shook their heads and turned away, muttering "this is a hard saying, who can know it?" The kind of faith that rests only on miracles dissolves easily. Again and again in the Gospels it is the Word that serves as the dividing line: "they believed through the Word which was spoken to them." And when the "hard sayings" were uttered, those who stayed by Christ stayed because "thou hast the words of life" (cf. John 6).

Why then the miracles? Why the healings? Why the restoring of sight to the blind; of life to a sobbing parent's child; of strength to a crippled limb? Isn't it enough to take Scripture's point of view? "When he saw them, he was moved with compassion"?

The whole area of social concern (which we will explore further in chapter 20) demands an honest facing of issues. Dare we *use* people, by doing them good just so we can share the

Gospel with them? Mustn't we care about people with no strings attached? Why do we find it so hard to realize that when God plants His life in us, the fruit He seeks is at least in part justice and righteousness (Isaiah 5:7)? Why do we find it so hard to feel compassion, and offer ourselves freely; not merely holding out our good works as bait on the gospel hook?

In Christ these two concerns — the ultimate concern for a man's relationship with God, and the compassionate concern for a fellow human's suffering and need in this world — blend. They exist side by side, without conflict or contradiction, and both are freely and honestly expressed. Christ never "used" others, or used His love gifts to manipulate them. Such manipulation Christ rightly condemned as inhuman.

When the Gospel promises to produce Christian character and develop a new humanity, it promises to root out the empty selfishness within us, and replace it with an overflowing love. What is the old attitude toward others that must go?

> On one occasion when Jesus went into the synagogue, there was a man there whose hand was shriveled, and they were watching Jesus closely to see whether he would heal him on the Sabbath day, so that they might bring a charge against him. Jesus said to the man with the shriveled hand,
> "Stand up and come out here in front."
> Then he said to them,
> "Is it right to do good on the Sabbath day, or to do harm? Is it right to save life or to kill?"
> There was dead silence. Then Jesus, deeply hurt as he sensed their inhumanity, looked around in anger at the faces surrounding him, and said to the man,
> "Stretch out your hand!"
> And he stretched it out, and the hand was restored as sound as the other one. The Pharisees walked straight out and discussed with Herod's party how they could have Jesus put out of the way (Mark 3:1-6).

I confess that many who have claimed to be Christ's have exhibited pride and inhumanity; this should be no surprise. The Pharisees claimed to represent the God they crucified! Perhaps it should be no surprise that even believers at times act as cruelly as men of the world. How few of us have churches that are the transforming communities of Scripture! How few enjoy the rela-

THE COMMITMENT OF THE CHURCH   139

tionships with other believers in which mutual ministries are exercised. As we see our churches change into such communities, they will produce transformed men. And transformed men will reach out, with Christian love and concern, to all around them.

It is the same with our witness. How peculiar the concern of some that if we build a believer's church evangelism will die. "You have become a sounding board," Paul wrote, "from which the Word of the Lord has rung out, not only in Macedonia and Achaia but everywhere that the story of your faith in God has become known" (I Thessalonians 1:7, 8). Growth in Christ leads believers, by daily life and simple personal testimony, to share their faith in God. "The very spring of our actions is the love of Christ," Paul wrote. "We look at it like this: if one died for all men then, in a sense, they all died, and his purpose in dying for them is that their lives should no longer be lived for themselves but for him who died and rose again." Imbued with this motive and message, we realize that God has made each of us "agents of the reconciliation. God was in Christ personally reconciling the world to himself — not counting their sins against them — and has commissioned us with the message of reconciliation" (II Corinthians 5:14-19).

And so a knowledge of God, of His love and of His offer of a free salvation, will be mediated through transformed individuals. God's life will be incarnated in the lives of His children. *Love and life can be communicated no other way.*

What then is the strategy we must adopt to reach the world we live in? Not to shape as "the Church" a powerful institution, whose voice will be heard in the counsels of men, but to go back to the simplicity of community. To build again a church which will be *"the* Church": His body, a womb for nurturing relationships and ministries within which Christ can be formed in each and every one of us.

Part III

The Church in Transition

11

Change

Change is forcing itself on our churches. Congregation after congregation today is struggling with problems caused by new ways in today's new world: new patterns of life which simply don't fit a church whose services and functions are carried over from a horse-and-buggy culture. In a new book, *The Impact of the Future*, (Abingdon), Lyle E. Schaller pinpoints some of the cultural trends that force change on our churches. These are trends that place stress on any church which views itself as a Sunday morning and evening cluster of agencies, with a weekday series of committees and activities. The stresses Schaller discusses range from changing patterns of housing to changing ways we use the increased time we have at our disposal; from our mobile, shifting populations to a greater demand by individuals for self-determination. Each of these forces, and many more, means change for our churches. Each force, projected into the future, foretells even greater stresses. Whether we welcome it or not, we are being forced into change.

Personally, I welcome these forces of change. To me the upheaval in our culture stands as a great opportunity for the church. This upheaval represents a great pivotal point in a human history which is rapidly drawing to a close: a point at which we are both invited and forced to rethink the pattern of life of the gathered church. What an exciting time this is! For we never live so vitally as when we live on the brink, or in a time, of decision.

It seems to me that there are only two directions a congregation can move these days. One is to struggle to patch up our contemporary churches, to retain all we can of traditional forms and patterns of life, and with all our might to resist the forces that cry for change. The other option is to accept the challenge of change, and to channel it — to seek to shape a church which will be a true expression of "the Church," yet uniquely suited to our twenty-first century world. Both these limiting considerations are important.

I do not believe we are to build again "the New Testament church." We are not bound to reproduce the institutional forms (7 deacons, a Widow's List, etc.) of that church. I am convinced, however, that the New Testament gives a clear revelation of the nature of the church, and of the function of churches. These distinctive biblical features are to guide us as we reshape the life of the gathered church today.

Within the framework provided by these features (discussed in the last six chapters) we have freedom to work out a structure which fits our new and changing world — one which blends into a culture built on the car and the jet, on the TV and the moving van; not one built on the old gray mare. We can, in each of our congregations, work out patterns of church life which will be fully responsive to the patterns of life of our members.

You may have noted that I speak here of individual congregations. I am not thinking of "the church in America," or of a denomination or association. My focus is, purposely, on individual local congregations. Why? Because I believe that we can not, and dare not, work out "the structure" for local churches, and impose it. I am convinced that in each local situation full freedom must be given a congregation to respond to its own unique conditions, to work out its own problems responsive only to the guidance of the Holy Spirit. Thus change is something for each congregation to deal with — and something each congregation must face for itself. It can resist change, and fight to maintain the status quo. Or it can accept the need for change, and seek God's help to guide and channel it into patterns of life which will be both biblical and creative.

Guiding Change

Change is a fact of life our congregations are being forced to face. And so it is important to understand how one can prepare for and guide change — ways to channel change into biblically valid patterns of congregational life. This is the role of this section of the present book. To deal with the practical question of, *How?*

In developing the general guidelines on how to meet and channel the areas of change that are contained in chapters 11 through 16, I was guided by several personal presuppositions. It is best to spell these out at once as all my suggestions fit only within the limits these presuppositions permit.

(1) *We must work within our present congregations.* Some who urge renewal demand that we desert today's churches. It is too slow to try to change them. It is too difficult. It cannot be done. This whole way of thinking seems dreadful to me. It is dreadful, because it is a denial of everything that evangelical renewal is about. For such a course of action is to deny the very principles on which renewal must be built — such basic truths as these: that the Body of Christ is one; that each believer has a spiritual gift needed within the Body; that the ordinary Christian is the key to vitality in our churches; that each of us can be transformed in a church which fulfills the functions for which it was intended.

Thus the Christian who holds to the traditional is still one with us. How dare we separate ourselves from Him, tearing the Body apart in our eagerness for change? Paul's evaluation of such schism is succinct: while you divide yourselves from your brothers and deny the unity God asserts, "are you not unspiritual?" (cf. I Corinthians 1:10; 3:3).

How can we assert that each layman possesses a spiritual gift to be used in mutual ministry, and then abandon men and women whose gifts we need?

How can we assert the primacy of the layman, and say the purpose of the renewed church is to encourage full development of the life of Christ within each of us — and deny the opportunity we say renewal alone provides to those we leave behind?

Everything written in this book is predicated on the assumption that each congregation of believers, possessing the Holy Spirit and partaking in the life of Christ, *can* grow and change. That each congregation can experience renewal of its own life.

(2) *The leadership of our churches must provide opportunities for creative change to take place.* This statement reflects my perception of twin dangers which face the leadership of all our congregations. The one danger is that, under pressure from some, leaders will resist all efforts to innovate and introduce change in church life. The other is that, convinced of the necessity of change, they will move unwisely — that leaders will attempt to force change, and to direct its course themselves.

This latter course is not only extremely perilous, it is self-defeating. Unless the biblical principle of full participation by the congregation in seeking God's direction, and in fulfilling His will, is followed, churches will be split and individuals injured. And the changes so forced will last only until the leadership pressure which caused them is removed. Forced change is never lasting.

This is why I used the phrase, "provide opportunities for creative change to take place." This seems to me to be *the* role of leadership in times of change. Not to direct change, or to force it into predetermined channels, but to work flexibly to create opportunities for change to take place.

(3) *The success of change depends on the personal spiritual growth of the church members, and on their sense of freedom to take part openly and honestly in the change process.* Helping people grow, and freeing them to become honest participants in any social process is closely related to the church becoming the church. That is, to developing those close personal relationships between believers as a context in which the gifts of the Holy Spirit can be exercised. In a context of such relationships, individuals will find freedom to be themselves, and, as the gifts of the Spirit are exercised in a mutual ministry, all can grow spiritually. Thus a *primary concern* for a church in change must be the provision of opportunities for such a mutual ministry.

(4) *The results of change in a given congregation will be unknown.* Specific predictions about resultant forms or structures

of congregational life cannot, and should not, be made. Each congregation will need to solve its own problems having to do with place and time and frequency of gatherings, and with education of children, ways of communicating Christ's Gospel and His concern to the community, etc. Such resultant forms are always to be left open ended when a change process is initiated.

This *open endedness* should not (although it will at first) seem threatening. It stands rather as an evidence of our commitment to the Lordship of Christ. We leave Him free to direct us, His people, and we leave ourselves free to respond to Him. And so we go out into a country we know not where.

It is within the framework of these presuppositions, then, that all my suggestions are to be offered.

I have tried to select issues which seemed crucial in setting up conditions for change, and for taking maximum advantage of these conditions. Thus chapters 12 and 13 deal with group life: the development and encouragement of mutual ministries between believers. Chapter 14 discusses the involvement of the church in goal-setting, a subject crucial in the implementation of consensus decision-making in the church. Chapter 15 discusses the integration of group life with church structure, and some of the transitional problems involved. Chapter 16 looks at the role of the pastor or other church leaders in change.

The material in these chapters is suggestive, not exhaustive. It doesn't contain "four steps to renewal" that can be taken by any church. But it does present handles which, grasped under God's guidance, may be useful for the church facing the prospect of change or involved in it.

12

Introduction to Group Life

Many ministers today have become concerned about their effectiveness in communicating the Christian message. Some of the concern has stemmed from sad experience: how many believers in our churches seem to have been reached and transformed by the teaching-preaching ministry of the pulpit? Part of their concern has stemmed from communications research, which has shown basic inadequacies in mass, one-way communication. While the traditional sermon may potentially communicate blocks of information, the very form of this communication makes it difficult to receive feedback from listeners (to see if they have really understood what has been said, and its implications). More significant still, this form of communication has been shown most unlikely to change attitudes and values, and consequently, behavior. Preaching seldom leads to whole-hearted response.

As a result many ministers have been experimenting with forms of communication which make the layman a participant in the communication process, by giving him a chance to respond and contribute to the sermon and to fellow believers.

Several books and articles have been written to suggest ways to take preaching out of the realm of mass communication (a one-way process of transmitting messages to a large group), and add dimensions of interpersonal communication — to make preaching the Word of God a two-way, rather than one-way, process. The movement toward dialog in preaching (encouraged by such books as Howe's *Partners in Preaching* and Reid's *Preaching and the Nature of Communication*) is an encouraging sign of progress in our churches toward the development of a group life — that is, toward the drawing of a congregation together as those who recognize a deep commitment to each other and an identity with each other in Christ.

This kind of group life is a distinctive mark of the true church. When we experience it we recognize our unity in Christ, our oneness, and we truly love one another. But group life is not only important as a mark of the church. It is essential to the functioning of a group of believers *as* a church. For only when we realize the *community* described earlier will we find ourselves free to be honest with each other, free to share openly our life in Christ. And only in this sharing of ourselves with others do we minister to each other.

Now, I do not believe that the trend toward participation in preaching can bring us to community, but I am convinced that such participation can be an important factor in developing a sense of group life in a congregation. As such, it is an approach to renewal which every concerned pastor should consider very carefully.

In Minneapolis, pastor Al Windham has helpfully summarized techniques pastors can use to encourage participation. Here are some of the suggestions he catalogs, many of which he has used in his own ministry.*

What to do before the sermon. Advance assignments may be given to encourage intelligent listening. A series of sermons may be developed around a significant book, and the congregation encouraged to read selected chapters and Scripture passages before each sermon. Or thought questions on a biblical segment can be included in the Sunday bulletin for study before the next week. Other techniques involve the congregation in sharing.

---

*Windham, Albert. *Preaching is not a One-man Show.* Unpublished Master's thesis.

Prayer meeting night small groups can discuss the passage on which the coming Sunday's message is based.

A variation of this is the *sermon seminar*. Several from the congregation are asked to serve as a sermon sounding board. They meet with the pastor early in the week. He briefly introduces the passage from which he will preach, asks the group a key question, and permits them to discuss at length. He listens, while they talk, for their ideas and insights which he uses in sermon preparation. Those who serve in the seminar are changed every three months, permitting the whole congregation to take part. Discussion in such groups not only helps the minister prepare but helps develop the sensitivity of participants to each other and provides an opportunity for mutual ministries to take place.

What to do during the sermon. Verbal response is seldom encouraged in present morning services. Yet many do use involvement methods Sunday evenings. These may range from a dialog sermon, in which two or more discuss from the platform, to an open forum — when those in the congregation may be invited to raise hands during the sermon when they have questions. Or the pastor may raise questions, encouraging the congregation to answer and discuss them together.

What to do after the sermon. There are many ways for a congregation to participate after a sermon has been delivered. Some pastors open their homes Sunday evenings and invite whoever wishes to come and discuss the messages of the day. Others have church board members serve as discussion leaders for small groups. These meet over coffee in the church basement or the leader's home. A question-and-answer session is the simplest form of after-sermon involvement.

Another option is the *talk-back sermon*. Here the pastor preaches Sunday morning, and the congregation is asked to respond Sunday evening. That evening the pastor summarizes the morning message and divides the congregation into small groups. These discuss such questions as, "What was useful in this sermon?" and "How might I apply it?" Pastor Windham writes of this method,

> In my own experience this method has proven exciting and profitable. On one occasion a college student called to ask if our denomination had any written statements that would help

him secure a conscientious objector's classification. For the first
time it "got through to me" that some of the college, university
and working young people in the congregation I serve were
struggling with the problems of war, peace, Vietnam and military
conscription. After a week of study; visits to Bethel College,
the University of Minnesota, the Friends Counseling Center;
and several interviews, I preached a message on "The Christian's Responsibility for Vietnam." My purpose was twofold: to
show the young men in our congregation that I was anxious to
help them think through the draft question; and to emphasize
the need for Christians to accept responsibility for the consequences of whatever position they take on Vietnam. The evening was given over to a talk-back sermon. I summarized the
morning message, and the people talked. Seldom has there been
such animated, yet charitable conversation in the church service
itself. Opinions differed, but they were expressed. We learned
from one another. Young people expressed appreciation and
told of receiving guidance. Adults spoke of being made to think.
One man said, "If Christians would discuss questions like this
more often, maybe our country wouldn't be in such a mess."*

A final variation is the *feedback group.* Here a group of six or
eight people, a cross section of the church membership, are invited to discuss the sermon in depth. This discussion is tape recorded for later listening by the pastor. The group discusses
such questions as, "What did the preacher say to *you?*" "What
difference do you think this sermon will make in your life?"
"How might the message have been of greater challenge?" etc.
The membership of this group also can be rotated, to involve
ultimately the entire congregation.

In a variety of ways, then, without significant change in the
traditional form of church meetings, a pastor can encourage congregational participation, and create opportunities for Christians
to become aware of their unity in Christ.

And there are other simple avenues to a sense of group identity.
One is a church newsletter, featuring "God at Work" columns in
which members of the congregation share ways God is using
them or has been speaking to them. I have seen a brief five
minutes on Sunday morning or evening used to interview a layman and give him an opportunity to share some recent experi-

*Ibid., p. 93.

ence with Christ, bring a new sense of unity to a large congregation.

But as important as these approaches to building group life are, they will not, by themselves, lead to the development of true community in our churches.

The Small Group

From the first year of my serious involvement in renewal thinking, the small group has seemed to me to be the basic building block of the life of the gathered church. This initial judgment has been deepened and confirmed by experience and also by the many helpful books and articles which have appeared on the subject. Among the most helpful (important reading for those who seek renewal in their churches) are Keith Miller's *A Taste of New Wine,* Clyde Reid's *Groups Alive: Church Alive,* and an older classic, John L. Casteel's *Spiritual Renewal through Personal Groups.*

It seems significant also that the behavioral sciences are assigning numerous roles to face-to-face groups. Today therapy-group training is seen as a basic tool in business and management, and in working with organizations of all kinds. Therapy groups are used to help those with personality problems or serious mental illness. Group counseling is often used with troubled families, as well as with alcoholics, dope addicts, and weight watchers. Of course the "small group movement" has been perverted, as are all movements. Some so-called "sensitivity groups" have engaged in all sorts of excesses. But the excesses shouldn't blind us to the discovered facts about human nature and our need for one another. These the Bible has always reflected in its structuring of the church.

Yet the well-publicized excesses have led many Christians to be suspicious of all small groups, and of all "group" movements. So at this point it might be well for me to state what I mean by "small groups" in the church, and also to suggest how these groups are to function.

I suggested in the first part of this chapter that "group life," as I use the term, refers to the experience in a local congregation of their oneness in Christ. As such it means a drawing of believers together; a shared sense of identity as a body; a deep love for and commitment to each other. It is obvious that this atmosphere permeates few churches today. No longer do outsiders say in wonder, "see how they love one another!"

How then are we to rediscover the group life that the church has lost? I suggest that the starting point almost *has* to be the small group. In our culture, larger meetings of the congregation draw men and women together who seldom see each other during the week. They do not truly *know* each other. They can not truly love, because they are not involved in each other's lives. In a larger congregation most of us must remain strangers. Few have opportunity to share themselves. Few would feel free to be truly honest. The Bible suggests that Christians should even "get into the habit of admitting your sins to one another, and praying for one another" (James 5:13). How many of us trust the larger congregation to the extent that we would admit our sins — and if we did, how many in that congregation would pray, and how many would gossip?

The small group in the church. To learn to trust, and to become trustworthy — to learn to love, and to become loving — we must become deeply involved in the lives of others, to whom we commit ourselves in Christ. To develop this kind of relationship we need to share ourselves with others, and they need to share themselves with us. All of this demands time. More than this, it requires a face-to-face relationship. A relationship we can have only with a few others at one time. And thus a church is forced to move to a small group structure.

"Small," then, suggests a size which permits and encourages face-to-face relationships. It is not so large that any will be cut off from deeply and personally sharing himself with others, and in turn receiving them. How large is this? Some research in group dynamics suggests that five may be the optimum number! But often groups of eight or twelve are suggested for church fellowship groups, and this range seems to have many advantages.

Now, simply throwing eight or twelve Christians together does not make them a group. Nor will it, in itself, insure that they will develop group life. Members may, over a span of many meetings, remain strangers who share nothing more significant than what each thinks the others want to hear. A small group which functions as the church needs to develop group life. Without initial guidance and help, or without an understanding of how the group can become the church for its members, a small group may move far off course.

Such a group has several vital functions. These functions, with their relationship to secular "group" terminology and to the theological issues discussed in Section II, are shown in the circles in Figure 7.

(1) As members of the small group develop concern for the needs of each participant, and minister to each other, the Holy Spirit works through their gifts to nurture the members to ma-

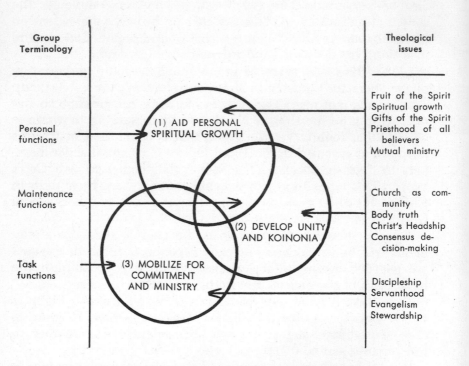

Aspects of the Small Group as the Church

Figure 7.

turity. Thus the small group is a vital aid to personal spiritual growth. If this, the sharing of personal concerns and feelings, becomes the *only* function of the group, it ceases to act as the church. It then takes on characteristics of the therapeutic group, and the focus shifts from Christ and others to self.

(2) In the small church group, concern is also expressed for the development of unity. In the process of sharing their lives with one another, the members become aware that they are more than an association of individuals; they become aware of a group identity. They develop a loyalty and commitment to the group, and a strong sense of belonging. This dimension of group life can also be perverted. The group can become so completely the source of an individual's identity that he becomes dependent on it rather than on Christ. He lets the group become God for him in making his decisions, and plotting his life.

(3) A third dimension of group function is the mobilization of members for ministry to those outside the church. A group can become ingrown. The group experience can become so significant to a person that he *shuts out* others, seeking to preserve what he has found. Yet the group that is committed to Christ's purposes as revealed in the Word will tend to mobilize its members to *draw in* others. They will seek together to live God's Word. This tends to mobilize individuals to share their faith in Christ, and to let their awakening love flow out to others whom Christ would love through them.

When a group is functioning as the church, these three elements will be in balance. As each function is fulfilled, excesses are guarded against. Such a small group will accomplish the basic tasks of the church, the Body of Christ.

This, then, is what I envision for the "small group." Eight or twelve believers gathered to minister to each other, to grow in their sensed love and unity, and to encourage one another to full commitment to Christ.

Why the small group? The need to know others intimately in order to become the church, while a basic reason for the small group, is not the only one. Another reason lies in the nature of the spiritual growth we seek. For spiritual growth cannot be understood merely as a change in ideas, or in belief systems. It must be understood in terms of character change — transformation of attitudes, of values, of personality.

In discussing such change in people, Matthew B. Miles writes in *Designing Training Activities,*

> The "inspirational" speaker often used in larger conferences is unlikely to bring about permanent attitude change in any intended direction (although he may be able to produce a temporary glow or negative counter-reaction). If the speaker is unusually non-threatening, symbolizes an important reference group, and can help learners analyze their attitudes thoughtfully, then a talk by him may help in changing attitudes. Not many speakers meet these three criteria.
>
> If attitudes, feelings, opinions, and the like are the basic things which are to be changed, some research evidence suggests that it is important to provide a situation of low threat, where a person can tentatively shift his attitudes without feeling defensive or threatened. In addition, other studies indicate that most attitudes are socially anchored. That is, a person holds attitudes as a part of his membership in specific groups (such as a school staff) and more general reference groups (such as "effective English teachers"). The durability of a new attitude is probably mostly a function of whether the learner feels approved and rewarded by an individual or group important to him when he expresses the attitude, either covertly or overtly. In general the success of appeals to emotion, fear, prestige, or credibility as a means of opinion change (as in some films and mass media) is variable. A frequent finding is that the "sleeper effect" occurs. Initial opinion changes are not durable; opinions often revert to their original level after some time has passed.
>
> If attitude change is the main desired outcome, it is probably appropriate to choose as a training method small open-end "off the record" discussion groups where the person feels unthreatened. To the degree that these discussion groups are important or valuable to the person, attitude changes are more than likely to be durable.

Attitudes, values, character. These *are* socially anchored. These are learned in our association with others throughout our lives. Now, as Christians, we need a social anchor for an entirely new set of attitudes, values, and behaviors. We need the church, a group important and valuable to each believer, which will give expression to the nature of God. We need a community in which the Word of God is made flesh, and its authoritative message studied and obeyed *together.*

"A whole series of studies," says the *Handbook of Small Group Research* by A. Paul Hare, "shows that if one wishes to change attitudes and the subsequent behavior of a group, discussion and decision where all members participate as directly as possible tends to be more effective than 'enlightenment' or 'persuasion' by the lecture method" (p. 287).

In giving this vital role to the small group I am not in the least suggesting we diminish the role of Scripture. Rather we place Scripture as central to the life of the small group, as will be developed in the next chapter. I do point out, however, that our normal method of teaching God's Word (by sermon) has both communication limitations and also serious limitations on life-impact. Certainly I do not deny that the Holy Spirit uses the preached Word. I only insist that He is much freer to use the Word in a small group where it is studied and discussed together, and that this is one of God's purposes in creating the church.

Thus four "impressive values" of group study and discussion can be realized in the small church group. These suggestions are listed by Halbert E. Gulley in *Discussion, Conference and Group Process*:

(1) There is clearly stronger commitment to a decision when those affected have participated in its formulation.

(2) In most situations, groups apparently produce higher quality decisions than do an equal number of equally able individuals working separately.

(3) Group discussion participants gain increased understanding of other persons and learn to get along better with others.

(4) Members learn about collective responsibility and irresponsibility, group action and inaction, and similar matters.

(pp. 366-369).

For all these reasons, then, the small group is vital to the church facing renewal.

In no other way can we move so quickly toward becoming the church. In no other situation can the functions of the church be so fully carried out. In no other context can the Word of God be communicated with so much impact on lives. The church today, as the church of the New Testament, needs the "church in the house." We need the small group.

A Context for Ministry and Growth

Recently I talked with a man who had an unhappy experience in a small group. For a year he and his wife had met with three other couples. They wanted to study the Bible together and to find a deeper relationship with Christ. They began by deciding who would lead the group (the host in whose home they met that week) and what they would study. They all felt a little uncomfortable, not being experts in the Bible. Soon they discovered that they disagreed on their interpretation of various passages. This made them very uncomfortable. They continued to meet, but the sessions seemed less and less significant. Often the leader was unprepared, or someone would dash in late and mumble excuses about having to leave early. More and more the meetings became simply social times when they politely discussed all that was peripheral in their lives. Understandably this man was unimpressed when I suggested that the small group is the ideal context for ministry and for spiritual growth. For him the small group had been a total waste of time.

What makes the difference between this kind of group experience and an experience of *group life?* What is it that transforms the small group into a vital experience of Christian nurture? The answer to this question hinges on the answer to another.

What qualifies us to minister? Too often in our churches today ability to minister seems contingent on training and Bible knowledge. ("How many years did he have in seminary? Greek, and Hebrew too! Wow! He'll be a *great* pastor!") The problem with this view is that it is both naive and unscriptural.

Biblically two factors seem crucial in the ministry of believers to one another. The first of these is the spiritual gift. We know that each Christian has been given a gift by God, a special ability to contribute to the growth of other believers. Thus *everyone* in the church has been equipped for ministry, no matter how extensive or how limited his training.

Another factor seems to control the exercise of gifts. This factor is seldom understood, or even considered. Yet the whole New Testament concept of the church shouts it, and Paul's own ministry often gives expression to it. One of these places is the introduction to his second letter to the Corinthians.

Thank God, the Father of our Lord Jesus Christ, that he is our Father and the source of all mercy and comfort. For he gives us comfort in our trials so that we in turn may be able to give the same sort of strong sympathy to others in theirs. Indeed, experience shows that the more we share Christ's sufferings, the more we are able to give of his encouragement. This means that if we experience trouble we can pass on to you comfort and spiritual help; for if we ourselves have been comforted we know how to encourage you to endure patiently the same sort of troubles that we have ourselves endured. We are quite confident that if you have to suffer troubles as we have done, then, like us, you will find the comfort and encouragement of God (1: 3-7).

Here Paul relates our ability to minister to others to our own experience of trouble! "If we experience trouble we can pass on to you comfort and spiritual help." Somehow being human, and subject to all the pressures of human existence, is basic to being a spiritual help to others.

The problem my friend experienced in his small group can be located right at this point. For these men and women met weekly to *conceal from each other the very needs and problems which must be expressed if we are to help each other!*

It is tragic if we believe that to minister necessitates our having "arrived" spiritually — that we have to be "victorious" Christians. None of us have arrived. All of us are subject to loneliness, to frustrations, to failures, to despair. These, as well as the peace and joy of the Gospel, are our lot. When we struggle to hide our humanness from each other we build walls instead of bridges. We cut ourselves off from one another, hiding behind masks. When we hide from our brothers we can only fear them, not love them. We can never invite them to share our lives, or expect to share theirs. Throw such people together in a small group and the strain of hiding themselves drives them apart. They cannot be drawn together.

But is this really what Paul means when he speaks of "troubles"? Or does he mean things *outside,* circumstances a believer is to override with joy? The next paragraph shows that Paul not only encourages the Corinthians to share their inner selves; he shares himself, too.

We should like you, our brothers, to know something of what we went through in Asia. At that time we were completely overwhelmed; the burden was more than we could bear; in fact we told ourselves that this was the end. Yet we believe now that we had this experience of coming to the end of our tether that we might learn to trust, not in ourselves, but in God who can raise the dead (II Corinthians 1:8, 9).

Paul wrote this letter to a church in which his apostleship was being challenged. Even so he did not hesitate to reveal his true self. Only as he met these people as a man, and shared his own inadequacies, could he lead them to discover the adequacy of God.

If spiritual gifts are to be exercised in mutual ministry, we in the church must also be willing to expose our real selves — to admit our humanness and our need, to receive encouragement from others who share our common lot, and to encourage them in turn.

Toward Openness. There are many barriers to such openness in our culture. Blake, Mouton and Blansfield have summarized several cultural forces that tend to block openness and honesty in our relationships with each other.

(1) There are cultural norms that protect the feelings of other persons. Such sayings as "don't say anything if you can't say something nice" reflects them. We particularly are taught to hide hostility.

Hostility is very difficult for a Christian to handle. We know we're supposed to love each other. So when we feel angry we hardly dare admit it, much less express it! Yet in any small group hostilities do arise. And the only way to handle them is to bring them out in the open. Repressing even unacceptable feelings about others means hiding ourselves. Such a retreat into ourselves cuts us off from ministering and being ministered to.

It is important to get this idea in perspective. The church is a *transforming* community, it is not a *transformed* one. It is made up, not of perfect people, but of sinners who are struggling to experience the life of God that is within them. Our acceptance by God is not based on perfection. God knows us and loves us and receives us *as we are.* So we must learn to accept, and love, *imperfect* people in the church — including ourselves! As we learn to be honest with ourselves and with each other, God can deal with our sins and our imperfections. He can transform us. But for this we must open ourselves up to God and to others in the church.

There is another fact to recognize about hostility. When we express it, we say nothing about the person who is its object. We tell only of ourselves. Thus hostility is *our* problem: not the other person's. Sharing it we open ourselves to the ministry of the group, and even to the ministry of the one with whom we are angry.

So even hostility toward others in the small group must be faced, must be expressed and dealt with. The cultural norm which demands we hide from others must be replaced by a biblical norm which demands that the Christian *care* enough about others to be honest with them — even when it hurts.

(2) There are cultural norms designed for self-protection. One reason we hesitate to be honest is that we fear the backlash. How will others respond? Will they resent us? Criticize us for being too honest? Will they gossip about what we reveal? Will they lose respect for us?

All these are possibilities. But we must take the risk. We must learn to trust our fellow Christians, and to trust God to change them. We must take the risk because such honesty is the only pathway to deepened concern and love.

As a young husband I was afraid to be honest with my wife. I tried to hide all the things about myself that I thought would disappoint her, would make her think less of me. I discovered that all I succeeded in doing was driving a wedge between us. All I succeeded in doing was to make her feel unwanted, and unneeded. It was not until God freed me to be honest, to share my feelings and my real self, that a potential tragedy became a home. There is no route to unity, in a home or in the church, except the open and honest sharing of real selves.

(3) There are norms that suggest feelings only cause troubles. So we often hesitate to talk about what we *feel*, and say only what we *think*. This too cuts us off from others. We are not disembodied minds. As whole persons, sharing ourselves demands expressing our feelings. Paul considered it important for his Corinthian brothers to know how he *felt*: "completely overwhelmed." To no church does the Apostle write with stronger criticism and command; yet to no church does he reveal himself

and his feelings more fully. He tells them that when he came to them he felt "nervous and rather shaky" (I Corinthians 2:1). In the fullness of his self revelation he says, "Oh, our dear friends in Corinth, we are hiding nothing from you and our hearts are absolutely open to you." (II Corinthians 6:11).

We must accept this as God's way. We must reject the pattern of our culture, the way men think about living, and see God's view. For the small group to function as the church, and for renewal to take place, openness is demanded.

In an excellent book by Schein and Bennis, *Personal and Organizational Change through Group Methods*, this same point is made concerning secular learning groups.

> Let us emphasize this point by saying it another way. A person cannot learn about himself and others in a group unless he gets certain categories of information which are not readily available. And, he cannot get these categories of information unless his attitudes change about which kinds of data are relevant, which data he is willing to reveal about himself and which data he is willing to pay attention to in others. To put it even more concretely, *the learning process at the onset, hinges upon a person's becoming willing and able to reveal his own feelings and reactions, and upon his becoming willing and able to listen and pay attention to the feelings and reactions of others* (p. 273).

Thus the success of the small group, and the freeing of individuals to exercise mutual ministry, depends in some degree on the openness and honesty in sharing the group achieves.

And this is God's way in the church: to accept ourselves as fully human, in need of transformation and not yet transformed; to share our trials, so that we can pass on to others comfort and spiritual help. This is what it means to be the church.

Starting a Small Group

There are a number of ways to start a small group in the church. Often a specific goal is set. This draws and holds members together until group life can develop. In evangelicalism this goal has usually been evangelism.

An example is a recent county-wide movement among the evangelical churches of DuPage County, Illinois. Under the name of *Tell DuPage* the effort has drawn many together in small groups for prayer and Bible study. After twelve weeks of preparation, witness is begun, and the groups are maintained as centers for prayer and encouragement. The ultimate goal of drive leader Gary Henley is that these groups might discover the life of the church and serve as sparks of renewal in the area churches.

In *Integrity of Church Membership,* Pastor Russell Bow tells how a call to higher Christian commitment bound groups together and encouraged the development of group life. Pastor Bow challenged his members to covenant to live as disciples for one month (with the covenant renewable each month). Those who did want to commit themselves promised to read the Scripture daily, to meet weekly in small groups, to pray for other members of their groups daily, to tithe, and each day to share something of their faith in Christ with those outside the church.

A group of eighteen men and women in the Rockford (Illinois) Evangelical Free Church were commissioned to study the life of their church and to make recommendations to the board. Their study led them to Scripture to redefine the nature and functions of the church, and led them to question many practices of the contemporary church. Committed to this common goal the group held together in spite of early and strong disagreements. In their final report they stated that they had *experienced* in their committee what they felt the church should become: a transforming community.

These are all possible roads to group life. But all of them rely on the force of an external commitment (to evangelism, to discipleship, to reexamining church goals) to hold the group together until an internal cohesiveness can develop. Often groups which begin in these ways fail to develop group life. Like the group my friend described, its members stay on the surface of their lives, and never find the freedom to be honest.

The freedom to be honest. In a significant article in *T-Group Theory and Laboratory Method,* Jack Gibb suggests that there is a pattern in the development of the life of any group. He suggests four concerns which must be resolved (Figure 8).

In his article Gibb suggests that "the deepest and earliest concerns arise in the following order: acceptance, data-flow, goal formation, and control. Development of each factor in this order seems to facilitate subsequent development of the other factors."

Concerns in Group Development

Primary Modal Concerns	Derivative Modal Concerns	Symptoms of Unresolved Concern	Symptoms of Resolved Concern
Acceptance	Membership	Fear Distrust	Acceptance Trust
Data	Decision	Polite facade Caution strategy	Spontaneity Process feedback
Goal	Productivity	Apathy Competition	Creative work or play
Control	Organization	Dependency Counterdependency	Interdependence Role distribution

Figure 8.

Growth in each dimension is contingent upon growth in each of the dimensions higher in the hierarchy. Each factor in the hierarchy provides a pace-setting or boundary function for the factors lower in the hierarchy. A free flow of data is possible only within the limits of trust formation. A free flow of data is possible only with antecedent or concurrent reduction of distrust and fears. Defense mechanisms and organizational demands prevent functional processing of data beyond the trust limits. A person can look at his goals only as he begins to trust himself. This growing self-trust makes self-awareness possible. Integration of group goals occurs only as rapidly as members build sufficient trust and awareness to verbalize openly their intrinsic goals. Premature goal formulation beyond the trust and data boundaries leads to unrealistic, overaspirational, or formalized goals, the pursuit of which or lack of pursuit of which leads to apathy and various other forms of resistance (p. 283).

The significance of this statement is understood more clearly when we realize that what Gibb is speaking of as acceptance, trust and data flow is exactly what we have been discussing in terms of *openness*. In our small groups we must *first* come to trust and accept ourselves and others. Only when we do will we be free to share our real selves, and be free for mutual ministry.

Another chapter in the same book suggests that the development of trust is a freeing and dynamic experience. To me this seems to describe the *internal cohesiveness* so essential to our life together in the church.

As a learning group is constructed with a high level of trust, individuals are able to lower their defenses and develop satisfying relationships with others. They become freer in expressing and accepting caring feelings. Because it satisfies and rewards the individual, each venture toward accepting the reaction of others and expressing helpful feelings toward others reinforces the next venture. As the group grows in its capacity to support experimentation, risk taking becomes easier (p. 202).

Thus two roads to small groups in the church seem open to us: (1) we can set a goal external to the development of group life to draw and hold participants together, trusting that they will in time work through trust and data flow levels, or (2) we can begin by helping participants break through their natural reserve, and develop quickly a dimension of trust and love.

An approach. My own feeling is that the latter approach is best. This feeling has been reinforced through experience recently at Honey Rock Camp in Wisconsin. There 32 pastors and other church leaders gathered for a seminar in "The Small Group in Tomorrow's Church." In the initial phase the participants were divided into small groups and worked together toward trust formation.

The initial phase of the seminar can be adapted to a retreat format, and used in a local church to start small groups. The retreat schedule, which follows, is designed only to *initiate* participants to group life. Further development is necessary for fulfillment of the functions described on pages 171 ff. Sources for resource materials referred to in the chapter so far are listed at the end of the book.

The retreat is designed to be the first step in establishment of small groups in a church. Only those who express a willingness to participate in a small group for a definite length of time (at least three months of weekly meetings) should be invited. It is important that the retreat take group members out of their familiar surroundings and give them opportunity for uninterrupted involvement. If possible, a two-and-one-half day program, with time in the afternoons for recreation or reading, is desirable. If necessary, this may be condensed into two days by limiting recreation and free time.

Participants are divided into groups of eight or twelve (keep-

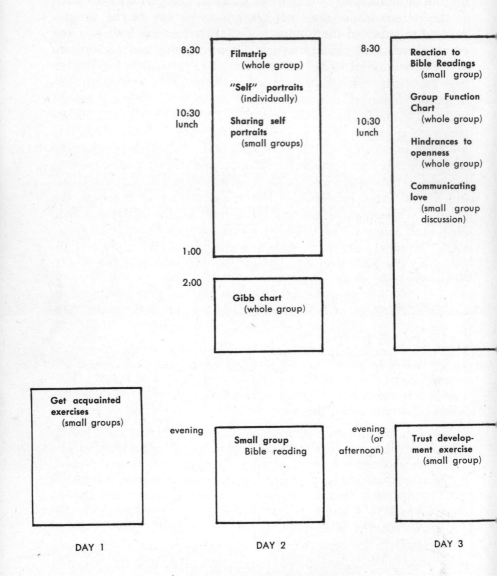

Trust Formation Retreat

Figure 9.

ing the number even). A number of small groups may take part, as the retreat leader does not participate in any of the groups. And no member of the groups is designated as the leader. Concerning such leaderless groups, *T-Group Theory and Laboratory Method* comments, "Our many years of experience with 'leaderless' groups in various settings led us to feel that maximum participative behavior is attained more readily in training groups without trainers than with trainers" (p. 298). This leaderless structure is particularly important in the church, where believers are seen as interdependent units of a body, in which relationship each believer has a ministry. The retreat, then, is designed to initiate certain processes in small leaderless groups. But the working out of these processes is the responsibility of those in the groups. Throughout the week the retreat leader introduces concepts and suggests experiences which should help each group work through to trust formation. *But the leader does not infringe on the autonomy of a group, or take responsibility for its life away from its members.*

The Retreat

First Night (2½-3½ hours)
The leader briefly states the purpose of the retreat: to form small groups and help get off to a good start in the experience which will extend over the next several months.
Two hours (or three, if group sizes are 12 or above) are used in initial get-acquainted exercises.

(1) Pair the members of each small group. One of each pair is to tell his partner "all he needs to know" to understand him as a person — in three minutes. Then these roles are reversed.

(2) The small groups then come together, and each person has 1½ minutes to help the group understand his partner as a person. Everyone is free to interject questions and comments, and the groups should be permitted to run well over the suggested time limit.

(3) Each small group member is asked to check his perception of other members, by saying what he thinks they were like at age seven. One of the group is selected as first subject. Each then shares his impression of the subject as a seven-year-old. The subject is then invited to tell what the group saw correctly, and incorrectly. In the process he begins to share himself. The process is repeated with another person as subject.

For this exercise too the group is encouraged to ask questions, make comments, etc.

(4) When about half the group have been described as seven-year-olds, interject and ask them to imagine the others as seventeen. Ask the group to describe how they think these members would respond in this hypothetical situation: At seventeen they have developed serious questions about their faith. How would they handle their doubts? Would they share them? With whom? Would they hide them? Why?

This experience encourages each person to reveal how he feels about others, and to express how he feels about revealing socially unacceptable thoughts and feelings. Here too conversation within the groups is to be encouraged. The more informal and personal the group experience, the more effective it will be.

(5) The leader concludes the evening with a reading of II Corinthians 1:3-11. He points out the importance of being ourselves and expressing ourselves if we are to minister and be ministers.

Second Day (Morning)

(1) The whole group views the filmstrip, *Members One of Another,* and discusses it for half an hour.

(2) Each person is given a large sheet of paper and crayons. He is asked to draw, or express, his *real self.* This may be done pictorially, with swirls of color, etc. But each is urged to try to capture and express the person he feels he is *right now.* Participants are asked not to disturb others or to show their pictures around.

Coffee break: 20 minutes

(3) All return to their small groups, and each is asked to explain his picture to the others. Again, all are urged to enter into discussion, with the goal being to understand one another as fully as possible.

(4) If discussion lags, or groups tend to move through exercise 3 "on the surface," the leader may inject a Scriptural thought, such as the idea in Colossians 2:11 f. that sharing in Christ means "the miracle of rising again to a new life." How does the picture of each person show him in this process of rising? How would each like to see Christ fitting into his life?

(Afternoon)

(1) The Gibb chart (p. 164), showing priorities in group development, is explained to the whole group. This will help them

better understand the purpose of the morning's activities, and give them insights into what happened in their groups.

(2) Assignment is made for the evening meeting: review any portions of Scripture which have been particularly significant to you the past few months.

Free time is then provided for recreation and rest on the retreat site.

(Evening)

(1) Small groups meet for about 1½ hours. Members are to read, *without comment or discussion,* passages of Scripture which have been significant for them. After this the group disbands without further conversation.

Third Day (Morning)

(1) Small groups meet for one hour. Members are asked to share their reactions to the choices of Bible readings made by others. Did these choices suggest any insights into the life of other members? Free discussion is to be encouraged.

(2) The chart of small group functions (p. 154) is presented to the whole group. Relevant material from Scripture (Part II of this book) is introduced as appropriate. The whole group is invited to raise questions and discuss.

Coffee break

(3) Cultural hindrances to open communication (pp. 160-162) are discussed with the whole group. The importance of openness and honesty is stressed, and the need for knowing how what you say and do affects others (feedback) is explained.

In particular the importance of viewing hostility as (a) natural, and (b) the hostile individual's problem rather than an attack on the other person, should be brought out.

(4) The small groups are asked to spend at least an hour in discussion of this question: "Our cultural norms against openness often keep us from showing love as well as showing hostility. How can we show support and acceptance to others in this group?"

(Afternoon)

(1) If possible a two hour break for rest and recreation should be permitted. This may be curtailed if departure plans demand.

(2) Each small group is given three envelopes, numbered 1, 2, and 3. The groups are instructed to open each *in order*, and follow the directions given.

Each group is urged to spend all the time needed to work through each question to the full satisfaction of each group member.

Here are the contents of the envelopes.

1. Discuss: Where is our group in terms of the acceptance issue brought out yesterday?
2. First. Each of you feels *most comfortable* with one person in the group. Tell the person with whom you you feel most comfortable why you feel this way about him or her.

   Second. Each of you feels *least comfortable* with one person in the group. Tell the person with whom you feel least comfortable why you feel this way about him or her.
3. Discuss: How did it make you *feel* to be "teller" and/or told in each of the last two situations?

In my experience this structure has led, particularly in the culminating activity, to an intense sense of involvement in and commitment to the group. It has helped the group members learn the rewards of being open with one another, and created a context in which mutual ministries can take place.

13

Development of Group Life

One of the most significant of trends in the secular approach to organizational change is the increasing emphasis placed on helping *people* in an organization grow and change.

I suggested in an earlier chapter that to approach change in the church as a simple matter of manipulating the format of meetings and other structures is both naive and harmful. When we change externals without concern for the people involved we seriously upset patterns of expected behavior. And we set up strong forces of reaction. Such changes will always be viewed by most members of a church as threatening and they will respond by struggling to get back to the comfortable "normal" church life they have known. Sadly, many who are concerned about renewal have initiated changes for which people were not ready. The intense reaction against them has discouraged many from making further attempts, and has forced others to leave their churches.

One chapter in *The Planning of Change* (Bennis, Benne, and Chin)[1] describes a family of change strategies that rely, not on changes in organizational structure alone, but on "normative re-

[1] Warren G. Bennis, Kenneth D. Benne, and Robert Chin, *Planning of Change* (New York: Holt, Rinehart and Winston, Inc., 1969), p. 44. Used by permission.

education." That is, these strategies focus on the "attitudes, values, norms and the external and internal relationships" of the interpersonal system that constitutes the organization. Such strategies recognize that successful change "may require alteration or re-education of these," and thus pay primary attention to the people in the organization (p. 44).

The concern with people is twofold. (1) To involve the people in the organization in working out their own solutions. This requires setting up structures which permit them to work together to define their goals and solve the problems that arise in trying to reach them. It also necessarily involves helping the people in the organization learn to discuss openly their feelings and ideas about the changes that are being worked out. (2) To help the people in the organization develop personally: "releasing and fostering growth in the persons who make up the system to be changed" (p. 48).[2] The same text suggests that

> . . . movement towards innovation-producing organization requires processes of personal and interpersonal re-education so that more of us develop the qualities of independence and capacity for autonomous interdependence earlier attributed to the ideal innovator (p. 525).[3]

Thus to successfully change an organization this school of thought insists that change in the people *within* the organization is crucial.

It is at this point that the small group becomes a key factor in change strategy. This approach to change uses the small training group (T-group) to help members of an organization better understand each other and feel more free to give, and to listen for, attitude and feeling data that must be considered if changes are to be made successfully. Thus the small group is increasingly seen as a context for growth and change; a context in which to free people to become involved in the process of change within an organization.

I inject this here because I want to underline, again, the utterly crucial role the small group has in renewal.

All the freeing forces of the small group, now recognized by

---

[2]Ibid., p. 48.
[3]Ibid., p. 525.

the social sciences, have been inherent from the beginning in the church. God planned His church to be in harmony with His nature, and also to be in full harmony with human nature. The natural power of group relationships, and the overriding power of the Holy Spirit operating through gifted individuals, frees, transforms, and opens up believers to one another and to God. *Renewal in the churches demands renewal in the lives of believers.* For this, the church must become "the Church," and the small group is the ideal context.

What can we expect to happen when people are renewed? How do they view change? I was particularly impressed by this paragraph in the report of a church survey committee, made to the church board — the committee which also reported that in their struggle to evaluate their church they had experienced what "the Church" is.

> Those who have read "Tomorrow's Church Today" [the title under which the first eight chapters of this book were first published] are no doubt wondering how much like this we will become. Again, we don't know. However, we feel it would be unwise to attempt to duplicate it — to super-impose this image on us. We must be who, and what, God wants us to be. And we feel He will lead individuals into those ministries that fit His plan, if we are open and flexible. Thus our structures, forms . . . organization will be shaped by these called people . . . exercising their specific ministries.

I was impressed, because this group came to the point that everyone in our churches must come to — the point of saying, confidently, "we don't know." We don't know, but "if we are open and flexible" God will lead us into His plan.

I am convinced that before we demand broad changes in the structure of the churches (which are most certainly needed!) we must become a freed people who can face change just as the men and women of this committee did. Thus our *first priority* in renewing the people of God seems to me the development of small groups, to be the church *within* our churches.

In the last chapter I suggested some functions of the small group, and how group life might be initiated. In this chapter I want to move on from the initial retreat and look at the *development* of groups that are started. These groups will not include *all* members in any of our churches. How will they fit into our traditional structures? What are some of the problems our small groups will discover, and have to solve, to build an on-going and meaningful life? If church change requires changed people, and the small group is our strategy for freeing them, we need to pay close attention to these questions.

Small Groups in the Traditional Church?

Bob Roxburgh, young British pastor of Calgary's Killarney Baptist Church, wrote me recently, "We have developed a pattern for change in which the 'traditional' coexists alongside the contemporary in harmonious relationship."

Pastor Roxburgh was called by a church that recognized the need for change. How, the people wondered, were they to make an impact in a rapidly growing, changing city of 400,000 on one of Canada's industrial and economic frontiers? Roxburgh accepted the call, promising to introduce change, but not to eliminate the three "basic" services of the church (Sunday morning, Sunday evening, and Wednesday prayer meeting). Changes have come and with them new people.

The main point of change has been in the introduction of small groups, called CADRE groups at Killarney, as an alternative to prayer meeting. At present there are about 120 members in CADRE groups; the other 130 members of the church are free (and urged) to support the more traditional meeting they seem to prefer. Through it all the people have maintained a strong sense of love and unity. Both traditionalists and contemporary groups accept, and value, each other and see themselves as members together in one church. This, to Bob Roxburgh, is the key to their vitality in this growing and excited church.

Often the suggestion is made that traditional services be adapted to a small group format. Why not meet in small groups *during* the traditional prayer meeting time? Why not break down larger Sunday school classes to get them to function as fellowship groups? Isn't the present structure of our churches, with modifications like these, well enough adapted to the small group?

This hasn't been the experience at Calgary, where groups meeting in homes are an accepted alternative to "in church" prayer meeting. I doubt that such suggestions present a meaningful option. I do feel that occasional group experiences within the present framework are a healthy thing, such as, a 4- or 6-week series of small group Bible studies as part of prayer meeting. Or, introducing an adult elective in the Sunday school which features aspects of the small group approach. (Very workable materials are available: i.e. *Growth by Groups* booklets, from Huntingdon, Pennsylvania.) Nevertheless, group life has several distinctives which make it difficult to squeeze into our traditional church agencies. The factors that trouble me most are these:

(1) *Preparation.* Throwing a few men and women together and calling them a "small group" hardly equips members for the quality of participation that group life demands. I feel that most "small group" prayer meetings, and "small group" Sunday school classes, fail to break through the polite facade we adopt to hide from one another. In many cases such sessions can disappoint, and have the same negative impact as the experience reported early in the last chapter. Experiencing group life requires preparation of members for openness and honesty, or the structuring of group experiences to encourage their development — each of which is difficult to do in traditional situations.

(2) *Commitment.* In most programs which attempt to foster group life, a minimum level of commitment is demanded of each participant. Normally this involves attendance at each session of the group, and some preparation before sessions, so that responsibility for success of the sessions is shared. Our traditional services simply do not require this kind of commitment. Attendance is sporadic, and preparation is nil. Traditionally both Sunday school and prayer meeting services revolve around a single leader (the teacher or the pastor), who alone is responsible to prepare. This is deadening to group life. For group life development regular attendance by all members is essential; so is a sense of personal responsibility for the life of the group. While an elective Sunday school class can be structured to call for such commitment, it is unrealistic to expect commitment in organizations which have not traditionally called for it.

(3) *Time.* This seems to me the most serious objection of all. The churches traditionally fit their services and activities into a rigidly circumscribed time schedule. Meetings are to last for an

hour. Then we go home. Such pressures on a small group are extremely destructive to its life and development.

Group life should be built around an *experience*, not packaged in a time block. This means that participants must be completely concerned about the meaningfulness of their shared experience — and completely unconcerned about the amount of time spent. Actually, three hours is a far more realistic amount of time to allot than one!

Small group experience by nature often takes an hour to work through the "strangeness" that a week apart has introduced in the fellowship — to sense again the oneness that was known before. Only then, in the fullness of our fellowship, are we able to move to Bible study, mutual ministries, and prayer. Thus when a small group meets, it is vital that its members *reject* time as a limiting factor.

The time factor is one compelling reason why renewal must ultimately involve restructuring of the church activities and agencies. Ultimately we must rediscover the vitality of our life together as the church in experience-oriented rather than time-oriented structures.

For all these reasons, while we can and should inject a variety of group experiences into our present church structures, the small group will not fit them. While we can and should introduce more participation in our sermons and Sunday school classes, this cannot replace the small group as a center of renewal. And the small group needs a place, and time, of its own — a place like the one at Killarney, where it exists alongside the traditional, not as a threat but as an option. A place to develop in its own unique way, unrestricted by the limits imposed by the rigid, unyielding structures of present church forms.

Ongoing Life

Let us accept then, the premise that small groups require an opportunity to become themselves — to develop in their own ways. And let us leave the problem of relating traditional and renewal people and forms in the same church until chapter 15. Focus now on the distinctive issues the small groups will have to face if they are to develop and grow. How does a small group "become itself"? How does it become "the Church"?

Basic conditions for growth. I have already discussed one of
the basic conditions for the growth of group life. (1) The group
must learn to share Christ's life in mutual ministries characterized
by openness, self-revelation, concern and prayer. I suggested a
retreat in which the focus is placed on encouraging trust development, to free group members for openness.

Two other conditions seem basic if a small group is to function
as "the Church." (2) There must exist a mutual commitment to
Christ and a responsiveness to Him as He speaks through His
Word. And (3) there must be a commitment to accomplish
God's will as it is revealed.

The role of Scripture in small groups in the church is much
disputed. Some renewal writers see a need only for those who
come together to have a general commitment to "Christian values." Some see the small group as a vehicle of evangelism. Thus
it is cast as a neighborhood Bible class, or, on the other extreme,
a group in which the Bible is seldom mentioned but believers
invite alienated individuals to experience, through them, God's
love and acceptance. Others see the small group in the church
as a prayer cell; others as strictly a place for sharing. To these
people the Scripture has an important, but background, role.

The small group is a useful vehicle for any of these purposes.
But in this book I am concerned only with the small group functioning as the church — that is, as Christians-in-relationship,
with the spiritual growth of believers the primary concern. For
the church, as described in Scripture, is not *directly* concerned
with evangelism or social action, but with the nurture of its members. If, then, the small group as the church is to function as the
church, we must ask, What is the role of Scripture in the church?
The answer to this will determine the place we must give the
Word in our small groups.

In chapter 10 I developed the concept that the Word of God
stands to the church as the revelation of God. As His objective
truth it gives us insight into the way God views us, our life and
life-situations, and eternity. As such it is intimately related to the
personality transformation task with which the church is charged.
For this transformation involves reshaping the believer, to bring
him into harmony with God's way of thinking, feeling, and being.
The Word of God, which uniquely reveals what that way is, is
essential to the task of the church. Because Scripture alone, with

its source outside of human culture and experience and brought to us by supernatural revelation, can give us an objective check on the mind of God, the church is commanded to "hold fast to the pattern of sound words."

Yet in its insistence that it is revealed truth, Scripture never loses sight of its nature and mission in transformation. Because it is truth, it accurately portrays reality. Because it is given for transformation, we are not merely responsible to *believe* it. We are responsible to live it. Thus in our approach to Scripture in the church our primary concern must always be, How am I to respond in view of this new understanding of God's way? We are to center our study of the Word on its experiential impact, not on construction and defense of a doctrinal system. We read it, not to pinpoint the time of the Second Coming, but to know what God seeks in me in relation to His return.

Please do not misunderstand this. I am not in any way questioning the eternal, objective, absolute nature of God's revelation. But I am insisting that the eternal relate to us in time; that the objective be made part of our subjective experience; that the absolute be absolute for me, here and now — and not merely absolute as some abstract truth "out there." The Word is to be central in the ongoing life of the small group in the church, but it is to be studied primarily to discover its impact on present experience.

Unfortunately we evangelicals have been trained to think of and to read Scripture in terms of "truth to be understood" rather than "reality to live." One problem most small groups in the church will face is tied directly to this. How can the study of the Bible be *meaningful* in our group? For this many of us will have to re-learn our approach to Scripture.

A simplified framework for meaningful (in the sense of experientially relevant) Bible study is expressed in the following diagram.

Normally (Λ) will be done at home, though it possibly could be done in the group. (B) will be discussed in the group, and a consensus understanding of the meaning of the passage will emerge. (C) is necessarily a group activity. To the extent that openness is maintained, and real needs shared, the Bible will become compellingly relevant as deepening bonds of love and prayer develop.

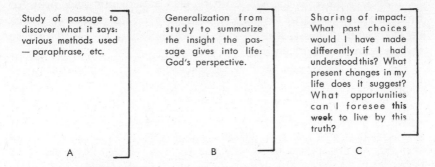

Figure 10. Pattern for Group Bible Study

Small groups often have difficulty in determining how to select Bible portions for study. Several ways are open. The first is to select Scripture on the basis of needs discovered in group sharing. This is probably the most exciting way to live together as the church. We share ourselves, until we bring to the surface a question, problem or need that has real meaning for us. Then we turn to God, to search His Word, and discover in the ministry of the Holy Spirit His reality, as He speaks to us and gives us wisdom.

Many small groups feel uncertain about this approach. At first a group tends to look for a leader who "knows the Bible" and can point them quickly to answers. When a group is willing to take full responsibility itself, and willing to invest time outside the group meeting in personal Bible study, this "disadvantage" becomes a highly motivating impetus to personal study and growth.

A second approach is to select a portion of Scripture arbitrarily, and work through it week by week. Each individual in the group studies an assigned portion (A) at home. The group then discusses the meaning of the passage (B), and shares its impact (C).

A third approach is to adopt materials which are designed to "help" the group. Too often materials selected are of a "fill in the blank" kind, which hop all over Scripture seeking a proof text here and a proof text there, to force the student into the pattern of thinking of the writer. As you may gather, I am not enthusiastic about this approach. It severely limits the freedom of the group, and *freedom* is the genius of the church. Freedom requires a minimum of structure and a maximum of flexibility, permitting an unpatterned group to respond spontaneously to the leading of the Holy Spirit.

I might say a word here about a common fear, expressed to me by many. Doesn't this approach (the "turning loose" of a small group without a "trained man") lead to doctrinal deviation? More than one pastor has been upset by the idea of the small group, and expressed a desire to protect his people by making sure that the only teaching they receive is "pure" teaching — from him! My response to this is to point out that this whole pattern of thinking is a return to pre-Reformation Catholicism. Luther could contend that the meanest peasant with Scripture was mightier than the greatest Pope without it — but we are unwilling to turn the Word of God over to the best educated generation of Christians the world has ever produced! Even worse, in our fear to trust the Holy Spirit to faithfully interpret His Word, we deny the Word we claim to protect for Him. For that Word says "the man who really believes in the Son of God will find God's testimony in his own heart," and "the touch of His Spirit never leaves you, and you don't really need a human teacher. You know that His Spirit teaches you all things" (I John 2:27).

When Paul established churches he left them to God, with only the Word he taught and wrote. And God was faithful. God taught them, and they grew strong. How tragic if we can no longer trust God: if *we* insist on teaching them. No wonder today we are weak, no wonder we need renewal!

The Word of God, then, must have a central place in the small groups we establish, if they are to function as the Church.

The third condition (3) I mentioned reflects the responsibility of the group to sense and to do the will of God. It relates to leading into the particular role each individual, the group, or the church as a whole is to have in filling Christ's ministry in the world. A commitment to *do* God's will as He leads frees God to coordinate the various groups in the congregation to form a harmonious whole. It permits Him to *be* Head of His Body, the church. This sensing of God's leading is related directly to consensus decision making and goal-oriented thinking, and will be discussed in the next chapter.

Solving emerging problems. Even when a small group has discovered the meaningfulness of honest sharing and has developed skill in relating to God through the Scripture it will face a multitude of problems. When will the group meet, and where, and for how long? How will new members be integrated into the life of the group? How can shared leadership be most effective for us? How do we help all members of the group meet the standards we work out for the most meaningful experience? What specific goals, action goals, should be set for our group and our whole church? There may also be a number of problems in working out various process problems.

The National Training Laboratories, pioneers in the field of group work and publishers of a number of excellent books and pamphlets, suggests symptoms of a number of group process problems in its booklet, *Group Development* (p. 42-45).

If
- every suggestion made seems impossible for practical reasons,
- some members feel the committee is too small,
- everyone seems to feel pushed for time,
- members are impatient with one another,
- members insist the group doesn't have the know-how or experience to get anywhere,
- each member has a different idea of what the committee is supposed to do,
- whenever a suggestion is made, at least one member feels it won't satisfy the larger organization,

Then
- the group may have been given an impossible job and members are frustrated because they feel unable to meet the demands made of them, or the task is not clear or is disturbing.

If
- ideas are attacked before they are completely expressed,
- members take sides and refuse to compromise,
- there is no movement toward a solution of the problem,
- the group keeps getting stuck on inconsequential points,
- members attack one another on a personal level in subtle ways,
- there are subtle attacks on the leadership,
- there is no concern with finding a goal or sticking to the point,
- there is much clique formation,

Then
- the main concern of members may be in finding status in the group. The main interest is not in the problem. The problem is merely being used as a vehicle for expressing interpersonal concerns.

If
- the goal is stated in very general, non-operational terms,
- members take sides and refuse to compromise,
- each member is pushing his own plan,
- suggestions don't build on previous suggestions, each member seeming to start again from the beginning,
- members disagree on plans or suggestions,
- members don't listen to one another, each waiting for a chance to say something,

Then
- each member is probably operating from a unique, unshared point of view, perhaps because the members are loyal to different outside groups with conflicting interests.

If
- there is a goal which members understand and agree on,
- most comments are relevant to the problem,
- members frequently disagree with one another over suggestions,
- comments and suggestions are made with a great deal of vehemence,
- there are occasional expressions of warmth,
- members are frequently impatient with one another,
- there is general movement toward some solution of the problem,

Then
- probably, members feel involved and are working hard on a problem. The fight being expressed is constructive rather than destructive in character and reflects real interest on the part of members.

APATHY — an apathetic membership is a frequent ailment of groups. Groups may suffer in different degrees from this disease. In some cases members may show complete indifference to the group task, and give evidence of marked boredom. In others, apathy may take the form of a lack of genuine enthusiasm for the job, a failure to mobilize much energy, lack of persistence, satisfaction with poor work.

Some ways in which apathy may be expressed:
a) frequent yawns, people dozing off
b) members lose the point of the discussion
c) low level of participation
d) conversation drags
e) members come late; are frequently absent
f) slouching and restlessness
g) overquick decisions
h) failure to follow through on decisions
i) ready suggestions for adjournment

j) failure to consider necessary arrangements for the next meeting
k) reluctance to assume any further responsibility.

If
— questions may be raised about what's really our job, what do *they* want us to do,
— members fail to follow through on decisions,
— there is no expectation that members will contribute responsibly, and confused, irrelevant statements are allowed to go by without question,
— members wonder about the reason for working on this problem,
— suggestions are made that we work on something else,
— the attitude is expressed that we should just decide on anything, the decision doesn't really matter,
— members seem to be waiting for a respectable amount of time to pass before referring the decision to the leader, or to a committee,
— members are inattentive, seem to get lost and not to have heard parts of the preceding discussion,
— suggestions frequently "plop," are not taken up and built on by others,
— no one will volunteer for additional work,

Then
— the group goal may seem unimportant to the members.

If
— there are long delays in getting started, much irrelevant preliminary conversation,
— the group shows embarrassment or reluctance in discussing the problem at hand,
— members emphasize the consequences of making wrong decisions, imagine dire consequences which have little reference to ascertainable facts,
— members make suggestions apologetically, are over-tentative, and hedge their contributions with many *if's* and *but's*,
— solutions proposed are frequently attacked as unrealistic,
— suggestions are made that someone else ought to make the decision — the leader, an outside expert, or some qualified person outside the group,
— members insist that we haven't enough information or ability to make a decision, and appear to demand an unrealistically high level of competence,
— the group has a standard of cautiousness in action,
— numerous alternative proposals are suggested, with the group apparently unable to make a decision,

Then
  — members probably fear working toward the group goal.
If
  — no one is able to suggest the first step in getting started toward
    the goal,
  — members seem to be unable to stay on a given point, and each
    person seems to start on a new tack,
  — members appear to talk past, to misunderstand one another, and
    the same points are made over and over,
  — the group appears to be unable to develop adequate summaries,
    or restatements of points of agreement,
  — there is little evaluation of the possible consequences of decisions
    reached, and little attention is given to fact-finding or use of
    special resources,
  — members continually shift into related, but off-target, tasks,
  — complaints are made that the group's job is an impossible one,
  — subgroups continually form around the table, with private dis-
    cussions held off to the side,
  — there is no follow-through on decisions or disagreement in the
    group about what the decisions really were,
  — complaints are made that you can't decide things in a group
    anyway, and the leader or somebody else should do the job,
Then
  — the group may have inadequate problem-solving procedures.
If
  — the view is expressed that someone else with more power in the
    organization should be present in the meeting, that it is difficult
    to communicate with him at a distance,
  — unrealistic decisions are made, and there is an absence of sense
    of responsibility for evaluating consequences of decisions,
  — the position is taken that the decision doesn't really matter be-
    cause the leader or someone outside the group isn't really going
    to listen to what we say,
  — there is a tendency to ignore reaching consensus among mem-
    bers, the important thing being to get the leader to understand
    and listen,
  — the discussion is oriented toward power relations, either within
    the group, jockeying to win over the leader, or outside the group,
    with interest directed toward questions about who really counts
    in the organization,
  — doubts are voiced about whether we're just wasting our efforts
    in working on this program,
  — members leave the meeting feeling they had good ideas which
    they didn't seem to be able to get across,

Then
— members feel powerless about influencing final decisions.

If
— two or three members dominate all discussion, but never agree,
— conflict between strong members comes out no matter what is discussed,
— dominant members occasionally appeal to others for support, but otherwise control conversation,
— decisions are made by only two or three members,

Then
— a conflict among a few members is creating apathy in the others.

INADEQUATE DECISION MAKING — getting satisfactory decisions made is often a major struggle in the group. These problems are discussed in detail in the article "Decisions . . . Decisions . . . Decisions!" beginning on page 69 of this publication. Here is a list of common symptoms of inefficient decision-making.

If
— the group swings between making too rapid decisions and having difficulty in deciding anything,
— the group almost makes the decision but at the last minute retreats,
— group members call for definition and redefinition of minute points,
— the discussion wanders into abstraction,

Then
— there has been premature calling for a decision, or the decision is too difficult, or the group is low in cohesiveness and lacks faith in itself.

If
— the group has lack of clarity as to what the decision is,
— there is disagreement as to where consensus is,
— a decision is apparently made but challenged at the end,
— group members refuse responsibility,
— there is continued effort to leave decision making to leader, subgroup or outside source,

Then
— the decision area may be threatening to the group, either because of unclear consequences, fear of reaction of other groups, or fear of failure for the individuals.

All this may lead us to ask, what controls do we need to set up in the church to make sure problems are successfully solved? To see the myriad of potential shoals that seem able to wreck the small group, how can we best protect our groups against them? On this subject I find a paragraph in *T-Group Theory and Laboratory Methods* particularly significant.

> We found that groups tended to take over direction of their own processes and move more quickly along the dimensions of growth when given the greatest freedom and least prescribed structure. Groups built their own attendance norms and reduced absence to nearly zero as they arrived at group generated goals. Groups found they needed data and constructed their own instruments, which were in many cases more imaginative and certainly more relevant to emergent daily concerns than were the instruments provided by the staff in earlier years. Groups organized for work built internal and distributive leadership structure and worked with interpersonal data that were more significant and at greater depth than those dealt with in conventional trainer groups.

In other words, *the freedom to be responsible* is critical in group growth and development.

This does not mean that a group will be deserted once a retreat initiates its life. Or that there is no role, as counselor, for the church leadership. It does mean that development of a strong, ongoing life requires that church leadership trust God and the group, and that group members learn to trust God and each other.

What can church leadership do, specifically? (1) Make sure that the small groups understand the role and place of Scripture in church life. (2) Be sure the group members understand that they are both trusted and responsible for group life development. (3) Provide as resources some of the excellent materials that discuss group life and group problems (see bibliography). (4) Encourage a conference of small groups, in which questions and problems can be shared and discussed. (5) If invited, visit a group meeting to help restore the members' confidence in themselves. (6) But primarily realize that healthy growth and development of the small group and the church demands that responsibility for group life be placed squarely on the group members themselves — and left there.

14

Involvement in Goal Setting

One reason why many approaches to planned change focus on the people within an organization lies in the growing awareness that change, to be successful, requires that those involved be given a role in guiding the changes made. The small group, discussed in the last two chapters, is used to help people learn to listen to each other. They need to learn to accept all the relevant data — which means valuing people's feelings and reactions as well as "the facts." As members of an organization openly and honestly discuss their goals and ways to reach them, changes made are more likely to accomplish desired ends.

One of the premises on which this book is based is this: change in our churches must be an open, and a local, process. By *open* I mean that we can not change *toward predetermined ends.* The leadership of a church must not attempt to manipulate the people, and so force change into patterns set beforehand. Rather, the people of a church must be fully involved in the total process: in setting the goals, and in working out ways to implement them.

This necessarily introduces an uncertainty factor into change. When we structure a process of change, we can never know for sure just where it will lead us. And so church change is open ended. Change is *local* because each congregation must work through its own problems. With this presupposition it is impossible for me to set down four or five steps to "easy renewal." At most I can isolate and discuss key aspects of the change process.

In the last two chapters the focus was placed on the small group because this to me is crucial in effecting renewal. In this chapter the focus is placed on another crucial area — the involvement of the people of a church in the process of change. Within this area I want to look at three factors: (1) the decision-making process best adapted to change, (2) the encouragement of goal-directed thinking, and (3) the approach to reaching set goals.

Decision Making in the Church

In chapter 9 I suggested that Scripture, and the nature of the church, indicate decisions in the church should be arrived at by *consensus*. I suspect this was misunderstood by some, and disliked by others. Yet there are many reasons why this is the only method for use in church renewal and change.

The nature of the alternatives provides some of the strongest arguments for consensus. Consider, for example, autocratic rule — change imposed by authority. I object to this as a serious distortion of the role Scripture assigns to leaders in the church. It is difficult to *impose* change on any voluntary organization. The armed forces can require changes and enforce them militarily. Employers can require changes and enforce them economically. But how can the church require or enforce? What sanctions can be applied to command conformity?

Interestingly, even military and business structures find it difficult to impose changes. Departments, offices, and individuals all display an "informal organization" (pattern of behavior) which differs from the "formal organization" expressed on charts and in procedure manuals. Thus people in the organization are successful in thwarting, blocking, or sidestepping officially prescribed ways of doing things. Really, the autocratic method of decision making is not only unscriptural, it is not even effective in situations where machinery exists for enforcement.

The most common approach to decision making in voluntary associations, in our culture, is the vote. I suggested earlier that this also runs counter to the nature of the church. The vote tends to divide, not to unite. During pre-election campaigns in our country people are divided into Democrats and Republicans — and Independents. The whole process of electioneering tends to make these differences appear more significant than they are — as witnessed to by the ease with which, after an election, we settle back into being just Americans. The divisive effect of the vote is one which cannot be tolerated in the church, for the church is uniquely one. *It cannot be forced to take sides and remain true to its nature.* The vote approach to decision making must always do just this: it must force individuals to argue and attempt to convince, rather than help them work together to reach mutually agreeable solutions. The vote just is not an option for the church.

Consensus is the better way — arriving at a decision agreeable to all members of a group, which all will support. There are several advantages to the consensus approach. It emphasizes the unity of the group and tends to increase cooperation. It encourages creativity as group members are stimulated to find new solutions (rather than to campaign for the old). Consensus tends to emphasize the goal toward which a group is working. Thus each individual considers the good of all, rather than only his own. And consensus succeeds at the very point at which the other methods fail — in drawing out commitment necessary to follow through on a decision. Members view the decision made as *their* decision and feel responsibility for acting.

What is a consensus? And what does consensus decision making involve? A consensus is *a shared conviction that a particular decision is the right one.* Steps to be taken in achieving consensus can be stated simply — but each group has to work out its own style of reaching and recognizing consensus. The essential steps are:

> Everyone participates fully in discussion of the problem. Each member of the group is responsible to state his ideas and feelings as various factors and possible choices are brought out.
>
> No one agrees "for the sake of harmony" or to please a friend. If a suggested course of action disturbs a group member, he is to express his viewpoint, his feelings, his reasons. This is data a group *must have* to reach a true consensus.
>
> When a person honestly feels that he can agree with one or more courses of action (even though they may not be his first choice) he so expresses himself.

When all relevant data has been brought out and discussed, and everyone in the group is satisfied that a particular decision is the right one, consensus has been reached.

It is clear from this description that reaching a consensus takes time. Actually, however, this process is much more effective than the others in the long run. Other methods of decision making may lead to quick decisions (and even right decisions), *but the implementation of the decision will lag*. For the execution of a decision depends on the cooperation of every member involved. And cooperation is difficult to achieve by other means. To judge the success of decision making, one should not look at the time required to reach a decision, but focus on the length of time between the definition of the problem and its solution.

Figure 11.

Decision-making Processes

While a consensus decision may seem to take longer to reach, the solution of the problem (the real goal) comes most quickly using this approach.

```
                                          consensus
                                          decision
problem o_____O_____o solution

              imposed decision
problem o_____O_____o solution
```

Another important consideration, buttressed by considerable research, is that the *quality* of a consensus decision is nearly always higher than that of a decision reached by other means. More information is gathered, and more factors considered, in the consensus-reaching process. As a result, decisions are more likely to be good ones.

Closely related to this is the fact that a consensus approach provides a context in which conflicting views can be considered within a context of oneness. In other situations resistance to change is often misunderstood and fought against. Actually resistance and disagreement provide just the kind of information necessary if changes are to be made effectively. In *A Leader and the Process of Change*, Thomas A. Bennett[1] suggests several values that are always inherent in resistance (adapted from p. 8).

[1]Thomas A. Bennett, *A Leader and the Process of Change* (New York: Association Press n.d.), p. 8.

1. It forces us to clarify the purpose of change, and the results to be achieved.
2. It discloses inadequate communication processes and an insufficient flow of information — both of which must be corrected.
3. It encourages us to examine more carefully the immediate and long-range consequences of change. This may lead to revisions which increase the effectiveness of the change effort. Thus resistance provides clues to bring into the open unexpected consequences of a decision.

In other approaches to decision making, resistance is often seen in a negative light. In a consensus situation, resistance is good. Members of the group are invited, and urged, to express doubts and problems. And this behavior is viewed by all as helpful. Thus resistance forces can be handled without destroying the unity of the group, or the mutual commitment of the group to its goals.

For all these reasons, consensus decision making is a must strategy in working toward church renewal.

Encouragement of Goal-directed Thinking

Recently a friend challenged the idea of consensus decision making. His view was that most of the people in our churches have thought so little about the basic issues of church life they simply could not reach an intelligent decision! To some this may seem a compelling reason to abandon consensus. To me it is a compelling reason to *insist* on consensus!

Suppose that a church board did force through changes in church structure without the full understanding and cooperation of the members. How well would the changes work? Not at all! Successful changes hinge on the understanding and cooperation of those involved. Members who neither understand nor agree with changes resist them. Or, at best, are indifferent and withdraw. And so the changes would be meaningless. They could never accomplish the purposes for which they were made.

Change demands an involved and committed group of people. What better way is there to call out commitment than to involve the people of God in a serious search for His will, and in making decisions which will reflect it?

At the same time, it is discouraging to see the lack of goal-oriented thinking in our churches. We live by habit. Even boards and committees charged with making policy decisions focus far more on organizational trivia than on their goals and objectives. I have found too that when questions of goals and objectives are raised, our tendency is to think immediately of methods. For instance, it is a clear biblical principle — and thus should be one of our objectives in the church — that the home is to be the center of Christian nurture. This responsibility is *never* given to the church. But suggest this, and our reaction is to ask, "But how will we do that?" And if we cannot see the how, we reject the whole idea out-of-hand. How tragic for the church!

It is necessary for renewal to focus thinking in our churches on goals — not on means. When the goals are defined, and our objectives are stated, God can lead us into creative ways of working them out. How can this be done in our churches? One of the small groups at Honey Rock Camp developed a short list of approaches (Fig. 12). In addition, I would like to comment at greater length on the approach used at Rockford and on two other approaches I have used recently.

Figure 12.

Helping Our Churches Think in Terms of Goals

1. A six-month strategy:
   a. Committees to study purpose of church; calling in resource individuals outside church; reporting to entire church
   b. Pastor devotes a series of sermons to scriptural foundation, with interaction and participation
   c. For one quarter, all Sunday School classes, High School and above, engage in in-depth study and discussion.
2. Leadership of church on week-long retreat, involving group training, discussion of goals.
3. Renewal books made available to members, reported on, etc.
4. Discussion groups meet to review renewal reading.
5. Hold conference (like missions conference) on Nature of the Church.
6. Provide and use evaluation tools:
   a. Mennonite Brethren, 4824 E. Butler, Fresno, Cal.
   b. Fuller Seminary, Church Growth Institute
   c. Church Growth, South Bend, Indiana
   d. American Baptist
   e. Methodist "Planbook"
      etc.

7. Involve families in developing a list of priorities.
8. Pass out pamphlets, etc.
9. Share articles from magazines.
10. Discover what other churches are doing, via **interCHANGE** (p. 208), visits to nearby churches, visits from churches where change is taking place.

The survey committee. When the First Evangelical Free Church of Rockford, Illinois, felt the need to examine its ministry, an 18-member committee was appointed. The committee was to report on three questions: Where are we now? Where do we want to go? How can we best get there? The first two meetings were spent interpreting the assignment, which they defined this way (as contained in their final report, dated May 23, 1969):

1. FIND THE BIBLICAL PATTERN OF THE CHURCH
   We felt it was necessary for us to determine from God's Word what was the reason for the church's existence: Why are we here? What was God's purpose in establishing His church? What did God intend His church to be and to do?

2. ESTABLISH GOALS AND OBJECTIVES
   Once we formed the biblical picture of the church we then established our long range objectives and goals for reaching these objectives, all based on the biblical picture or pattern.

3. DEVELOP A STRATEGY AND PLANS FOR ACHIEVING THESE GOALS AND OBJECTIVES
   The Bible-based information thus acquired would not only give us direction but would also give our church bench marks against which to measure our performance for God, both as a congregation and as individuals.

These men and women were laymen — not theologians and not deeply immersed in renewal thinking. Yet their assignment led them to focus on the nature and purposes of the church. They began to think in terms of goals and objectives, and *then* think in terms of how to reach them. As the committee went through this process of goal-oriented study they themselves were gripped and changed.

This is one way to help our people think in terms of goals — to challenge boards, committees, classes, and individuals to work out answers to similar simple, but penetrating, questions.

The evaluation guide. Recently I have worked with several church boards, using an evaluation guide to raise questions concerning the goals and objectives of their church. Because this tool has seemed effective I include it here, and extend permission to any who wish to duplicate and use it. Part II of the guide is adapted from a tool developed by Elmo Warkentin of the Evangelical Mennonite Church.

The questionnaire does not provide answers. And it reflects an "agency structured" rather than renewed organization — because that is the structure of churches who will use it. Yet it has, whenever I have used it, focused attention on basic biblical goals, and raised serious questions about "the way we're trying to do it now."

The questionnaire is best used when a significant block of time is available (3 to 4 hours), and when the whole questionnaire will be worked through at one sitting.

Local Church

SELF-EVALUATION GUIDE

It is important that a church periodically sit down to evaluate the purposes to which Christ has called it, and the ways in which it has attempted to obey His call. This is particularly important any time a church faces decisions which may affect its life and future ministry.

This tool is designed to help in making such an evaluation, and in clarifying church goals. When goals have been clarified and agreed on, then and only then is a church prepared to make major decisions.

Contents

   I. We evaluate ourselves
      a. Our Christian education ministry
      b. Our ministry through the home
      c. Our ministry of outreach
      d. Our personal spiritual growth
  II. We gather information
 III. We clarify goals

I. We Evaluate Ourselves

Read through the items in each of the four areas in this part of the guide. (1) On the basis of criteria suggested (in parenthesis with each item) decide whether or not your church is accomplishing what is indicated. Discuss and decide this together. It is important to spend enough time on each item to *come to agreement* on whether

to check Yes, No, or Question. (2) Then discuss and decide together
how important this is to your church. Indicate in the columns to the
left whether you consider this a Must, or an Optional.
Each item should be discussed by the whole group, and a consensus
arrived at, if this self-evaluation tool is to be of real value.

A.   Our Christian Education Ministry

Yes	No	?		Must	Op-tional
			1. We periodically attempt to discover and meet the needs of all age-groups in our church. (How is this done? When was it done last? What changes were made as a result of the study?)		
			2. We have *in writing* long and short-range goals for our various agencies and activities. (Where are these goals stated? How recently were they evaluated, and set?)		
			3. We have a board or committee responsible for setting Christian education objectives, and seeing that they are met. (If so, is the board functioning in this way?)		
			4. The responsibilities of our CE workers are clearly stated and understood. These include responsibilities to students, and the homes from which they come. (Where are these stated? Are they understood by those who serve? Do workers fulfill their responsibilities?)		
			5. We realize that the starting point of Christian education is the home, and coordinate our agencies and their ministries with our homes. (How? What is the relationship? What do parents do? Church workers?)		

Yes	No	?		Must	Op-tional
			6. Our teachers and leaders receive training to equip them for their ministries. (What training was provided last year? How many participated?)		
			7. We plan in specific ways to help learners translate the Bible content taught in our church agencies into vital daily experience with God. (How is this done? What does helping learners live Bible truths involve?)		
			8. Designated leaders in each agency supervise to maintain the quality of ministry provided in our churches. (Who is designated? How do they supervise? How do they measure, and improve, the quality of ministries?)		
			9. We periodically evaluate workers in our agencies to see that they are ministering effectively. (Who evaluates them? By what criteria is effectiveness measured?)		
			10. We realize that reaching and teaching adults is the key to church growth and vitality, and do not overemphasize a ministry to children. (What makes adult ministry the key? What percent of effort is expended with various age-groups?)		
			11. We are effective in reaching *families* for Christ through our agency ministries. (What contact is made with homes of the unsaved? What percent of the decisions recorded are children? What percent adult?)		
			12. We carefully maintain contact with those who make profession of faith in Christ, and nurture them in their		

Yes	No	?		Must	Op- tional
			new faith. (How? Who is respon- sible? Who checks up on new con- verts? What happened to children who made profession 5 years ago? 3 years ago? To adults?)		
			SUMMARY Jot down any questions this evalua- tion has raised about your Christian education program.		
			B. Our Ministry Through the Home		
			1. We constantly stress that the pri- mary responsibility for Christian nurture rests on parents. (How is this done? How is this principle implemented in the church pro- gram?)		
			2. We provide training and other helps to equip parents to teach and guide their children in the Christian life. (What training is provided? What helps? How many in church par- ticipate in such activities?)		
			3. We view the Sunday School as an aid to the home, not a substitute for it. This view is reflected in the cooperation of Sunday School and home. (How do the two cooperate? What information on SS studies is provided for the home? How do SS teachers work with parents?)		
			4. We encourage our members to con- duct meaningful family devotions. (What helps are provided? What problems do our families have? How do we help solve these prob- lems?)		
			5. We view the home as the basic unit of the church, and encourage families to witness in their neigh-		

Yes	No	?		Must	Op-tional
			borhoods. (How is this encouraged? Are adults witnessing to neighbors? Are they involved with others as a family?)		
			6. We encourage parents to nurture their children in the Biblical pattern (defined in Deut. 6:5, 6) by applying Scripture to their daily lives, not just saying words. (Do parents understand this kind of sharing? How have they been trained for it? Is it being carried out?)		
			SUMMARY		
			Jot down any questions this evaluation has raised about the ministry of your church to and through the home.		
			C. Our Ministry of Outreach and Witness		
			1. We have made realistic efforts to reach the unsaved in our community. (What have we done? Who have we reached? Are we going out to them, or waiting for them to come to us?)		
			2. Newcomers find it easy to become involved in the life of our church. (How do we welcome them. Of those who visit, how many stay?)		
			3. Our church members maintain close friendships with non-Christians in their respective communities. (How many close non-Christian friends do *you* have? What kind of things do you do together? How much time do you spend together?)		
			4. Our church members are members of various community groups in which they can both serve and come		

Yes	No	?		Must	Op-tional
			to know others who need Christ. (What groups are represented in our church? How much time do our people give to such activities? How many have come to know Christ through such associations?)		
			5. Our outreach ministry is reflected by the presence of those won by us to Christ this past year in our church. (How many adult converts have joined the church in the past three years? How many others have made profession of faith?)		
			6. Our church members are consistently witnessing to others, and share such experiences with one another. (In the past month, how many have asked prayer for people they are witnessing to? How many have shared witnessing experiences?)		
			7. We are aware of those who move into our communities, and contact them within a few days.		
			SUMMARY		
			Jot down any questions this evaluation has raised about the outreach and witness of your church.		

D. Our Personal Spiritual Growth

% Yes	% No	?		Must	Op-tional
			1. Our people know how to study the Word of God for growth and enrichment, and do so regularly. (What percent do regularly study the Word? How do they study the Bible — what methods have they been taught?)		
			2. Our people effectively solve personal problems, applying the Word of God in the Spirit's strength. (How do we go about problem-solving? Who do we rely on and go to in times of trouble?)		
			3. Our people are growing spiritually, as adults minister to each other, sharing their experiences and problems, and victories won in Christ. (What occasions are given for this kind of sharing? How well do we know each other? What do we talk about when we converse? How victorious are we?)		
			4. Our people daily share their faith in Christ with friends and neighbors who do not know Him. (How many of our people are actively witnessing? How many have we won to Christ this year? How many are we praying for now?)		
			5. Our members are deeply concerned about others' needs, and express this concern by giving of their time, money, and themselves. (What needs are we aware of? How are we meeting them? How many of us are significantly involved in the lives of others?)		
			6. Our people are dedicated to the goals and purposes of the church. They take an active role in guiding its course and fulfilling its ministries.		

% Yes	% No	?		Must	Op-tional
			(How many "just come"? How many are involved in church life? How many are aware of the present goals and objectives of this church?)		
			7. Our people form a community within which Christ's command to "love one another" is daily fulfilled. (How do we show that we love one another? Is our love a practical or theoretical one? Do outsiders know us, as Christ said His disciples should be known, by this mark: "how they love one another?")		
			SUMMARY		
			Jot down any questions this evaluation has raised about the personal spiritual growth stimulated by your church.		

II. We Gather Information

The following charts should be completed with information from church records. If information is not available, those present may estimate.

This information will provide a check on the evaluation of current activities. Should you wish, in light of this information, go back and discuss any item on Part I.

A. Membership/Sunday School Chart

B. Involvement List

C. Age-span Analysis

A. Membership Chart

MEMBERSHIP	1955	1960	1965	1966	1967	1968	1969	1970	1971	1972
Church members (end of yr.)										
Gained by conversion										
Gained by transfer										
Lost by transfer										
Lost by death										
Lost by other										
Total increase or decrease in church membership (end of year)										
SUNDAY SCHOOL										
Total enrollment (end of year)										
Av. attendance per Sunday										
Increase or decrease in av. Sunday school attendance										

B. Involvement List

How many are active as officers and workers in the following agencies of the church?

Church Boards_____   Church Committees_____

Church Choir_____   Sunday School_____

Club Work_____   Women's Organizations_____

Men's Organizations_____   Youth Sponsors_____

Home Bible Class Ministry_____

Visitation_____   Other_____

Total of all workers_____

Less duplications _____

Total deduction _____

Net total church members serving _____

Total church membership _____

% of members serving _____

% of members not serving _____

C. Age-Span Analysis

	Sunday School	Church
Ages 1-12		
Ages 13-19		
Ages 20-40		
Ages 40-60		
Ages over 60		

III. We Set Goals

At this point you are ready to clarify the goals toward which you believe your church must work.

Discuss each item, and agree on the importance of the specific goal, in view of your evaluation of your present situation and the tasks to which Christ has called you.

Rank no more than five items as of No. 1 priority.

1 2 3 4 5

1. We need to have each member personally active in daily witnessing to friends and acquaintances.
2. We need to provide training and support for our members in personal evangelism.
3. We need to strengthen our follow-up of absentees.
4. We need to place priority on reaching the following for Christ, and bringing them into the life of the church.
   a. Children (under 13)
   b. Youth (13 through high school)
   c. Young adults (20-40)
   d. Middle adults (40-60)
   e. Older adults

```
  1  2  3  4  5
| | | | | | | |
| | | | | | | |
| | | | | | | |
```

5. We need to involve more of our members in the ministry of the church.
   a. To be workers in our present agencies.
   b. To take part in boards and committees.
   c. To become actively involved with others and to win them to Christ.

6. We need to free working members of the church from responsibilities which do not contribute to the attainment of the real goals of this church.

```
| | | | | | | |
```

   a. From working on more than one organizational responsibility.

```
| | | | | | | |
```

   b. From working on a committee or in an agency which is not sufficiently contributing to attainment of goals.

```
| | | | | | | |
```

7. We need to reduce the number of evenings we are involved in church meetings in order to meet people and win them for Christ.

```
| | | | | | | |
```

8. We need to encourage our members to share their needs and experiences with Christ with one another.

```
| | | | | | | |
```

9. We need to help each member become vitally involved with the Word of God, and to practice daily Bible study.

```
| | | | | | | |
```

10. We need to provide better training for our Sunday School teachers and other workers.

```
| | | | | | | |
```

11. We need to fix responsibility for planning to reach the goals of the church.

```
| | | | | | | |
```

12. We need to develop a strategy for evangelistic outreach.

```
| | | | | | | |
```

13. We need to involve all members in the achieving of our church goals.

```
| | | | | | | |
```

14. We need to concentrate on developing the spiritual life and dedication of our adult membership.

```
| | | | | | | |
```

15. We need to define responsibilities and functions of our existing boards and committees, in relation to achievement of our goals.

```
| | | | | | | |
```

16. We need to discover and understand God's purposes for us in family relationships.

```
| | | | | | | |
```

17. We need to discover how to make the home the center of teaching and evangelism.

```
| | | | | | | |
```

18. We need to express concern for the social needs of our time and our community.

```
| | | | | | | |
```

19. We need to provide more opportunities for developing personal relationships with each other.

1 2 3 4 5
| | | | | | | 20. We need to provide more opportunities for de-
veloping personal relationships with those outside
of Christ.

| | | | | | | 21. We see the primary tasks of our church as:
winning the lost
becoming a community of believers who *live*
the Word. . . .

An evaluation guide like this one is just a tool: just a starter to help focus thinking on the nature and goals of the church. But it can be used in a variety of ways. In Trinity Baptist Church of Grand Rapids, Michigan, it was the first step in a morning session with the church board, and cleared the way for introduction of revolutionary ideas about church life. Chicago's Riverdale Baptist Church used the guide as basis for a summer series involving the whole congregation. Adult and youth Sunday school classes spent eight weeks in 1969 discussing the questions raised by the guide, section by section. The program culminated in a weekend retreat featuring a resource person who could give illustrations of directions churches are taking today to solve problems the series brought to the surface.

In ways like these such an evaluation guide can become a powerful educational tool to involve broad segments of church membership in working together to discover the nature and needs of their own fellowship.

Modeling the church. This is another approach which helps people focus attention on basic questions and on Biblical principles. At Honey Rock I provided each small group with all sorts of materials — rubber bands, scotch tape, thread spools, construction paper, tacks, colored string, scissors, glue, paper clips, razor blades, crayons, wire, erasers, keys, chenille wires, light bulbs, etc. I asked the groups to use these materials to portray the church as they know it. Their models were to reflect everything that they saw as significant about the way churches work — their decision-making processes, activities, communication patterns, interpersonal relations within the church, roles and responsibilities of members and leaders, the pastor's role, etc. Each group came up with a very creative portrait of the church as it is.

I then asked the groups to revise their models. What would happen if we applied one biblical principle, the priesthood of all believers, and truly worked it out in church life? If we actually lived by this principle what might the church look like?

Groups spent most of one morning discussing the meaning of this doctrine for the church. Then they struggled with its implementation — how would we work it out? Finally they reworked their models — startlingly and totally revamping church structure! And that evening, after comparing results, each group was asked to discuss this question: What other biblical realities should have an impact on church life and structure?

Whatever approaches are used, renewal demands that we focus our attention on goals and objectives — goals and objectives that flow from a truly biblical understanding of the nature and purpose of the church.

Reaching Goals

Goal-setting is the first step in planned change. Ideally we want to involve the whole church in a consensus process to define and establish goals and objectives. In the last section of this chapter I described possible "starter" activities to help a group focus on goals. *It is meaningless to speak of "how to get there" until "where are we going" has been established.* But then the *how* becomes extremely important.

What would be involved in working out the "how" of church change? The general procedures are suggested by the well-known "problem solving approach."

1. Goals are clearly defined, and agreed on.
2. The present situation is studied thoroughly. All relevant facts and feelings are brought out, discussed, and recorded.
3. Problems which have to be solved if goals and objectives are to be reached are carefully defined. The most significant of these are located.
4. Many possible solutions to these problems are suggested. Each is then discussed and evaluated in terms of the overall situation and in terms of goals.
5. Decision on what to do is reached by consensus, and all cooperate in carrying this out.
6. Progress is continually reviewed, and the group follows the same approach in solving new problems that emerge.

In this problem solving process, practical issues are extremely important. Here "How do we do it?" is *the* relevant question. Unfortunately, data on "how" is often unavailable. Fortunately, current books and articles on renewal contain more and more helpful information. Nevertheless, information on what other churches are doing in solving their problems is not generally available.[1]

Often visits to nearby churches who are solving old problems in new ways is a help, or inviting their members to share what is happening with your congregation. All this helps. Ultimately each church must stand as responsible to its Lord, and "work out your own solutions with a proper sense of awe, knowing that it is God who is at work in you to will and to perform His good purpose" (Philippians 2:12, 13).

Renewal, then, requires that churches involve their members in studying and setting goals and objectives — goals that reflect the biblical portrait of the church. Objectives that are in keeping with the ways in which God has ordained His purposes are to be carried out. Renewal demands that change come slowly — by consensus, by working things out *together*. Finally, renewal will require all of us to step out in faith, to try new ways, new structures to reach goals God sets before us. In each church renewal will be a different adventure with God.

There can be no shortcuts to this process, for there are no shortcuts to a renewed people of God.

---

[1]In an attempt to provide better communications within evangelicalism, my office at Wheaton College is now serving as a clearing house for renewal information. A renewal newsletter, *interCHANGE,* was begun in 1969, with the idea that those in our churches who are experimenting with change, or who face various problems, might have a place to write and exchange ideas. Every six weeks questions and reports from participants are included in a 6 to 8 page letter, and sent to *interCHANGE* members.

Anyone who wishes to participate is to send me $1.00 (for postage and materials), c/o Wheaton College, Wheaton, Illinois, for the first year of *interCHANGE*. Include renewal experiences or questions. This may be one way in which practical ideas can be fed into churches facing change, to help us all solve the many problems of "how." There are other avenues to this kind of information.

15

Integration of Group Life

A frustrated church member sat with me and told of the small group of fellow church members who met weekly with him and his wife. And he told of his attempts to talk with the pastor and various board members. He wanted to share the meaningfulness of the group experience, and he wanted to share his concern for directions the church seemed to be taking. For one thing, he cares deeply for young people and knows them well. The all-too-obvious failure of his church to make Christianity vital and relevant to them disturbs him deeply. He has seen the people who stream in and out of church Sundays — and knows their weekday lives. He has served on boards and committees, and felt deeply the failures to focus on the goals of the church.

The members of his group had discussed all these things. They were disturbed and critical, but underneath the criticism they all shared a deep concern for a congregation they considered theirs. And they had tried to communicate. They talked to the pastor, to board members. They wanted to share the new vitality they had discovered in meeting together, and to raise the questions they had been asking about their church. They felt that they had failed; they felt cut off. Though people seemed to listen, no one apparently really heard. And so the feeling grew that they had no power to influence the life of their church. Now, convinced of the futility of their efforts, they were planning to leave the church.

It is tragic that an experience of renewal (for so my friend viewed the spiritual change in himself and his friends) can divide, but it can. It can force members who feel cut off from the mainstream of church life to leave a congregation. Or, when the movement is larger, it can split a church wide open.

I do not feel either of these are *necessary* results of renewal. We can find churches, like Killarney Baptist, where traditional and contemporary live together in love and unity. I am convinced that we *must* not let such differences divide: that the church is *one,* and each church family must work out the issues they face, together. We can give no thought to a "divorce" by reason of incompatibility.

Yet when renewal influences enter a church, tensions are always created. Small groups, so basic to renewed life, will develop. If these are kept unrelated to the organizational life of the congregation, the tendency will be for them to spin off as they feel more and more alienated from their brothers. If these are related organizationally, other tensions arise. For the organizational forms needed to support a group-oriented church and our present agency-oriented churches are in direct conflict.

It is important, then, in thinking of renewal to understand why conflict will come and to spell out some of the organizational implications of church renewal.

Structural Change — A Certainty

Recently a professor friend of mine told me that he had done an organizational analysis of the restructured church I describe in chapter 2. He found that it would take about as much administrative machinery to run it as to run the church of today. I am not sure that this conclusion is correct; in any case to me the time involved in administrative details is not necessarily relevant. Instead the issue I see is this: does the organizational structure of the church (which we might liken to a skeleton or nervous system) support group life, or meetings? Is it designed to improve the functioning of the Christian in mutual ministries and group life, or is it designed to carry the weight of agencies and larger congregational functions?

Unfortunately, church organization today grew up focusing on large-group, impersonal activities, and on agencies which were developed to take over the functions of the Christian home or individual. This kind of structure simply cannot support the kind of life described in Section II as the life of the church.

In saying this, I am clearly stating my conviction that a renewed church requires a structural reorganization. That change must be far more sweeping than many of us envision. Why is this? What is the effect of current organizational patterns on church life? A recent study by Inter-Varsity Christian Fellowship shows what happens when a movement grows, and when consequently emphasis shifts from small-group to large-group orientation. This study is particularly significant because, while IVCF urges students to be active in their own churches, IVCF chapters do function as "the church" for students. That is, Inter-Varsity is concerned with fulfilling the functions of the church described in Section II of this book, and in the biblical way! Through mutual ministries Inter-Varsity seeks personality transformation and enthusiastic witness to Jesus Christ.

Within this framework, striking parallels exist between Inter-Varsity chapter organization and church organization. And the conclusions reached by key Inter-Varsity staff members concerning what has happened in their movement, as reported in the November, 1968 His Magazine, seems to me particularly relevant to understanding renewal of church life.

Five levels of chapter growth, and the resultant organization of life, were discussed in the articles written by Paul Fromer (see Figure 13). The following selections from the articles reveal problems faced by any group as it grows — problems for which a solution must be found in the church.

Level two (ten members) Personal relations are of course very high because people know one another well. Let's call this group of ten an action group because of its vigor. It has no formal exec or chapter-wide committees, and the center of attention is not the weekly meeting but "we" . . . the center of attention is people, not a meeting. The group is still people, not an organization.

Considering the size of the group, the number of people to whom the gospel is explained in the course of a year is high, perhaps thirty, as is the number saved, say four. This group is moving along and there is no stagnation in the picture.

Level three (thirty members) Relations are less personal in the group than when there were only ten, because people don't know each other as well as in those early days.

Four or five people on the exec, however, are just as personally related as the old nucleus of ten, and because of their capacity for closeness and ability to do work, they form a sort of modified action group.

Demand on the leaders is now increasing because chapter activities like the weekly meetings have to be organized for the core of ten and the fringe of twenty. Notice that the core is about the same size as at level two, but the fringe has increased notably — from one to twenty.

The number of people who hear the gospel from the members of the chapter may be larger than at level two, but not by three times, though the chapter size has increased that much, from ten to twenty. It is as though energy is beginning to leak from the chapter. It can't seem to harness all the available energy so it can't do three times the work of level two.

Level four (one hundred members) The size is up over three times from the previous level, but the personal relations are suffering, so that the chapter is less personal than at either level three or level two. . . . Further, the personal character of the exec may be down slightly because twelve officers and chairmen are a good deal larger group than the five at level three.

As the group gets larger, the center of attention more and more becomes the weekly meeting, and the demand placed on the leaders by it and the other chapter-wide responsibilities is up sharply from the days of thirty people. . . . Just getting enough chairs to set up for the weekly meeting takes a lot of time.

The core of the group, counting the exec, now numbers around twenty, with a fringe of eighty. Notice the radical change in proportion of the core to fringe. At level one it was nine to one; at level three it was one to two. Here at level four it is one to four. To get anything done, or effect any change, the exec has to move an apathetic block comprising eighty percent of the chapter!

Level five (two hundred fifty members) Because of the increased size, the personal character of the chapter has nose-dived. Twenty-five new people could probably come into a weekly meeting without the group knowing it. The exec likewise has problems, numbering perhaps twenty students, which almost equals the size of the total chapter at level three. The personal character of the chapter is no longer conserved in the exec, which by this time has ceased to be a modified action group. It is only wheels within wheels.

Such a chapter may have fifteen committees. . . . The center of attention is a walloping chapter meeting. This is about the only sense of identity the chapter has left, and it's not very sharp.

The average person's sense of mission is less than the chapter had at level four, which was pretty low. Probably less evangelistic work is done here than at level four. Energy simply isn't channeled to do effective witnessing so the number saved drops.

Parallels to local church life are too striking to develop. With growth comes a loss of personalness, a loss of sense of mission and identity, an organization geared to bigness instead of smallness, where life can be shared and nurtured. In Fromer's analysis he wrote: "I see four basic problems: a drop in personalness, sense of mission, and evangelistic work achieved, and an immense rise in demands on leaders." And thus organization which arose to support the bigness of the group cut into that which was it's genius — smallness.

What solution does IVCF suggest to its chapters? Fromer goes on to describe an effective chapter strategy which the leadership believes is the answer.

> Professionalism and meeting-centeredness can lead to a defective chapter strategy. Properly (1) the big meeting should serve the small group rather than vice versa, and (2) the small groups should be shown how they are the key to both penetrating the campus evangelistically and helping the individual student grow personally.

I am convinced that this analysis holds for the churches as well. That for renewal our emphasis must shift from the large meeting to the small group. Only here will we rediscover our identity, and only here will each one become able to accept a full share of the mission of Christ on earth.

Making the small group the basic unit of congregational life will not be easy. Such decentralization goes contrary to the centralizing structure that has grown up. And because the two trends are not compatible, to the extent that small groups become basic in church life the total church organization will necessarily change.

Why? The center of church life today is the meeting and the agency. Mr. Fromer pointed out the energy expended in an IVCF chapter of any size to simply obtain chairs. Do we need to point out the energy expended in our churches on getting and maintaining a building? On staffing and supplying agencies? On running committees? Because this *is* an energy-consuming concern, nearly all church machinery is designed to support such activities. The organization is designed to put on a central meeting or series of meetings. Such an organization cannot adjust itself to tasks it was never created to carry out.

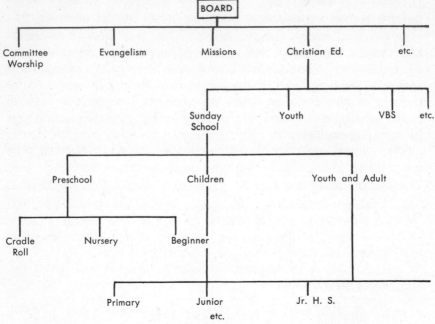

Figure 13.

A look at the organizational structure of a typical church illustrates this fact. Note that lines of responsibility and communication run between various boards, committees, and agencies. These are charged with responsibility for the activities and meetings of the larger church.

Where in this organization is a relationship shown between church structure and the *people* of the church? *There are no direct relationships between the members and "the church," except as members happen to fill organizational roles!* The organization is designed to keep the meetings running, not to personalize participation in the life of the congregation, or to provide direct lines of communication between church members and official-dom.

The experience of my friend, reported at the beginning of this chapter, is not surprising because current church organization is not oriented to people. The official machinery does not encourage communication, but discourages it. True, he could talk to people in official positions. But his viewpoint (running counter to the whole organizational strategy and commitment of the church) was disregarded. He had no indication that his view-point was ever expressed or discussed in an official meeting.

In the final analysis, organizational structure both responds to and shapes the life of any group. Our present organizational structures testify to a church which finds its identity in buildings and mass meetings and its mission in the work of its agencies. If the life of the churches shifts significantly toward the biblical frame of reference, with our identity as the church experienced in our relationship with other believers, and our mission in the world carried out as transformed individuals, organizational forms must change to reflect and support that new life.

And it is important that we face the changes that are needed now, that we realize, as tensions between the traditional and biblical concept of the church grow under the sweeping pres-sures of renewal, that a choice must be made. The old wine-skins simply cannot hold the new wine.

Organizing New Life

In the church, as in ivcf, organizational structure tends to dis-tract us from our purposes, dissipate our energies, and deper-sonalize our communities. In saying this I am not criticizing organization as such. Nor am I suggesting a "no church" move-ment, in which small groups are the only form of gathered life. I am suggesting instead that the church must be reorganized. That we need new structures which will support group life and give form to a deeply personal, mutually ministering association.

It is possible to specify some of the characteristics of such an organization. I would suggest that, whatever forms are finally developed, they must have these qualities:

(1) *Church organization should promote communication.* Organization must provide and keep clear channels for sharing experiences and concerns throughout the church. These channels should be as direct as possible, for distortion of communication is in direct relationship to the number of relays in the communications net.

It is also important that the communication channels be designed to handle all kinds of communication. Present church structures can deal with such information as "We need a new Primary Sunday school teacher." There are, within the communications net, designated stations to which such messages are channeled — the Sunday school superintendent, or the Personnel Committee, etc. But when my friend wished to tell of his small group experience, and suggest new approaches to ministry, the organization could not handle that kind of data.

The communications net for the renewed church will have to be able to handle *personal* as well as organizational messages. Without such a communications system, capable of sharing the real life of the church, the sense of unity with other individuals and groups in the church will be lost. Small groups and individuals will be unable to influence the life of the congregation, and will feel alienated from it.

(2) *Church organization should encourage maximum participation.* The structures of the renewed church need to encourage consensus.

Present organizational structures force decisions *up,* to the top. That is, if an individual in the organization has a problem he cannot solve, he is encouraged to take it to his organizational superior. Say that a dispute arises in the Young Teen Department over what Sunday school materials to use. Some of the teachers prefer one publisher's materials; some prefer another's. The problem is taken first to the Sunday school Superintendent. If he does not come up with "the decision," it then goes to the Christian Education Committee. The problem is *not* solved by the teachers who use (and thus should best know) the materials. Nor are those most affected (the young people) given a voice. Church organization serves to force decisions *up* the structure, away from the point of problem, and to cut down the voice of those most intimately involved in resolving it.

Consensus decision-making requires an organizational structure which tends to move issues *down* the chart, not up it. Rather
than taking decisions out of the hands of the many, and giving
them to the few, a consensus concept insists that issues be resolved by the full participation of those involved. This clearly
demands a structural revision for renewal churches. Present
structures actually work *against* consensus. .

(3) *Church organization should facilitate feedback.* The en-
trenched and rigid structures of today's churches do not encourage feedback, and they tend to resist rather than respond to
dissent.

The renewed church must remain flexible and open, eager for
feedback from every member and group, and ready to respond.
The renewed church needs an organization which permits *it* to
change, rather than demanding change and conformity in its
members.

Only as the church listens to the reactions and expression of
needs of every member can we work as a body to implement
God's purposes. Only as accurate information is received from
individuals can the church be sensitive to the impact of decisions
and actions on its members.

Thus revised organizational structures must be designed to
stimulate feedback, not cut it off.

(4) *Church organization should encourage innovation.* It is
vital that our churches retain the ability to discover and implement new ways to solve problems that arise in our changing culture. Church organization today is fixed, committed to a strategy
of big meetings and agency-centered activity. The weight of its
organizational machinery does not permit it to be responsive to
people within or without.

The Sunday school is a prime example. For years it has been
seen as *the* answer to the question, "How do we nurture children
in the Christian faith?" For all its contributions, we have to
recognize the limitations on the heavily transmissive, limited time
approach it takes. Yet when problems became evident, the church
did not reexamine the biblical concepts of Christian nurture. It
took the position that we merely needed more time. So boys and
girls clubs, children's churches, released time classes, etc. were
added. Committed to an in-the-church, agency-centered ap-

proach to Christian nurture we were not free to innovate — to reexamine our foundations, and come up with new, more biblical answers. And regardless of the mounting evidence of institutional education's ineffectiveness the church continues to commit its efforts to the agency approach.

How can organizational structure encourage flexible responses? How can it help us avoid falling into ruts? In part the answer lies more in our attitudes than in our organizational forms. We must continue to hold goals sacred, and view all means as expendable. We must retain our sense of freedom to innovate — recognizing that the check against change for change's sake does not lie in unwieldy and unresponsive organizational structures, but in the nature of the consensus process by which each change decision must be reached.

At the same time, organizational structures will reflect this attitude. For one thing, *permanent* additions to the basic structure of the church will not be made. Short term agencies or activities will replace them. We may plan and hold Sunday school for nine months. Then we may try family schools where all family members are involved together. Or we may try a period of exclusively home-centered teaching, in which all parents are equipped to teach their children creatively, and do so each week. Or we may see concentrated periods of Bible training, as a church takes over a camp for a month during the summer and works intensively with its own children.

In the same vein, committees will probably be *pro tem,* to research intensively problems facing the church, and report for congregational discussion and consensus. Meetings of the church as a whole will serve the small groups, not vice versa. Training classes may be held, retreats, etc. But again these will be temporary, planned to meet a need that arises in the life of the congregation, and dissolved when that need is met.

Thus the organization will reflect the value the group places on innovation, and will encourage innovation by resisting the establishment of meetings and activities which might, in time, become an end in themselves.

These, then, are some of the characteristics of a church organized to support small group life. And if we honestly do come to the point where we consider the small group the basic unit of the church, organizations with these characteristics must develop.

They must develop, because these characteristics are in harmony with the distinctive life of such a church and are essential if that life is to be supported and encouraged. Other kinds of organization must finally strangle renewal.

Tension in the Church

Renewal and traditional thinking and organization must always, by their very nature, exist in tension. What are various ways of handling these tensions?

On the one hand, renewal thinking may lead to establishment of small groups *outside* the organized church. Such groups may draw those who find them meaningful away from their churches. This is unacceptable to me. The church is *one,* and our unity in Christ must be maintained. Differences in viewpoint do not justify rending that unity. Again, small groups may spring up *inside* an organized church. In this case any church has two options: (1) to ignore them, or (2) to attempt to integrate them organizationally.

What if a church attempts to integrate the small groups into its organizational structure? This depends on the nature of the integration. Some churches attempt *token* integration. The church leadership wants to keep an eye on the group activities, and so may create a "Coordinator of Small Groups" to sit on the Christian education board. This is not true integration, for it is clear that those with the group viewpoint still have no power to influence the direction of church life. As group-life develops, group participants will still feel cut off and alienated from their church because of communication and influence gaps.

What if group-oriented members are given true representation? One church board, made up of older men who were strongly traditionalist, realized that the younger couples (who were deeply involved in group-life) needed to be heard. They invited the executive committee of the married couple's fellowship to join the board as full and voting members. This action gave renewal and traditional people equal representation on the board. And the very gracious act of the older men set the pattern for cooperation and concern as differences in thinking surfaced and were worked out.

This was full integration. The renewal people were not only

given the opportunity to be heard, but also the opportunity to influence the course of church life.

Of course, it is possible to have *informal* integration of the two viewpoints. This happens when part of the present power structure (board members, committee members, etc.) hold renewal viewpoints, and are themselves involved in the church's small fellowship groups. The integration in this case may be unofficial, but is nevertheless real as communication and influence lines are open.

It should be clear that the best chance to work through tensions exists when there is a maximum opportunity for both "sides" to be fully represented within the organizational structure, and when each viewpoint is understood and respected and everyone is determined to face issues openly and in love.

But even such ideal conditions will not remove the conflicts which arise from the meeting of two such divergent concepts of church life. The tensions must actually increase, as the practical implications of the two ways of thinking about the church (as people gathered for mutual ministries, or as large meetings and agency activities) become increasingly clear. Ultimately the very issues discussed in this chapter will surface. Each church will realize that it must choose between traditional and renewal structures, *for neither of these can support the life forms of the other*. The churches must ultimately accept the small group as the basic unit of its life and re-form itself accordingly, or must retreat to the traditional emphasis that present forms were devised to support.

In saying this, that conflict is inherent between traditional and renewal life-styles, I am not expressing pessimism about change. Nor am I saying that when the traditionalist makes room for the renewal-oriented he sets up conditions which will force him out of his church. In the transition period in the early church, many Jewish believers held tightly to Old Testament traditions. And they were accepted by the growing Gentile majority. We are in a period of transition now. It may be that many will decide to retain the traditional. They should be allowed to do so, and be fully accepted and respected. It may be that some churches will remain like Killarney, with traditional and renewal organizations coexisting. But in most churches, complete reorganization will take place — soon.

For there is something vital about new life. It breaks the old wineskins and forces the dead leaf from the tree. Its very vitality causes it to grow, and in growing to become *itself*. And so it will be with the church of Christ. As more and more of us rediscover the reality of the church in relationship and ministry to one another, we too will be freed to shake off the dead husks of a ritualized church life and be shaped by the Spirit of God into forms that permit us again to become "the Church."

16

The Role of the Pastor in Change

Renewal raises many questions for and about pastors. Is the role given the pastor in today's church Scriptural? Yes, and no. Yes, in that certainly any church can select and support one or more leaders, so they can give full time to the ministry. No, in that many of the time-consuming, organizationally oriented activities forced on modern pastors stray far from the biblical pattern for leaders. Yet renewal raises far more pressing problems. How is the pastor to function in the process of change? He is denied by Scripture the role of directing church life. How then can he guide change? He is not to impose his ideas on others in the church, or to manipulate them, or to control change in other ways. How then is he to function? How is he to *lead?*

There is no doubt that today the pastor is a leader. Usually he is the key to church change. If he resists renewal trends, rejects the small group, and uses his influence to restrain objections to the way things are being done, he can probably stifle renewal of the church organization. This course will, however, likely lead to the loss of a growing segment of his church population, and abandonment by the younger generations.

On the other hand, even if the pastor is oriented toward renewal, change will not come automatically. A pastor can easily alienate those oriented to tradition. In trying to lead the church into new forms and patterns of life, he can cause reaction against the changes and against himself. "It is a well known fact," write Benne and Bernbaum, "that change in an organization is often followed by a reaction toward the old pattern, a reaction that sets in when pressure for change is relaxed" (p. 330). In a time of such tension, forced to "take sides," a pastor may find himself the focal point of a battle that divides the very congregation he was seeking to unite in a new and deeper fellowship!

Nor is "neutrality" an option for the pastor. For one thing, he will not really be neutral. And to be true to his calling, a man of God must be an open, honest person. He must "speak the truth in love."

So the pastor who resists change can usually hold his church back from renewal. On the other hand the pastor who seeks change may not be successful in achieving it.

Nevertheless, the pastor in today's church does have a key role to play in renewal. His leadership style will either facilitate a smooth and effective transition, or make change a traumatic and damaging experience for the church. Because of this, the questions asked earlier must be discussed. And each pastor who yearns for renewal will have to determine his function in change, and decide how he is to lead.

The Pastor's "Moral Force"

One of the great responsibilities of church leaders is to model Christian character for the church. In any discussion of the pastor's role in church change, this aspect of his ministry must be examined first.

It is unfortunate that the nature of this moral force is misunderstood by so many in our pulpits. Too many men associate leadership with "being right," and in the pulpit and in relationships within their congregations they seek to hide their humanness. "Don't make personal friends in your congregation," I was told in seminary. "Always keep a distance between you and the people." And I was also told, "Don't use too many personal illustrations."

I have had time since then to observe the results of this course of action. I have one pastor friend, whom I admire and respect more than any other, who never used personal illustrations from the pulpit. To me, for I knew him personally, he was a warm and intensely human man, one who suffered with his weaknesses, and gloried in the grace of his God. But to the people in the pews he seemed a distant, impersonal, and often condemning voice. If he had shared himself with them as he did with me, I believe his ministry would have been appraised in an altogether different way because knowing him as a man, people could have known God much better through him.

In chapter 12 I discussed briefly the significance of openness and self-revelation. Our shared humanity provides the context for ministry. I am convinced that the pastor who would help his people change must be this kind of person. He must be a living example.

Sharing our humanness may be misunderstood. Particularly in situations where we have learned to hide our true selves from others. So self-revelation may, at first, seem to hurt rather than help. But there is no other way. We need to see and touch and observe the kind of person God wants us to be; we need an incarnation of His character if we are to trust ourselves to change.

Another question is raised. In encouraging change, should not a pastor keep some of his views to himself? Isn't there a danger in telling too much, before people are ready for the startling and sometimes threatening revisions renewal seems to indicate? Here too I feel we must be open and honest whenever questioned. We can never act to deceive.

It should be noted here, however, that there is a great difference between sharing renewal opinions in the context of self-revelation and in the context of persuasion. I can sit down with a church board member who is violently traditional in outlook, share my views and listen to his. As long as I remain gentle and concerned, such sharing need not lead to conflict. But if my attitude is one of superiority; if I listen only to find fault with his ideas; if I am so certain of my own position that I cannot hear his ideas, the whole situation changes. My attitude communicates itself to him, and he clearly sees that I am pitting myself against him. Then everything I say earns his hostility, and more and more he rejects both me and my ideas. Sharing, then, even of opposite views, is possible as long as the attitude described in Philippians two is maintained. I am revealing myself, trusting him to understand and accept me even though we disagree — considering him in this even better than myself, and demonstrating my respect by trusting him in this way.

While much more could be said, it seems to me that a pastor exerts a moral force which opens up the possibilities of change when (1) he becomes a human being to his congregation, (2) he trusts his real self to them, sharing his problems, his feelings, his ideas, his convictions, his experience of God's love, and when (3) he learns to speak his convictions freely without attempting to persuade, and with no aura of superiority involved. On all these counts those of us seeking to encourage renewal should examine ourselves, for our effectiveness depends on what we *are* far more than we may realize.

The Pastor's Organizational Impact

Change in the church is not just an individual thing. Changes, especially those relating to renewal, necessarily affect the climate of the whole organization; the gathered life of the congregation. The whole interpersonal system and pattern of life will be altered. As changes occur, and stable patterns of action are broken, people are likely to feel threatened and insecure. Times of change are often troubled; and the experience of change may be traumatic for those involved.

How can a pastor work with the church, as a system, to facilitate change and reduce tensions? How can he serve as an agent of change without controlling and directing? Bennis, Benne, and Chin (*The Planning of Change*) suggest essentials in implementing planned changes which provide insights:

1. The client system — those involved in the organization being changed should have as much understanding of the change and its consequences, and as much influence in developing and controlling the fate of the change, and as much trust in the initiator of the change, as is possible.
2. The change effort should be perceived as self-motivated and as voluntary as possible.
3. The change program must include values, and emotional as well as cognitive (informational) elements for successful implementation.
4. The change agent [the one working with the group to facilitate change] can be crucial in reducing resistance to change.

As long as the change agent acts congruently with the principles of the program, and as long as the client has a chance
to test competence and motives, the agent should be able to
provide psychological support so necessary during the risky
phases of change.

I believe that the pastor should view his role in the church
moving toward renewal as that of a change agent. As a person
who seeks to involve the congregation in a self-motivated and
self-directed change effort, and to reduce the tensions which
change will cause.

In this role as change agent he can encourage the development
of small groups. He can introduce participative elements into the
meetings he leads, and thus help the congregation develop a
sense of unity, as well as experience active roles. He can help
boards, committees, and the church at large to focus on goals. He
can encourage the expression of divergent viewpoints, and help
these groups learn to handle disagreement, thus moving toward
a consensus process. He can set a personal example of openness
and honesty that will help all in the congregation come to trust
him, even though they may not agree with all his ideas. He
can teach the Word of God, and help all the people look into
it to discover who they are and what they are to be as the church.

All these ways of working in a congregation have been discussed. Yet several very practical principles which can guide a
pastor's ministry need to be underlined.

The need for prior experience. All of us are threatened by
change. Change always creates uncertainty — in particular uncertainty about our ability to handle the new situations. This is
why suggested change of the Sunday school is highly threatening
to most parents. They may recognize the validity of the "home
centered" approach to Christian nurture, but not having known
this as children, or given it as parents, most will seriously doubt
their ability to teach and train their children for the Lord.

Often this kind of threat can be greatly reduced by careful
long-range planning. Recently a pastor told me of his attempt
to move from an "in church" prayer meeting to several smaller
home meetings. The groups formed were given to understand
that they would either stay permanently in small home units, or
return to the old pattern. In the first meeting in homes, influen-

tial laymen in each group strongly expressed their preference for the old pattern. And the attempt at change failed.

It is too much to expect men and women to move confidently into a new experience, so confidently that they would choose it over the old and the familiar. It would have been far better for this pastor to plan prior, and preparatory, experiences. He might have announced a six-week experiment and divided the people into small groups at the church, giving them guidelines on how to make these times most meaningful. After the stated time had elapsed, he could have returned to the familiar pattern. Later a similar series could have been planned, and followed up with extended discussions of the experience, and the advantages of each approach to prayer meetings. Having experienced the group approach, and being more confident of their ability to function in this situation, the people might have decided to move to the small group format. Or they might have agreed on offering an option, letting those who wished gather in groups, while the others assembled at church as usual.

Anything new and different is threatening. A pastor hoping to encourage change should provide experiences which will reduce threat, and help those involved feel able to succeed in the new situation.

There is a need for true communication. Often "communication" is misunderstood. It is viewed as a one-way process, in which the communicator acts on an audience. He says what he pleases, trying to convince or persuade them, or change their behavior. True communication is *transactional.* That is, it involves an exchange between two or more parties. In this exchange the parties are equal; each giving and taking, each profiting from the experience, and neither seeking to coerce the other.

Such communication is vital in renewal. It is vital for change. If a person is convinced that his voice will be heard, and that he has an opportunity to influence changes which concern him, successful change is far more likely. Lack of communication leads to alienation. When a two-way sharing of views is lacking, many in a congregation will feel that their needs are not understood or considered. They will resist change, and feel threatened by it.

To the degree to which all persons involved in a change feel that their view is understood and that they have power to influence the changes made, tensions and resistance will be reduced.

Need for a threat-reducing pattern of behavior. There are many reasons why change threatens. And there are many ways the sense of threat can be reduced. The pastor's style of leadership should reflect an awareness of the danger that many will feel threatened, and be patterned to help reduce this feeling as much as possible. One study group at Honey Rock suggested the following elements as characteristic of threat-reducing leadership.

Personally . . .

1. The leader is honest in communicating his own feelings and motives.
2. The leader creates an atmosphere of acceptance, in which people feel that they and their viewpoints "belong."
3. The leader avoids emphasis of negatives; he focuses his attention and that of the people on their goals and objectives.
4. The leader builds personal bridges; he loves his people and seeks to build up their sense of personal value and worth.
5. The leader is flexible, willing to respond and to change when others' needs so indicate.
6. The leader shows concern and understanding for opposing points of view, and love for those who oppose him.

Strategically . . .

1. The leader seeks to create and maintain options; he avoids either/or choices.
2. The leader seeks to provide an honest Scriptural basis for the goals and objectives of changes, and for the methods to be employed.
3. The leader sets time limits on new ventures, at the end of which they will be evaluated or called off.
4. The leader introduces most changes as experiments.
5. The leader makes sure that people have the training and help needed to succeed when new demands are made of them, and new situations have to be faced.
6. The leader gives opportunity for discussion and for explanation of all changes, involving all those affected.

There is a need for feedback. One of the most crucial points in any change effort is reached when the changes have been made, and their effects begin to be felt. It is important, *at that point,* to provide for feedback.

One writer discusses a business organization in which feedback on changes were planned for. He tells of . . .

> a feedback system which is immediately informative of the climate of the organization after an internal change has occurred and which is designed to accomplish planning for change in a matter of hours. . . . Representatives of all levels of organizational management meet together and exchange with each other the problems caused by the change made within the organization. Planning for action is done in smaller sub-groups which are concerned with a particular area. Plans are then presented to the total group, some are selected, and the proper resources are made available to put these plans into effect. All in 4½ to 5 hours.

This suggestion of feedback provision is made with the assumption that the original change plans were formed in a consensus process involving all those affected. Given a consensus decision, the group commitment to the change they directed should insure a problem-solving focus in the feedback session. Otherwise, it's likely that feedback at this point will serve only to reveal criticism, and to create added pressure for return to the old pattern.

Thus feedback, while an important factor in any change, will be most helpful when the group understands and has participated in the planning of change initially.

It is true that all men, and all situations, differ significantly. Thus each of us individually and each congregation will have to develop its own style of working toward renewal. But no pastor can fail to have some impact on change efforts. And no pastor can lightly disregard the factors discussed in this chapter and hope to guide people effectively through change.

Renewal Strategy

While situations and men differ, is it possible to present in simplified form a basic strategy of change toward renewal? I think so.

In this section on the church in transition I have attempted to focus attention on factors which are crucial in renewal. I have not given a set of detailed "how to do it" instructions. I do not believe any such instructions can be given. But perhaps the factors discussed in this section can be grouped according to priority, as in the following figure.

Figure 14. A Strategy of Renewal

Priority one:

A. *To "free" members.*

This means helping believers grow spiritually, and discover freedom in Christ to share, and to be, themselves. The primary context for achieving this goal is the small group. Secondary aids include the example of church leaders, and participatory methods in congregational services.

Priority two:

A. *Encourage goal-oriented thinking.*

This means helping church members focus, in all situations, on biblical goals and objectives, and helping them commit themselves to reaching these goals by whatever means God may direct.

B. *Encourage development of a "minister" image.*

This means helping each believer see himself as a minister of God's grace to other Christians, and responsible for fulfillment of the great commission. Small groups, participatory services, involvement in decision-making, all will help to change the average layman's understanding of his role in the church.

C. *Open up communication lines.*

This means involving all members of the church in transactional communication. Again, small groups are a vital element in achieving this goal. But achievement also demands organizational change to encourage participation in decision-making and feedback.

D. *Develop consensus decision-making.*

This means involvement of all members in making the significant decisions which affect the life of the church. This necessarily involves organizational change, but this style of making decisions will be learned in the small groups.

Part IV

The Church Renewed

17

Patterns of Congregational Life

There is something dreadfully unsatisfying about saying that church renewal is to be an open-ended process — and dropping it there.

For some, refusal to show in detail just where change leads may seem like a cop-out. For others it will increase fear; fear that in our rush toward renewal, what we abandon will prove far better than what we devise to replace it.

I don't feel that insisting on the open-endedness of church change is a cop-out. It is the only honest and reasonable position one can take. There are many options open to us, many patterns of life that may develop. And I certainly don't feel that open-ended change is threatening — if we use the safeguards provided for us. We have Scripture, which reveals the basic elements and goals of church life, and we have consensus, our great protection against radicalism and hastiness. With these, safe changes can be thought through and prayed through and worked through by members of every congregation. And so we can be assured of God's leading, step by step.

With this said, I must admit that it is fair to ask for more discussion of tomorrow's church than I have provided. To demand something more concrete, a sharper sketch of what the future might hold. Hence these last four chapters.

It is important to remember that these chapters are planned to show what may happen in renewal. The features which I have incorporated are valid options, but not the only options. No congregation ought to take these patterns as a model to reproduce. For valid change comes only through consensual discovery of God's will — and the change format in each congregation. But perhaps we can take these chapters as outlining a church that contrasts with today's church, and in the contrast demonstrate why we so desperately need change. For the new life of the church envisioned here is, to me, a far better life than we know today.

Each of the three previous sections of this book are written in a different style. This doesn't make for a stylistically unified book, but I hope each section is written in a way appropriate to its content and its purpose. In these last chapters I am driven to yet another style — a present tense, prophetic description. In these chapters we step into the future, to visit a church that has moved, through years of transition, into a settled pattern of new life. This church can mirror, though dimly, a future to which I believe renewal calls.

Visit to the Future

The helicopter settled down gently in one of the dozen or so garaging areas on the northwest side of Dunsea, a planned community of 100,000 about 40 miles north of Milwaukee. My host, Carl Ronstadt, quickly stowed his copter, and led me to the car where his wife, Estelle, waited. It had been a quick trip from the circular jetport, lying five miles out in Lake Michigan off Chicago, but Carl still seemed in a hurry.

Introductions over, we settled down for a short drive to join the group of believers with whom the Ronstadts met regularly. There were a dozen in this Home Unit now, Carl told me. The Unit had formed eight months ago with eight members, but had added one couple who moved to Dunsea from Denal, and two who had recently become Christians. This was the tenth Unit Carl and Estelle had belonged to in their thirteen years in Dunsea. Like the others, it was the center of their exciting Christian life.

I had selected Dunsea for this visit for several reasons. First, it is typical of the communities in which 75 percent of our population live these days. The trend toward decentralization had been noticeable even in the 60's, as shopping centers, businesses and light industries pushed out into the far suburbs and beyond. Today the Old Cities hold less than 12 percent of our population, and practically all of them are Disfrans. Thus the Dunsea church is quite representative.

Another reason for selecting Dunsea was that this church, after the transition years, has developed a stable pattern of life. And it has avoided the two most common overreactions to renewal: such an insistence on autonomy that the church splits into rival congregations and neodenominations, or such insistence on organizational unity that authoritarian structures develop, with centralized controls that stifle freedom and personal responsibility. I have seen many such failures over the years, but, thank God, far more successes.

A third reason for choosing Dunsea was personal. A student of mine from Wheaton, (where I taught in the 60's and 70's, before being called to the itinerant ministry that has claimed most of my life) lived in Dunsea during the church's early years. I was impressed by what he told me, so he called one of the Elders, who put me in touch with Carl. Two weeks later I jetted to Chicago, met lanky, red haired Carl, and was now driving through the Wisconsin dusk to share the Ronstadts' regular Tuesday worship.

"It's so exciting," Estelle was saying.

"I'm sorry. Afraid my mind was wandering. What's so exciting?"

"To have young Christians in the Unit." She tossed dark hair out of her eyes, and shifted in her seat to give me a happy smile. "Somehow the newness of their life helps to keep mine fresh. I really think I gain so much more from them than they ever gain from me."

Carl laughed quietly. "I remember when I was in college, angry because the churches seemed so irrelevant. I got in one of the fellowship groups that were springing up in those days. That's where I found that what I really needed was in other believers. That *we* are the church, and when I got to know others deeply, and we shared our experiences in the Lord, my Christian life became fresh."

"How many groups have you and Estelle been in together?"

"Nine, no, ten since we've been here. Of course, there have been others, ever since college. In the early years of our marriage we were in DesMoines, and we were part of the Church of Greater Las Vegas, too. So there have been a lot."

"How does the church here organize the groups — I believe you call them Home Units?"

"Oh, a number of ways. All Home Units have the same basic function, of course. But during every reorganization period some specialized groups form. Right now our congregation has family life Units, several evangelistic Units, and a number of service Units. You'll learn all about them. Wait till you see the schedule we've got laid out for you!"

Just then Carl swung off the road into a drive that swept up to, and around behind, an attractive condominium. "We're meeting at Jim Rhodes' place tonight. He's a teacher at Four Oaks High and spends a lot of time with our young people. The high school is just over there, beyond those trees."

All the members of the group had arrived by the time we came in. One of the new converts, a young fellow just out of high school, had been at the house most of the afternoon. We chatted a bit, and I felt right at home, a feeling that has become common to us now that we have learned to throw off our masks and become real to each other. The Unit had prayed about my coming the week before, and everyone was glad to share, so I began by running through a list of questions — questions that I have been asking through the years, and questions that some are still asking.

"Let's start with your Home Unit meeting. How often do you get together?"

A blond girl answered, "We see each other often. Some of us talk almost every day. But we meet as a unit just one evening each week."

"Some groups meet more often," said Jim. "The high school kids have daily prayer meetings, and some of their Units meet two, three times on weekends. Of course, teen Units are usually large. Four Oaks has eight units of 30 to 35 kids each."

"Any reason for the large size?"

"It's not planned, if that's what you mean. Somehow the kids keep even the big group real personal, and they seem to enjoy the larger grouping. They all are part of their family Congregations, of course, and some are also in Home Units with their parents."

"Not all?"

"No, not all. We used to think that they ought to be in the family Unit. But it doesn't always work out best. You know how most of their time is spent with their peers, anyway. Somehow kids seem to need each other more than they need us older folks."

"Not really, Jim." It was his young supper guest who disagreed. "We need you a lot, and all the other older Christians who are with us. You know how many times I've busted in on you these last few months!"

I was interested. "Are you a youth worker, Jim?"

Jim laughed. "Now there's an archaic term! No, we don't have any 'youth workers' in the church. A lot of us who teach, or who live near the schools, or who have teens in the family, do have a special concern for youth. So we open up our homes, go along on retreats, and well . . . just be available. It's usually a pretty full time thing. The kids are so enthusiastic, and they're really open to the Lord."

"Are you on the church payroll for this?"

"No, we don't have any payroll, or paid ministries. All of us use our free time for the Lord, one way or another."

"That's one thing about the church today," said Herb, an older man. "When I was young we Christians used our free time just like other folks. We took another job, or watched TV, or puttered around the yard. We weren't *involved* – not with people. Oh, we talked about being full-time Christians, but about all that meant was goin' out to church a couple nights, maybe serving on a committee, or spending 45 minutes Saturday night gettin' a Sunday school lesson ready. And maybe reading a bit of the Bible some nights.

"It's different now. At least, here in Dunsea."

"How do you mean, different?"

"Well, now bein' a Christian really is full time, that's all. It's not just a Sunday slice of life; our faith is our whole life. Really, there are parts of the Bible I never used to take seriously. Parts that seemed almost, well, fanatic. Like 'settin' our minds on things above,' and 'for me to live is Christ.' It used to be that for me to live was to have security and lots of leisure. Being a Christian meant being moral and middle class, going to church, and being real glad that when I died I wouldn't have to worry about the hereafter. But now, now living for Christ is the whole thing. That *is* life."

The others were nodding agreement as he finished. "That's just why we don't need 'youth workers,'" Jim said. "When the Lord dominates, and becomes the whole of life, we *care*. And caring, we give ourselves. Not just money, like it used to be."

"I guess that having individual Christians care and become involved with others has done away with the need for all those agencies and jobs the church used to think it needed."

I couldn't help grinning. "My, all this would have sounded pretty revolutionary back in '70, when renewal was just breaking out. You seem to be saying that the church today is totally unorganized. How can a church work without some planning and organization?"

"We're not disorganized, or unorganized," Carl responded. "We're just *re*organized, so as to do the job through *people* instead of agencies.

"I think they used to say that, since there are people in the agencies, it doesn't make sense to make distinctions between a 'personal ministry' and 'agency ministry' orientation. But they were wrong. Why, look how impersonal agencies can be. Like, well, collecting unemployment. You go into an office and talk to a person, all right. But he doesn't *act* like a person. He acts like part of the government. I mean, he asks you all sorts of questions, fills out forms, and sometimes gets rather nasty because he suspects you're not trying to find another job. You go out of there feeling that you're not a person, either.

"The same thing used to happen a lot in church agencies. People had jobs to do, teach, be a 'youth sponsor,' serve on a committee. And many got so busy doing the job that they never got around to being a person with you, or treating you like a person.

"We don't have any of that now. There aren't any agency ministries. It's all personal, all getting to know someone, and caring about him. And the whole church structure is reorganized to encourage and support personal ministries. Not the other kind."

"You say the whole organization supports personalized ministries. How about this supportive organization. How does it work?"

Carl continued now, sketching briefly the patterns of Dunsea church life. "Home Units are the key to our church life. We all meet at least once a week with our Unit, and sometimes more often. The Home Units in each neighborhood are organized into Congregations. We try to keep Congregations around two hundred and fifty adults, to make the meetings more personal. All the Congregations together make up the Church of Dunsea.

"Home Unit meetings are where we get to know each other most deeply, and get personal support and encouragement. We study the Bible together, and stimulate each other to total Christian living."

"What happens at a Unit meeting?"

"There's no set structure. But all the Units I've belonged to had a similar format. We begin with sharing. We talk about our lives and experiences since the last time we met, share answers to prayer and special problems too. Usually this lasts, oh, say an hour or so. In a way it's our warm up — we learn to know each other all over again, and sense our oneness in the Lord.

"Then we study the Bible. Sometimes it takes us another hour to agree on the meaning of a passage, and we might even take another hour to talk through how God's Word affects us. I've found one of the most helpful things we do is to go back to things we shared earlier, and think them through again in view of the passage. Then we pray together, about our lives and ministries, decisions we have to make as a Unit, etc. Usually we pray about an hour. Sometimes we're at it till one or two o'clock. It just depends.

"When I think of the *one* hour we used to give meetings in the old church, and then get upset if we were 15 minutes overtime! I'm afraid if someone then had said we'd end up with four or five hour meetings, renewal would have been off automatically! But now, well, we just meet together and with the Lord, and it's the *experience* that counts. Not the time."

"How long are Congregational meetings? Are they four or five hours, too?"

"No, not usually. But in some ways they're like the Home Unit meetings. Our Congregation meets Sunday, in the cafeteria of a local business. Some of the Congregations used to rent school buildings, before the Court said it was unconstitutional to rent public buildings. And of course now only the Recognized Religious Union can own property.

"That seems to leave out the children," I injected.

"Yes. The older children, from nine or ten, usually come to Congregational meetings. Families have different ways of dealing with younger ones. Sometimes one parent stays home, or an older child babysits, or congregations with different meeting hours exchange child-care. Three Congregations use our cafeteria, you know. But, you'll hear all about the children tomorrow.

"The meetings are informal at Congregation. We usually sing together for a time. Then two or three Teachers share from the Word. We talk over what they've said — sometimes in Unit, sometimes not — and all have a chance to respond and share. We close with a time of spontaneous prayer and worship, and with communion. Probably the whole thing takes about three hours."

"Are Congregational meetings always for teaching and worship?"

"Usually. Of course, we also hear testimonies and prayer requests. And sometimes an Elder will be invited to hold a Discussion. When we've got a special decision to make, we usually plan a Congregational retreat."

"Carl, you've used several titles I'd like explained. Like Teacher, and Elder, and Discussion. What are these, and how do they fit into church life?"

"Well, each congregation has several Teachers. These are men of the Congregation who have the gift of teaching and leading. In our Congregation two Teachers have no secular job, and two work. Besides leading our Congregational meetings, the Teachers sort of, well, pastor. They meet with us individually, counsel us and help us. If we have a problem, we may invite a Teacher to our Unit meeting. Or if we get into a doctrinal issue we can't work through, a Teacher may spend an evening with us on that too."

"They have authority to settle disputes?"

"Oh no. Teacher's don't tell us what to believe or how to conduct our Units, and they'd never try. I mean, they instruct us. We have to pray through our problems, dig into the Word for ourselves, and then reach consensus."

"Do Teachers have organizational responsibilities?"

"You mean like reports to fill out, or committees to attend?

Things like that? No. Not at all. Their ministry is *people*, just like ours is. They spend their time with us. Of course, Teachers of various congregations meet together, to pray and encourage each other and work through their problems. And to find out if there are any church-wide issues."

"Who are the Elders you mentioned?"

"They're men God has chosen to work with the whole church here. We have five just now, who give themselves to full time mission among us."

"What do they do?"

"That depends. They all teach, of course. Usually it's one of the elders who holds a Teaching Mission on Congregational retreats. They advise, and exercise discipline when a Congregation fails to. And of course they minister personally, just like the Teachers do."

"What's this Discussion you mentioned?"

"When a Congregation has a serious decision to make one of the Elders may meet with them. His primary role is to make sure we seek true consensus, and that in the process we miss none of the relevant Scripture. At times he'll speak authoritatively, but this almost never happens."

"How does an elder enforce an authoritative decision?"

"He doesn't. Usually those involved do what the Bible says, and 'obey them that have the rule over you.' If we don't, the Elder still doesn't have to do anything. God does it."

"God?"

"Oh yes. You see, now that we're living closer to the Lord, we've found that He is real — and really here among us. Today we *expect* God to act in the church, even in disciplining. And He does."

"You haven't said yet how often the Congregations meet."

"Usually just on the Lord's day. And then, of course, we have at least three Congregational Retreats, and a two-week Congregational camp. The retreats are up in Northern Wisconsin, in one of the facilities owned by church members."

"Has the Dunsea church ever owned any camp areas?"

"No. As you know, it's not legal now for any unrecognized religious group to own property. But even before that law, our church decided it would own no real property. We felt that would start a trend toward the old ways of organizing, and that ultimately that would stifle us. And we were sure that the Lord would supply what was needed."

"And He has?"

"Yes. All through Christians. You see," he added with mock seriousness, "even some rich men have come to know the Lord. And then what's theirs is available to the whole church."

"Are these camps and retreats family affairs?"

"Oh yes. And all come who possibly can. The camps are one of our most important times with the children, as you'll hear tomorrow when you meet Mrs. Stebbins. The retreats are times when we pray through issues facing our Congregation, or meet for special studies. And, of course, we start our Home Units on retreat."

"Each Unit starts its life together on retreat?"

"Yes. Usually we regroup Units every nine or twelve months, depending on their growth."

"Can you keep a Unit together if you want to?"

"Yes. No one tells us to change Units. If a Unit seems to become ingrown, and its members lose their enthusiasm for witness and service, the Teachers step in. Usually they try to help that Unit back to health, but sometimes they ask it to break up."

"So there are standards for the Units?"

"There surely are. Not formal ones, you understand. But the standard of 'spiritual health,' as measured by the Bible's statement of what a believer is to be and should be becoming. If we don't show spiritual health, the Teacher steps in. You see, they care about us."

"How do you handle finances in the church? With no property or organized programs, you probably don't have much of a budget."

Several snorted at that idea. "We don't *budget* money, but our giving is many times more than it used to be. You see, our money now is directly invested in lives, and we control its use. And, since many in the church have ministries that keep them involved full time, the rest of us give to free them to serve."

"How does it work?"

"Well, every Home Unit is also the giving center. We do as the Bible says, and every week give as the Lord has prospered us. There's no demand, and no pledges to fulfill. We're all individually responsible, just as the Word says in Second Corinthians.

"One of our Unit members, Herb in ours, keeps the money. As we learn of needs, and God leads us, we give. And of course, some of us give individually beyond what we've laid by."

"Where do your gifts go?"

"Herb," Carl asked, "can you give Larry a rundown on our gifts this last six months?"

Herb produced a small notebook, flipped through two or three pages. "Here we are. In January there was a gift to Harold Ranson, one of the Teachers. And to the Henleys — they live up at one of the camp grounds all year, to take care of the facilities.

"In February, nothin'.

"In March one of the families of the Congregation left for the Philippines. We gave them half our balance, and sent another $200 to a brother in Red Africa.

"In April we contributed $50 to the Newsletter."

Carl broke in here to explain that the church publishes a newsletter, sharing with Dunsea's Christians how the Lord has been working through them. This is put out every other week, and its 20 pages help keep the church informed of the needs of the brethren as well. "That's the thing that makes giving so real to us. The first Congregations decided against centralized giving, or setting up established funds — like the mission fund, education fund, Elder's fund, etc. All giving was to be through Home Units. But the Congregations did realize that we all have to *know* about each other if the Lord is going to lead us to give. So the newsletter keeps us informed of the Church around the world.

"You know, that Corinthians passage? The one that shows us how to guide our giving? It says that the purpose of sharing money in the church isn't to let some have it easy at other's expense, but so there will be 'an equality.' And in this context that means all of us being able to function effectively in the Body; able to do the job Christ gives us. And that's how we give in Dunsea. Each of us examines his own situation and his ministry, and before God determines how much he *needs* to function as a Christian. And he examines the needs of the church. When we know our needs and the church's needs, and can balance them together, we can determine our giving by God's will. So we do, and we make sure that Christ's work is going to get done.

"It's sure amazing how much more than the old 10 percent giving this New Testament pattern produces! And how unimportant all the things money buys are when we see how God uses our money through our brothers."

"In May," Herb broke in firmly, "we gave to a family in our own Congregation. The husband lost his job, and has some other special needs. And we gave to pay a debt.

"One of our Congregation had a dispute with a contractor over a bill, and refused to pay. Three men of the Congregation looked the job over, and since the contractor had fulfilled his obligation, told him he ought to pay. He refused. So our Congregation paid it. The man is under discipline now, but there's no reflection on the Lord because of his action.

"Now, in June, let's see. We haven't made any determination on that yet. So I guess that's it. Really, there are so many needs. When we're sure what the Lord wants, we'll decide."

"Then what you're saying is that the Lord coordinates your giving, and so you don't need organizational machinery to do the job?"

"Right," said Carl. "But remember, this isn't magical. We need to know about needs before we can meet them. And we need to live so close to the Lord that He can lead us. And that's what the church is organized to do, really. Help us see the whole Church, and help us live close to the Lord — so that the Lord can direct."

"And He does?"

"Yes. Absolutely."

"You know," it was Herb again, "I wouldn't have believed any of this when I was in the old church. Somehow, it just didn't seem logical. Or businesslike. Why, even the old 'faith' missions relied a lot on computers and all sorts of heart-touching letters.

"But I guess there's one difference. Today the whole church *expects* God to *act*. We really believe that God is alive; that we can know His will, and that He can be Head over all things in His church. We believe it so much that we live it. We let Him direct, and He does.

"Guess that's a funny thing about our 'disorganized' church here in Dunsea. It really is disorganized — from the old standpoint. Most of the controls that kept things working then are gone. But we have our own kind of organization. An organization that's designed to free God to act, and to direct individuals, small groups, and Congregations. We depend completely on Him. And you know, we don't need any of the committees or charts or pledges we needed then.

"It's really great. Living our life together, with God right back in the center of the picture. I really wonder why it took us so long."

18

Christian Education

The next day Carl turned me out of bed at 7, insisted that I eat a hearty breakfast (something all lean people insist the rest of us need), and outlined plans for that day. "I'll be dropping you off to spend some time with Mrs. Stebbins. She's, well, I guess you'd have to call her an 'education worker.' Our title for her is 'Mother.' I'll pick you up this afternoon, and tonight we'll visit an evaluation session of several Evangelism Units."

Mrs. Stebbins is a woman of 62, widowed twelve years. She has spent most of those years working with Christian families. Mother Stebbins (or Karen, as everyone calls her) lives in a small but attractive apartment. One whole room is full of books, pamphlets and manuals — everything from the secular Child Management Program Series from the University of Michigan, to children's study units produced by independent publishers like David C. Cook, Scripture Press and Gospel Light. After a cup of coffee, Karen sat me down to read two pamphlets. One was a historical survey of renewal's effect on Christian education, and the other one Karen gives to new families to outline Dunsea's approach to child nurture.

Because of their interesting content, I am quoting from both of these pamphlets, written by Harold Waggomen, one of the

Teachers in the Dunsea church. The following excerpts are from his pamphlet, *Renewal in Retrospect.*

The issue that caused the greatest turmoil in early renewal was the training of children in the Christian faith. Traditionally this had been attempted through various agencies, primarily the Sunday school. At the time renewal forces began to move in the church, every congregation owned its own building, much of which was educational space. Children of Christians and non-Christians alike came to Sunday school for one hour each week. During this one hour, usually broken down into "opening assemblies" and instructional time, a Christian layman attempted to communicate Christian truth to classes of six or eight or even more children.

Major criticisms of this approach to Christian education, aside from the basic fallacy of equating Christian nurture with the verbal communication of biblical ideas, were (1) the very short time period provided no opportunity to relate truths taught to experience; (2) the impersonal level of most classes, with neither teacher nor students knowing each other well; (3) the limited curriculum which far too often simply passed on some moralism through a Bible story media, often taking the story and the moral out of context; (4) the lack of training of teachers, who more often than not viewed teaching as saying words at their students; (5) the failure to involve parents meaningfully in co-ministry with the church. In point of fact, Christian parents abandoned the role of nurture to the church. Few knew what their children were taught in Sunday school, and fewer still understood how they *must* complete teaching begun at church through daily experiences within the family.

Renewal led to a variety of attempts to bridge nurture gaps. Some churches moved quickly to a three hour "total" program Sunday mornings. Others attempted a similar program weekdays. Still others moved classes into private homes, particularly under the ever-rising "Tax on Unregistered Religious Organizations," as all religious bodies not related to the Unified American Church and National Council of Religious Affiliates (NatCor) were classified in 1978.

The patterns of such classes were similar throughout. First there was a period of reviewing the week's experiences with the Bible truth taught last class. (Also diary sheets recording these experiences, called LifeLines, were brought by students old enough to keep them, and given to the class leader. He read them and returned them during the week, or planned private counseling sessions with the student.) The next part of the class was spent *intensifying.* This was an interesting term for a basic part of the developing educational program. Here the leader introduced experiences which would focus a sense of need for the truth to be studied. This might involve picture studies, tapes, movies, role play, discussion, hearing popular music, etc., to sharpen a "growing edge." When the students actually began to *feel* the problem, and see it in a personal way, Bible solutions were introduced.

Intensifying was one of the most significant departures from the older Christian education, in which a Bible story was merely told, and application was usually in passing. For normally (as children need much time to clarify and understand feelings and problems which do not grow out of direct experience), *intensifying* alone took longer than the old Sunday school had provided for the entire class period!

Subsequently the students were guided through Scripture to "see" the intensified problem from God's viewpoint, and work out possible responses which would be "in God's way."

The educational method used here, even with younger children, was that of *thought guidance*. This approach to teaching was developed from educational ideas of the 60's and 70's which the renewing church saw as in harmony with Jesus' method of teaching. One early book, *Teaching for Thinking*, a secular text by Raths, et. al., had a surprising influence. The distinctive teaching style which developed saw adult leaders serving not as tellers of God's truth, but as guides who helped the children work through to personal understanding. *Thought guidance* was used, with adaptations to fit children's developmental levels, with first graders on up through the teens, and some early materials attempted to apply its philosophy to a leaderless group-study for adults.

It would be wrong to discuss the transition years without mention of the role played by the independent publishers. Many factors made it difficult for them during those years. As old patterns began to break down, some customers clung fiercely to the old and demanded the traditional Sunday school lessons. Others, an ever-growing minority, demanded something uniquely different, that would fit the changing pattern of the adult Sunday morning service with its "three hour block," popularized by early renewal leaders. Courageously, first one publisher and then others began producing *two* kinds of materials. The financial drain was extreme, but those first All-Bible Experience Units provided the help churches needed, and proved a definite turning point in the commitment of many congregations to renewal.

Our Christian education today, far removed even from these then giant steps, owes much to those early pioneers who faced the problem of "what shall we do with the children" and willingly moved out to find new answers. Then this question seemed to many *the* greatest hindrance to significant change in church organization and life. How thankful we can be that men in those days found the grace to trust God, and to change, unsure of the outcome, but convinced of the need.

I jotted down several questions to ask Mother Karen while I read. Questions like, What happens to children at Dunsea when Congregations or Home Units meet? Is there anything like the renewed Sunday school today? Her answers may surprise you, but I found them understandable, if only one keeps in mind the basic concept of Christian nurture the church here has. This concept is admirably spelled out in another booklet, called *Sharing a Living Faith*, which I now reproduce in its entirety.

"Me? Teach my children! But, I know so little."

It's a common reaction. Especially when someone learns that this is exactly what the Lord expects — You, teach *your* children!

It's a little frightening, too, until you realize what teaching really means, and what resources we have to draw on. Then teaching our children becomes exciting, one of the most rewarding experiences we Christians can have. I hope that when you've read this booklet, and talked it over with others, any fears you have will be quieted. And only the excitement of it will remain.

Usually you will have some pretty challenging questions to ask before you are satisfied. Questions I would like to discuss in this booklet. Questions like, What does "teaching our children" really mean? Is there a biblical pattern for teaching? How do I do it? And, what help does the Church provide? Let's think about each of these, together.

First, what does "teaching our children" really mean? Too often, even today, a Christian's first thought when someone says "teach" is "convey biblical information." This is part of teaching, but only part. Actually, if this is mistaken for the *whole* of Christian teaching it invariably leads to a warped and lifeless Christianity. We here at Dunsea always think of teaching in a far broader way. Perhaps the synonyms *train, guide, discipline, lead,* and *share* will help to fill out its meaning. Especially when we add one transforming word — life!

You see, Christian teaching involves *training in a way of life.* Guidance in living God's life. Discipline in the pattern of God's life. Leading one another in the path of God's life. Sharing the life that God has shared with us. Content plays an important part, but *life* is the heart of Christian nurture.

This is why we stress the home as the center of Christian education. We are merely recognizing a long and well known truth — that it is in living with his family that a child learns how to live.

Take an illustration. Recently I have been troubled by the fact that both my boys make excuses. If anything goes slightly wrong; if they are called down for something they have done or criticized, immediately excuses flow. I know where they learned this — from me. For I too have a facility for explaining away the little things that I do.

Now, I certainly did not *teach* them this. That is, I did not instruct them in words. They did not even try to "learn" it.

No, my *way of life* became theirs.

Now, this is not to say that Christianity is merely imitating ways of life. Not at all. Christianity is new life, God's life, given us supernaturally when we come to know Jesus Christ as our Savior. But it is *life*. And any life, including God's, grows and develops in the pattern of life lived by others.

As Christian parents, our first concern is for the conversion of our children. Our second is that the new life they thus receive be developed and nurtured. And it is this, the development and nurture of a person's new life into the ways of God, that we call teaching, or Christian education.

There are many ways that our children must be taught, and much they need to learn to live as Christians. Here are several goals that the church believes are primary, and that we can reach as we "teach" in God's ordained way:

1. Christian education should provide the growing Christian with an accurate and relevant concept of God.

2. Christian education should equip the growing young Christian for self-directed maturity, and for self-chosen submission to God.

3. Christian education should enable the young Christian to continue in a deepening relationship with Christ, in a "by faith" walk. That is, translating his perceptions of God's will and his faith in God's power into a free and spontaneous life-style.

4. Christian education should free the young Christian to be an honest and *real* person, to express himself openly, and to accept and love others whatever their personalities or personal bondages.

5. Christian education should provide the growing young Christian with a deep concern for others, a reflection of God's deep love for all. And should help this concern grow into a loving responsiveness to human need which is both intelligent and selfless.

Look these over again. Can you conceive of *any* of these goals being reached simply by sitting children down to master biblical content? Even reaching the first goal demands more than Bible knowledge. True, it does require a perception of God that is accurate, and this demands a *biblical* understanding of His nature. But this goal also requires that our perceptions be emotionally and volitionally accurate too.

Think back a moment to my illustration of excuse making. Biblically I have always understood that God is truth. I accept the fact that providing things honest in the sight of men is important for a life in harmony with the Word. I can, and I have, passed on this idea to my sons. *But emotionally I have perceived certain situations far differently.* I have in fact seen, valued, and chosen momentary advantages to be gained by excuse making in preference to the real truth. That is how I have acted. And my children have followed, not what I told them, but what I *did.* What I communicated *so as to affect their way of life* was not my intellectual agreement with the biblical evaluation of honesty. I communicated by my life an evaluation that in certain circumstances, honesty is to be set aside!

Only now, as I have seen my actions for what they are, and openly shared this with my family and with God, and am seeing God reshape my responses, can I hope to communicate an accurate and relevant concept of God. *For the God I communicate is the one whose life I live. Not the one I merely talk about.*

Teaching my children, then, demands first of all that I live close to God. It means sharing Him with them as He shapes my life, and leads me to live His Word and conform with His ways.

As a Christian parent, the church seeks to help you teach *in this way.* Our whole structure is designed to help you teach, train, guide, discipline, and share Christ's life with your children. We do *not* attempt to teach *for you.* You must communicate His Word, both in word and by your life.

It is important to ask if this is the biblical way. For we recognize the full authority of Scripture as God's Word, and we seek our ways of life within it. The answer to the question is a certain, "Yes."

The New Testament, while silent on specific methods of teaching at home, does indicate that parents have that responsibility. And that in this nurture the Scriptures have a definite role. Like Timothy, "from childhood" young minds should be "familiar with the Holy Scriptures."

The basic passage on which we build our approach is Deuteronomy 6:1-6. Here, after the Exodus time of knowing God immediately through miracle and in the cloudy-fiery pillar, the people of Israel are given the task of communicating the reality of God to a new generation, through words. For this, the Bible tells parents, God's words are first to "be in your heart." And you are to "teach them diligently to your children."

The first responsibility of the parent is to have God's word in his heart. Not just on his lips. The words of God are to permeate our lives, to shape us, to transform us. Just so Paul writes to one of the churches, "you are my epistles, written not in stone but on the fleshly tablets of the heart, known and read of all." And so the primacy of *life* is established. The "teacher" must live the words he seeks to communicate.

And those words are to be taught diligently to the children. For the words interpret and explain the life. The words become the foundation for personal adult response to God, and thus the key to an ever-growing experience with God.

The Deuteronomy passage does one more thing. It locates the *context* of such teaching. And that context is daily life. "When you lie down, when you get up, as you're walking along the way." Living together provides the ideal context for sharing God's words. For several reasons. Perhaps the biggest is that the words of God show us how to live God's life in the world. Divorced from that life context, biblical teaching leads to deadened orthodoxy. Infusing experience, the Bible shapes our understanding of the nature of life itself. So the ideal way to teach is to bring into experiences we share with our families the perceptions of life God gives in the Word.

All this may seem rather terrifying. How can we teach a life we are only learning to live? How can we bring biblical truths to bear on daily experiences, when we know so little of the Bible? Many parents ask these questions. Perhaps you are asking them too.

But remember this. We are all learners. We all need to know so much more than we do. So God does not ask us to do what we cannot. He asks only that we share what we *do* know. That we live what we do understand. The Holy Spirit can use a yielded personality, no matter how immature. He can use a week-old Christian. What *you are,* God can use.

Perhaps this helps you see why our church centers its education on adults. The key to nurturing children is what the parents *are.* And our whole church is structured to help you be a growing, vital Christian. Not one of us has "arrived," but our aim is for you to be one who is daily living with Christ, and learning more of Him. Whatever you learn to live you can teach, by living it and talking about it, to your children.

I have tried, then, to answer the first two questions. *Teaching* is *sharing the life we live with God.* And this *is* the pattern given in Scripture for the nurture of our children. And I think I have answered the third question at the same time: the question of *how*. We teach by living the life we live with God with our families.

In most of our homes, this means a planned sharing time. It means prayer together, and words from the Bible. It means seeking to be aware of the experiences we can share daily, and relating these experiences to God's way. Skill in such sharing grows as we grow.

I haven't said anything about the help our church provides. Let me do that now.

You know, of course, that all Christians are expected to take part in Home Unit life. Some Home Units are made up of people who seek through their fellowship to help each other train their children. Perhaps you would like to become part of such a unit.

In addition, our church provides facilities for children's and family camps. The children of the church are encouraged to spend four weeks each year at one of the camps. There, in a decentralized program (with each group of five children living together as a "family" with a trained counselor), more concentrated teaching and life experience is provided than in two years of the old "Sunday school." The training varies with age, but includes grounding in biblical knowledge for all, and skills in relating knowledge to life-experience. And camp means fun and activities too. (Brochures describing the camp program, sports and activities, and "experience teaching" program are available.)

The family camp is an experience in family living. Three-family units, (which include all family members) live and play and worship together, working through common problems and seeking to develop unity within each family. Camp experiences are recommended for all families at least once every three years.

Also, Church Mothers are available to help you. Our church at Dunsea has recognized a number of women with this title and ministry. Each Mother has successfully raised her own family in the Lord, and received the testimony of her Congregation as to her gifts and love.

Mothers give full time to their ministry, and one will meet with you in your home, or with your Home Unit, whenever you wish. Each Mother has many resources to suggest for your use. These range from some of the better secular manuals on child guidance, to at-home Bible study units graded to your children's ages, to helpful discussion booklets for husbands and wives.

Each congregation has a list of Mothers. Please feel free to take a list, and call on one near you.

And remember. Your church will not bring your children up in our faith for you. Because it can't. But, by the grace of God, *you can*. And we stand ready to help.

That day with Karen Stebbins was a busy one. We visited homes of three families, and Karen talked with the mothers about their children and home life. In more than one home Karen ministers to the wife, counseling her how to love her husband and adjust to him. And we spent two hours at a woman's Home Unit meeting. These were ladies whose husbands are as yet unconverted, and who are trying to work through the difficult question of how a wife can live in submission to her unbelieving spouse. There I found Mother Stebbins has a firm and helpful grasp of the Word.

Another appointment was with a husband and wife who, as new Christians, were deeply concerned about reestablishing their relationship with their children. Karen helped them plan a series of studies, blending secular and Christian resources. The program she worked out with them includes study guides for the parents on principles of child guidance, family discussion materials designed to help adults and children work out better ways of living together, and several sets of graded Bible study material for the children.

It was clear that this couple were discouraged to discover so much was expected of them. Mother Stebbins encouraged them, and helped them work out a schedule that would provide time for daily study and discussion of their family life.

"You know," she remarked as we left, "one of the first lessons a new Christian has to learn is the lesson of priorities. We challenge those in our church to be Christians *first*. If we're really citizens of heaven, it doesn't pay, as Jesus said, to 'become entangled with the affairs of this life.' Sure it means giving up. But giving up what? That extra job? We can all get along on what we make four days a week. Usually one way you can tell believers from the unbelievers is that the non-Christians work at two jobs. We Christians work at being Christians, and are satisfied with that. And Christians first means giving up some evenings with the family '3-D.' But who cares about three dimensional shadows when we can be involved with flesh and blood people?

"Still, it's hard at first. But we learn. And when we learn, it's really exciting."

I wondered about the children, especially from the homes of new converts. Was all training given in the home, or did the church still have something like the old Sunday school?

"Normally the children over 10 attend Congregation with their parents. Younger children are sometimes pooled, and one parent in a Home Unit will stay with them each Sunday. More often Congregations exchange. That is, one family will keep the children of another family in a Congregation that meets at another time, sometimes for an experience-unit study. Often, by the way, a youth Unit will take on children of a neighboring Congregation for three months as a ministry, and as preparation for counseling at camp. Actually, the experience in youth Units and in the home prepares kids for the personalized kind of ministry we expect. But I do have regular training sessions with youth Units. I'm meeting with one tonight, to work on their skills in *intensifying*."

"What happens to the younger children when the Home Units meet?"

"Again, that depends. Children do take part in a very few of our Units. Usually we don't bring them in until Junior High age. Sometimes parents will hire a baby sitter, other times Units that meet different nights exchange sitting service.

"I hope you understand that we aren't really neglecting the children. We don't provide regular programs for them, but we work through their parents and both the family and children's camps. Our whole approach is to train and develop Christian *adults*, and these adults are then able and expected to guide their own children. So we simply refuse to go into the business of providing special agencies for children."

"Rather a hard-nosed view, isn't it?"

"Probably. But it works. And it never lets the parents feel that the church is responsible for their children. Parents are, and everything we do keeps that parental responsibility in focus."

Later I thought about what she had said, and jotted down what struck me as most significant. (1) Keep responsibility focused on parents. (2) Make Christians establish their own priorities in view of their responsibilities. (3) Provide specific and personal help designed to equip parents to meet their responsibilities. (4) Remember that the church is for adults, a community of transformation in which parents are helped to grow, so that they can share their growth with their children.

I was somewhat troubled by this fourth point, and so tried to pin Karen down on it. "This sounds like you're isolating the children from church life. From knowing adult Christians. Isn't this a mistake?"

"Well," she smiled, "it may sound like we isolate them, but we really don't. In fact, our children probably know adults better than any in the old church did.

"I remember how people used to say, 'Don't break up the family.' As if simply sitting beside adults in wooden pews was helping the family worship together! No, it's no physical proximity that marks togetherness, it's being involved together, so we share ourselves with each other.

"Well, today this is pretty much our way of life. Family Units often take retreats together. There, at one of the camps, all play together, work together, talk together. Children are treated like people; they can talk, and be listened to. On retreat they have more *personal* contact with adults who are not their parents than was provided in *years* in the old churches.

"And in Congregation, the children hear their parents and other adults, not just look at them, sitting there. A whole pattern of living with adults in a Christian community is established.

"Then, too, we often encourage play groups of younger children that rotate from home to home. We *want* children to know many Christian adults, and we want the adults to know and understand the children.

"And of course there's camp. At family camp we get two weeks of in-depth involvement. Not just the pious 'sit and talk' kind of involvement, but total life involvement. Three family units picnic, fish, swim, go on excursions, talk and pray together. In fact, most of our church children have more *significant time* with adults other than parents than many children have with their parents! And it's *significant time* we're always trying to provide, both at home and on retreat and at camp."

"What do you mean by 'significant time'?"

"Just what I've been talking about. Life involvement. For instance, sitting in a room and watching the family 3-D isn't significant time. Painting a room together, taking a trip, talking, swimming — all these can be significant time. Time when we share an experience, and not only share it, but communicate with each other about what's happening, and what it means to us. It's times like this that we share the reality of our life in Christ. When we share Him *through* sharing ourselves, and our whole approach to life as it is shaped by knowing and obeying Him.

"So, really, you can't say we don't provide for children. We do provide for them, in the only way that's meaningful. The only way that lets us share our faith as a living, vital reality."

I thought back to the days when my children were young, and remembered how discouraged my wife and I had felt as we struggled to do the kind of thing Mother Stebbins now called "normal" in the church. And I couldn't help praising the Lord that our children had grown up to know and love Him in spite of our deficiencies — and that today His church was providing the kind of help to other parents we so desperately sought. Renewal in the church of Christ, for all the difficulties, had proven fantastically fruitful. And I was thankful.

Before Karen and I parted, I had to ask her questions about the ministry to youth, something I have been especially concerned with for as many years as I have been concerned with renewal.

"Karen, do the young people fit well in their parent's Home Units, or have you another approach? And, how do they fit into Congregational life?"

"Normally highschoolers have their own Units. We look on the junior high years as apprentice years, when teens not only are introduced to group-life in their parents' Units, but are also involved in special discussions with their parents at home. In high school, nearly all the teens elect a youth Unit. Each Congregation has men and women with special interest in youth, and they share in the youth Unit.

"When it comes to Congregational meetings, the young people are considered as much a part as any other believer. They're free to share and participate, as God leads. You know, we're living on this earth to represent the Lord. And that means living out His love, sharing Him with others. Well, this is the focus for youth Units as well as the adult Units. And my, it's exciting to see what God does through some of these kids!"

"Do you have special activities for young people?"

"Oh yes. I mentioned that some choose to work with children in special teaching situations. And often highschoolers serve as counselors at our camps. Units are free to plan retreats, to develop special evangelistic or service projects, etc. Just like adult Units.

"We don't, of course, have teen Teachers or Elders. Actually, these ministries are open only to men who have served the Lord for years, and demonstrated gifts and faithfulness in the church. Even to become a Mother, I had to be known by the church for years, and all the Congregations of which I have been a member had to certify their recognition of my gifts and give their recommendation. Leadership in the church isn't something that someone 'fresh out of school' — even a seminary! — is given. We test a person's life and his gifts, and then only when God leads specifically will a person be ordained.

"But, really, that isn't an issue. Because, you see, there is plenty for every Christian to do. We each have ministries, and we concentrate on performing them. That's the mark of a healthy church — not its leaders, but its members. And our young people are full, ministering members of the church."

We were late getting back to Karen's home. Carl was waiting, ready to rush me to our next appointment. We took time to pray together and then I said good-by to Mother Karen Stebbins, a little woman with an exciting ministry in a truly renewed form of Christian education.

19

Evangelism

Carl swung his car out onto one of the elevated plastic highways that span Dunsea, and make travel in the planned communities so quick and easy. As Clearasel is liberally used, no railings or supports interrupted our view, and Carl pointed out many of Dunsea's points of interest.

Dunsea's administrative complex, as in the Old Cities, is in the center of town, surrounded by a 90-acre park. In the park is the city museum, community theater, art schools, and sports arena where football, basketball, and the more popular colosseum sports are played. This area is within six miles of any part of Dunsea and has acres of underground parking, enough for a good quarter of the community's cars. Carl explained that the colosseum games (revivals of the older Roman gladiatorial contests) are so popular that the community has been divided into color coded areas, and only those living in the zone selected by lot can attend them during festival days.

Other community services are decentralized. Each quarter of the community has an educational and shopping area approximately three miles from the center, and thus three miles from the Dunsea limits. Other businesses and light industries are, by law, at least a mile beyond the community limits.

The eight entertainment centers are on the edges of the community. These feature the Circarama theaters, licensed bars, and of course the community brothels. There are also eight Religion centers, staggered between the entertainment centers. Here are Recognized church and synagogue worship and counseling buildings. In these centers are located the medical buildings, too, some already being swallowed up in the Recognized church compounds, even as psychiatry and counseling professions have been for some years. And the community police maintain substations here.

It was strange, looking out over Dunsea, almost parklike with its planned clusters of condominiums, apartments, and scattered private homes, to realize that here one hundred thousand people live, marry, raise their children, do their work, enjoy their pleasures, and perhaps, die.

"Carl, how many Christians are there in Dunsea?"

"Somewhere around 35 percent of the population, I believe."

"That's a pretty solid percentage. A lot more than there were in the days of the old church."

"Yes, but there are many reasons. And even now we haven't reached the point the early church did in places. Wasn't it Tertullian who wrote that Christians in his day were 'all but a majority in every city'?"

"You said there were reasons you've reached 35 percent of Dunsea's population?"

"I can think of three pretty big ones. In the first place, evangelism today is a Christian basic. All of us witness. Part of our focus in Unit life is to share about the folks we're witnessing to, and pray for them. Mutual encouragement helps make witnessing more spontaneous and normal than in the old church. Why, there we never had much chance to share spiritually with other Christians! So how could we talk naturally about the Lord to outsiders?

"Then too, the paganization of our culture has helped make the difference between Christian and non-Christian sharper. You saw the tendency in the 60's and early 70's toward brutality and disregard of suffering, and toward the breakdown of sexual and other moral boundaries. All this has developed and so our culture has broken out of a 'Christianized' pattern of behavior. Why, didn't they talk even then about a 'post-Christian era'?"

I nodded.

"Well, today in our country many pagan values are the norm. So being a Christian really does offer an alternative — an alternative that many moral people of the old days couldn't see."

"Carl, I wish you'd define 'pagan' for me. That word has so many connotations."

"O.K. It's not that I mean 'without conscience,' or 'dirty,' or 'uncivilized' by pagan. I'm really thinking of life-style. The framework of values the culture accepts, and tries to find meaning in. Pagan people can be very moral, within their own meaning of the term. Not many cheat in business: honesty is still necessary for any society to function — at least, a minimum level of honesty. But there's a big difference in attitudes.

"A pagan has different ideas about values, about what's *right*. For instance, today most people think it's *right* to seek personal pleasure as an end in itself. And to use people. Like in the games. It's all right to go to the games to see a man killed, or lose an arm in Sword and Trident bouting. After all, he's being paid, and it was his choice to become a professional. And to a pagan it's *right* to use the brothels. After all, the girls there are paid, or at least select that kind of life in lieu of taxes or prison. And it's right to take up one of the college liaisons — it's just being 'sexually liberated.' To a pagan it's right to spend your life working for money, or for power. The whole pattern of values, of what seems right, is what is at issue.

"And today the pagan values are the ones the society accepts and supports, that's all. And that makes the difference between Christians and non-Christians so visible."

"What's the third thing?"

"It's related to what I've just said. Today most Christians really *live* the values we profess. I don't think we used to.

"I mean, as a group we've rejected, as meaningful goals in life, personal pleasure and money and power. We consciously reject *using* anyone; we seek to serve others instead. We build our lives on the Scripture, and we discipline members of the Church who fall off into pagan ways of life.

"You know, even though people think we're strange for being so different, they still are attracted to our way of life — because they see our joy. And they know that for all the time and money they lavish on themselves, their lives are without meaning."

"Carl, it sounds to me that you're saying one reason the Lord can use us today is that believers' lives lay the foundation for their witness."

"Exactly. The Christian has to mirror God's life, or what he says sounds unreal. I know that 'faith cometh by hearing, and hearing by the Word of God,' and that no one ever was converted just by watching another's life. But at the same time life and Word must correspond. They've got to be in harmony. And our church structures its whole life to help believers grow up in the Lord, to submit our lives to live totally for Him. When we live transformed lives, those lives win the hearing for the Word."

We had driven over Dunsea now, and Carl swung the car onto a road leading out to the country. "We're meeting at a farm tonight. The owner lets us use a barn he's converted for our meetings."

I had one more question to ask Carl before we arrived. "Carl, you said we were meeting with several evangelism Units tonight. I got the impression from what you've just said that the Church at Dunsea encourages *every* believer to witness. And that each Home Unit has some focus on witnessing. Why do you have evangelism Units then?"

"That's a good question, and rather hard to answer. Each Unit does stress evangelism as part of living God's life. And the Units you'll see tonight actually conduct their sessions much like the rest of us.

"But sometimes a Unit is in a special situation, and feels led to focus on evangelism in a particular way. When that happens the Unit registers as an evangelism Unit, and gets special help from the church."

"Carl, I'm afraid that hasn't helped much."

"Well, do you remember the old extra-church agencies? The ones that developed when it was clear the churches weren't reaching so many special segments of the population?"

"You mean groups like Youth for Christ, Inter-Varsity, Campus Crusade?"

"Yes, that's just what I mean. Well, there are still special groups in today's society. Often Christians who have close contact with a special group will want to get together in a Unit. For instance, one Unit at tonight's meeting is made up of Junior College Students; another of high school teachers. These groups were formed because the members wanted the support of others living in the same situation, facing the same problems."

"Are all evangelism Units homogeneous groupings like these?"

"No, not at all. Normally a Unit is formed on geographical grounds. Folks who live in the same neighborhood, and are part of the same Congregation. Some of these become evangelism Units, too. One Unit here tonight has become concerned about a rural town 70 miles west of here. They've been to the area, have a couple of home Bible studies started. In the next few months probably one or two of the Unit's families will move out there to live.

"Another Unit of six young married couples is planning a three-month mission to upper Michigan."

"So each evangelism Unit has some special interest that poses different problems than normal evangelism?"

"That's right. Normal evangelism is every member of the church sharing Christ with his neighbor, his co-workers, his daily contacts. The evangelism Units all are planning some special focus beyond this normal day-to-day approach."

For several minutes we had been parked behind a building that loomed darkly in the gathering dusk. Now Carl and I got out of the car, and went around to the other side of the barn where light shone warmly from windows in its modernized stone face. We slipped in and sat down.

The two rows of chairs placed in a huge circle were nearly filled. There were about 120 men and women. The meeting was about to begin.

That meeting (as most of the gatherings of the renewed church) lasted several hours so I'll only sketch what happened briefly.

The session began with spontaneous singing and praise, that extended over half an hour. Each person seemed free to begin a song, or lead in a sentence of prayer, and the atmosphere during this time was one of drawing together in worship around the Lord.

Then came a time of open sharing, during which I noted the same kind of honesty that marked the Unit meetings. A number told of experiences of the past two weeks, posed questions, and spoke revealingly of difficulties they had encountered. Problems that came out were recorded, for after a while an older man (whom Carl told me was an evangelistically gifted Teacher from the church) listed several of them on a large chalkboard. The topics, as I remember them, were:

Loss of interest of buddy. (I should explain that the church encourages a buddy system, with new believers closely followed up by the one who leads them to Christ.)

Personal failure seen by target. (This related to a situation where a high school teacher had been seen by a coworker to fall short of strict honesty.)

Leadership role in evangelistic Bible class.

Response to philosophical attack. (Posed by a junior college student.)

Approach to establish mission in new territory.

Introduction of convert to church life.

Each topic was discussed by the entire group. Various members shared personal experiences and insights from Scripture. The Teacher led the discussion, but made few comments. Those he did make were extremely penetrating and practical. He seemed to have an ability to sense consensus and express it, and to point the group to relevant Scriptures they might otherwise have overlooked.

The meeting was three hours old before the last topic had been discussed, and I had the feeling that while the Teacher probably could have snapped off the right answers to each problem in minutes, thinking the issues through had proven extremely valuable for the whole group.

Then, in clusters of three, we had a time of prayer.

I was unable to meet the Teacher, as Carl told me one of the groups would meet with him for counseling after the open session. And so we left, bringing with us a sense of unity and mutual concern, and a conviction that these men and women actually knew the Lord as a living Person. A Person who is active through them. What an exciting spirit this is!

Before we drove to the evaluation session I had written down several questions of my own about the evangelism and growth of the church. The discussion that night had helped to answer them, and I'll summarize what was said. Here are my questions, and the Dunsea answers.

How are new converts nurtured. Normally people are won to Christ by personal witness. (Very few non-Christians wander into

Congregational meetings.) Each believer is encouraged to build a special relationship with his converts, to meet regularly for prayer and help them get started in Bible study. Most new Christians are involved as soon as possible in the Home Unit of the person who brought him to Christ, and in their Congregation. Then, usually when the Unit breaks up, he is encouraged to join a Congregation in his own neighborhood.

There are no little "lists" of don'ts for members of the Dunsea church. Christians are well known for their high moral standards, and for their loving concern for others. So most new converts *expect* to live a holy life. (I was interested to learn that in Dunsea one nickname for the Christian is "a holy." This is a term both of ridicule and respect.) Each new Christian is nevertheless accepted as he is, and treated gently. A new Christian is encouraged to immediately make known his conversion. This tends to put pressure on him; pressures that make him feel the need for the church and the need of relying constantly on the Lord.

Evangelistic Units usually involve new converts in other Home Units. If there were many new Christians, the group's life would necessarily be focused on helping them with their personal and growing needs. And this would change the nature of the action-oriented evangelism Unit.

Oh, yes, the church does offer orientation retreats for new Christians. These provide some orientation to the Christian life, particularly to the Bible and to how to live in the presence of Christ and trust Him daily.

Retreat courses are not required of new Christians, and not all attend. The church in fact relies for the nurture of new converts on the intimate personal relationships that develop in the Home Units. And a surprisingly small percentage of those who profess Christ as Savior drift back to the world. Most are guided gently into disciplined Christian living.

How are new Congregations established? There are many Congregations in each American church. Dunsea now has about 140 of them, of which perhaps twenty have been established in the last two years. New Congregations are formed on the same principle as new Home Units. When a Home Unit grows during the year to fourteen or sixteen people, it is normal for it to divide in two. This way the closest of personal relationships can be maintained, and there is always a growth dynamic. When Congregations near three hundred, members begin to pray about dividing. They may divide into three Congregations of about one hundred, but usually there is a simple division into two. All Congregations in Dunsea, as in other renewal churches, form strictly on geographical considerations. They have no "favorite" Teacher they travel across a city to hear. They are all *one*, one around the world, and where they live determines the Congregation whose life they share. There is no room in the renewed church for denominationalism, or similar barriers to experiencing the unity we have in Christ.

Since each new Congregation is really half of an established one, its pattern of life is set. And it grows up as an organized part of the Dunsea Church.

I learned, by the way, that there were originally four Congregations in Dunsea when the community was being built, and that this pattern was worked out by them. As the city grew, and new Christians moved in, these four Congregations became twelve. Almost a third of the growth from that point can be traced to Christians moving in the community, and about two thirds to the evangelization of the unsaved.

What is the missionary vision of the church? Dunsea expresses its concern for other communities in a variety of ways. I told of the one Unit I saw at the evaluation meeting which was planning to spend three months "on mission." The team of young couples will work intensively in one area of upper Michigan for three months. During that period they will first seek to win several families to the Lord. Then they will concentrate on teaching these families to become a church. With the families functioning as the church, the couples will return. The new church will be visited now and then by a Dunsea Teacher, until after two or three years one of its own members will be ordained an Elder.

The other Unit I mentioned is sending two of its own couples to move permanently to a nearby rural town. They will become the nucleus for a new church. And the same general approach will be followed as in Michigan. After the church is established, it will be on its own, dependent completely on God. For, as you know, these churches are truly local churches, part of one body, but autonomous and responsible only to our Head, Jesus Christ.

It would hardly be fair to leave missions without noting the role of the Sent Ones, as they title their missionaries.

Each year Dunsea ordains those whom God calls to this special ministry. No one is lightly ordained, and all must have their calling confirmed by the Church. The ordination service takes place at one of the two regular yearly meetings of the whole church, when over 30,000 gather before dawn on the hills above the community to praise God together.

Those ordained are Dunsea's gift to the Church at large. Like others, they travel from place to place, teaching in some, establishing new churches in others, ministering as God leads. They are not responsible to the ordaining church or to any other body, but are of course considered a member of the local church wherever they may be. They receive no promise of support, but depend completely on God to move His people to provide for their needs.

Dunsea keeps no records of churches started by its Sent Ones, or by evangelism Units of its Congregations. There is no need. They are all independent churches, all part of the one great Church of Christ. I did learn, though, that Sent Ones from Dunsea are now ministering in many parts of the world as well as in this country. And that the newsletter carries their reports to the church. I particularly want to include this, because I remember that many feared renewal, with its growing rejection of traditional agencies and organizations, would lead to a loss of missionary vision. As if that had happened in the early church! Actually, the reverse has been proven true. And although the only mission organizations, so used by God in their time, no longer exist, the Gospel is sent throughout the world.

There was one question that was not answered at the evaluation, and so I asked Estelle about it when we got back to Carl's house. What about children?

In the old churches, evangelism of children had been a central feature of its life and program. Yet I hadn't heard a word in the Unit meeting, in my day with Mother Stebbins, or this evening, about child evangelism. "Doesn't the church care about children any more?" I asked.

Estelle started to answer, but Carl cut in with a vehemence that surprised me. "No, the church does not care about children any more. Not *directly*. You see, we're committed to a strategy that will work. And that strategy is, win adults. When we win parents, we reach the whole family. When the old church got children in Sunday school or Vacation Bible School, it might wring a profession of faith from some, but then it turned them back over to non-Christian parents. What a deadly, sinful thing that was!

"We care about children so much that we make sure they have a Christian home to grow up in. We go out and face adults, that's how much we care about kids. We don't sneak around and spend all our time with children because we're scared to death of grown-ups!"

"Carl's pretty wild on this subject," Estelle said seriously. "You see, he was won to the Lord as a child, in a day camp program. And then over and over he was told in Sunday school to talk to others about the Lord — but no one from the church ever got around to talking to his parents. Oh, they invited them to vbs closing programs, and things like that. But I'm afraid Carl feels their concern was slightly hypocritical."

"Oh Estelle, it's not that bad. I know they meant well. I just get upset thinking of that tragic approach to evangelism. I'm glad they reached me, and other children, too. But think how many might have been won if all that time and effort was given to sharing Christ with other adults."

Carl had been a child in the old church, but I was already deeply involved in Christian education, so I felt I had to break in. "Actually, it wasn't that simple. You see, talking to others about Christ never works as something done mechanically or because we have to. Witness today flows from our lives as we Christians live close to Him. We experience Him daily, and so our sharing is fresh and vibrant. Unfortunately, in the old church, too many hadn't grown much since their conversion. We didn't have the kind of fellowship you enjoy. We didn't meet in our churches to share and minister to each other; we met to sit and listen, or do a job. I'm afraid an awful lot of Christians in those days went to church with a sense of deep longing, and left with it unfulfilled. Christ wasn't real to us as He is now.

"So, however much we wanted to witness, we fell short in our testimony. So don't be too critical. You see, we had to *become the church* to each other before all the dynamic forces God built

into His church could work in our lives, to free us and transform us.

"Still, I'm afraid that this strategy of reaching adults, and
ignoring children, would make a lot of the folks in the old church
doubt your spirituality, and your love."

Here Estelle broke in. "Oh, we do love children! All Carl is
saying is that the church *focuses* on adults, and that it doesn't
make any special provision for children outside the family group.
So our concern for children isn't quite as obvious, but it's there.
And we see a lot of boys and girls from non-Christian homes become Christians."

"How does that happen?"

"Well, it's just natural, I guess. You know, I love children, and
they respond to me. So lots of neighbor boys and girls visit me,
to talk and eat cookies. And I do a lot of free babysitting for
mothers when they go shopping or to the beauty parlor. Quite
often I tell their children Bible stories, and we talk about the
Lord.

"I know that many mothers in our Congregation have the same
experiences. Their child has friends who play in their homes, or
go on picnics with them, and so they get exposed."

"Yes," added Carl. "And sometimes their parents don't like it,
either. Two days ago Helen Gregg burst in here and really told
Estelle off for talking to SuEllen about having Christ as a Friend.
She wasn't going to have her daughter becoming a Holy!"

"What did you do, Estelle?"

"Well, I really didn't know what to do. So I just said, 'Helen,
Christ is my life. I talk about Him to everyone.'"

Carl smiled. "Yes, Estelle's talked to Helen too, so she knows
it's true. She just stood there with her mouth open a second,
turned and went out.

"But SuEllen was over here playing today. She said her mother
said it was all right."

"What," I asked, "will you do if SuEllen becomes a Christian?"

"She'll be my responsibility until her parents are won to Christ.
I'll do all I can to teach her, and pray for her just as if she were
my own daughter."

"Then she won't go to Sunday school or classes or anything
like that?"

"No, she won't. But our Home Unit will pray in a concentrated way for her parents, and all of us will expect the Lord to open opportunities to win them for Him. And in the meantime, Sue won't just be a name on the roll of a succession of Sunday school teachers; she'll be our special responsibility, and we'll do all we can to help her grow as a Christian."

Really, as Carl stressed later, this approach is far more personal and meaningful than the Day Camp and Sunday school outreach of his childhood. For SuEllen would never be a hand, counted for report to denominational headquarters. SuEllen would be the girl next door, and there would be a Christian family nearby that cared, always seeking to guide her in Christian ways and always seeking to win her mom and dad to the Lord.

And so late into my second night at Dunsea, we talked about evangelism. About sharing a Christ who is real and living, so real to us that we can't help talking about Him to everyone. And it was good, to see a church where evangelism is a way of life.

20

Social Concern

The next morning I awoke before Carl, much to my surprise, for I am a good sleeper, and we had gotten to bed late the night before. But this was to be my last day in Dunsea, and an interesting one. I was to see how this church handled one of the most controversial of all issues for the evangelical. What is the Christian's response to social problems?

There is no doubt that cultural institutions and patterns either reduce or multiply human misery. And that the Christian is concerned for others — totally. But the question has always been, What do we do about it?

During the Reformation many insisted that the church command the secular, and enforce a righteous social order. Thus the Geneva experiment, and Cromwell's England, and many other attempts at utopia. But all have failed. Enforced righteousness cannot change the heart, and only righteousness that flows spontaneously from loving hearts can produce social harmony.

At the other extreme, Christians have withdrawn from society, denying responsibility for "the world." Its social systems have seemed at best to reflect "the lusts of the eyes, and the lusts of the flesh, and the pride of life." And there have been other reasons for withdrawal. Some, like the Anabaptists, were as much forced by their neighbors as by their convictions to take no responsibility for civil life. And, after all, social systems have seemed at best sand castles, which the waves of time and the purposes of God would soon wash away. "Make it your business to live at peace with all men, quiet and godly lives," men have read in Scripture. And this they have done, asking nothing but to be left alone to worship God, to live holy lives, and to share the good news of Christ's love. But not to change society.

Still others have been aggressively evangelistic, attacking those who in any way seem concerned for our human condition — unless the concern becomes a direct road to gospel witness. "Don't concern yourselves with poverty. Reject involvement in racial strife. Forget inequities in education, housing, and opportunities. What counts is that these folks hear the Gospel. When they're converted, then we'll have a basis for brotherhood! Until then, forget what is *right*.

"No, don't get involved. Send the missionaries out to Africa, and visit the slums to sell Bibles below cost, and talk to women on relief about how great it will be when they die. If they know Jesus. . . ."

Like the others, this approach has failed. Partly because everyone except those who take it can see that it is hypocrisy. If we love people, we care for them *totally*. Not just for their souls.

Of course, relationship with God *is* crucial. But if we love, if we love truly, it is "not in word only, but in deed." And we don't say to a hungry man, "the Lord bless you, brother. I hope you get some food and clothes." We feed him. And we clothe him. Even if he doesn't listen to us.

And we do all this because it's right, because God makes His rain to fall on the just and unjust, and because as His children we are also to bless all — with no strings attached.

And then there have been those who are socially alert and concerned. Some of them have said, Never mind relationship to God. Let's get these people fed. Even others, with a better theology, have tried to make the church an instrument of social justice. They've lobbied, and set up organizations, and tried to pressure other institutions in society to act in "Christian" ways.

Like the Geneva experiment, theirs have failed. For the same reason. Social justice doesn't change the heart. Social justice remakes the outside of things, and in many ways this is important.

But social justice alone doesn't free a person to love others. Social justice doesn't release anyone from the burning inner ambition to achieve, to *be* — no matter what the cost to others. Social justice isn't the Gospel, and only through the Gospel does God enter human life, wash away the twisted selfish desires that warp us, and fill us instead with love and true holiness.

So history has left us with the problem. We will always have it, until Christ comes and establishes His just and universal rule. Until then, what can we do? We cannot enforce the Christian conscience on those who do not have it. We cannot withdraw from our society, deny its existence, and deny the existence of need. We cannot be unconcerned about the life of men on earth, for this is part of life God would touch, and men are not just disembodied souls. Nor can we deny the nature of the church, rediscovered in renewal, and attempt with it to reshape society. We can leave that entirely futile attempt to the Recognized Church, which claims to speak prophetically on all sorts of political and social issues.

With all this in mind, I was particularly eager to see how the church at Dunsea responds to the problems created by the environment of our twenty-first century life. And find out I did.

Major Irwin, a retired police officer, was my guide that day. Major (his first name, by the way, not a title) is a gruff looking gentleman, with bushy eyebrows that hide his friendly hazel eyes. On our first jaunt, overland to Old Milwaukee, he outlined the philosophy on which all Dunsea ministries are based.

"We never give things apart from ourselves. Guess that's the clearest way to put it. People used to give money, clothes, food. Or go down to the ghetto one afternoon a week to tutor a child. Thought they'd done their duty, and could go back to their comforts feeling righteous. Everybody in the ghetto had 'em tagged. 'Do Gooders,' they called 'em."

"But," I objected, "they had good motives. These people really were concerned, in their way."

"That's just it — 'in their way.' But that way only made the gap between the ghettos and the comfortable seem wider. That way didn't communicate love. Christ didn't just drop into our world once a week to bring goodies, man. He got right down here in the dirt with us. He ate our food, coughed on the dust of dirt roads, wore scratchy robes, and smelled unwashed crowds. He communicated love, because He become one of us. And we knew Him. Now, *that's* the only way."

"You're saying then that the church today follows that pattern? That Christians actually move into the areas where conditions that cause suffering exist?"

"Exactly. And that's what you'll see."

I did.

Old Milwaukee has suffered the same blight that destroyed many of the Old Cities of America. Decentralization first meant a movement of the middle classes, now over 75 percent of our population, to suburban and semi-rural areas. Later automation, with its startling changes in our employment, further reduced job opportunities in the cities, which were already suffering from the removal of most service and sales organizations to the suburbs. When planned communities came along, with their balance of business and creative industries, the distance between suburb and city cultures widened. Now the Old Cities have become ghettos, and hold a vast number of men and women who are cut off, by lack of education and training, from the mainstream of educational life. And, while racial considerations are less significant than educational ones, the educational opportunities for non-whites have always been limited.

Of course, the government hasn't forgotten the people of the cities, even though the Black Rebellion led to disenfranchisement of most of those who now live there. A wealthy society can afford to support millions, and does, providing minimum doles of food, clothing, and amusements. Enough, in fact, to have made the old reliefers feel wealthy indeed! But as a society apart, the Old Cities have developed their own cultures. As a people without work and without hope, their inhabitants have fallen victim to the worst traits of mankind. Filth, drunkenness, and crime have become a way of life.

It was into this world, so foreign to most of our daily lives, that Major Irwin drove me. And it was in this world that I met Carol and Marie, young women who have voluntarily given up the franchise to live in a dingy apartment across from a cemented park.

For five years Carol and Marie have lived in the Old City. They told me that there are nearly a hundred Christian couples, some with children, who have come to live here. Not all are from

Dunsea; members of many churches have come here. "Of course," Carol explained, "we're no longer members of the Dunsea church. We're part of the church where we live — Old Milwaukee."

The girls told me about their early days in the city. They were distrusted and hated because they came from the outside. Even the news that they had given up the franchise hadn't affected their neighbors' attitude. For the first two years the girls had merely lived their love. After scouring their own apartment, they had gone to work cleaning the halls and stairs of their building. They had nursed sick children, who often were placed outside apartment doors on cotton pads, lest they infect others in the family. One night they'd dragged in a hulking brute who had been cut in a knife fight, and for their troubles were later beaten by him. More than once they were threatened, and in serious danger. Through these days, when they could see no response in any of their hardened neighbors, they had prayed to God for His grace. And they had gone on living His love, encouraging each other in weekly gatherings of the small church.

Today, they told me, the church is nearly a hundred times larger than the day they took their apartment. And it's composed mostly of "disfrans." While it's much like other renewed churches of today, it has developed several patterns that reflect the unique life in disfran culture.

On the way out of the city, I asked Major if this was all Christians could do about the disfran situation. Did he believe that the church's only role was to reach people of the cities for Christ? Should we attempt to touch the social causes of the situation?

"Two things to remember," he explained in his blunt way. "First, the church has no voice. We are not an organization, and no one speaks for us. Second, we do care about the disfran and other social problems. We study 'em and pray about 'em in Congregation, and we ask God what we Christians can do. As franchised citizens, we've got a right to speak out, and we do, too."

"But," I wondered, "what can individuals do?"

"More than organizations, really. God has believers in every level of society. And most of our young people select occupations where they can serve — social work, teaching, medicine, government. We do what we can as citizens, and we do whatever we can wherever God places us in society. To be an influence for what's good and what's right.

"I think Refranchisement will pass Congress, and be ratified in most of the states. If it does, one big reason will be the Christians, who've written letters, studied, gotten into government, and made themselves heard.

"And Christians in key places will have a lot to say about how Refran is applied. So, we don't take a back seat. We do what we can, and there's a lot we can do."

I asked Major about the service Units of the Dunsea church. While Carol and Marie had been in the prayers of the church, they really weren't members. What did service Units do?

"A Home Unit registers as a service Unit when its folks feel led to serve others in some special way. The Units share their concern with others in the Congregation, and we all pray for 'em. And give, to help their ministries, when we're led. But service Units, like all of us, depend on God. Not on a dole from the church."

That afternoon I visited with members of two service Units. Mary Kane is a woman of about 50, a little worn, but cheerfully at home amid 35 bustling preschoolers. Her day nursery, 1½ miles southeast of Dunsea, is called Second Home. It's near one of Dunsea's creative industries, a small art-light factory. I asked Mary how Second Home got its start, and how it is related to the church.

"A few years ago," Mary told me, "a divorcee with two small children moved into our apartment block. She had to find work and really didn't have enough money to hire a sitter. So I offered to watch the children the days she worked. Later in my Home Unit we got to talking about all the divorced people with children that we knew, and about other mothers who wanted to work. We wanted to help, so after praying about it we registered as a service Unit and studied how to start a day care center."

"Did the church sponsor your center?"

"Oh no, the church doesn't sponsor anything like this. And, of course, not being a Registered religion, the church couldn't own property anyway.

"But lots of people helped. We all checked around the community to see where the greatest need was, and what I had to do to get a license, and how much it would cost to get started, and, oh, all sorts of things. I really had no idea how complicated it would be!"

"But it looks like you made it."

"Yes, finally. We were led to this property, and I bought it, so it's in my name. And I took some special University courses and passed my licensing exam. Now we have 58 children who come regularly, with about 35 each day. We're open six days a week, you see, and with most of the girls on four day shifts, we can rotate attendance nicely."

"Is this service provided free?"

"Oh no. Everyone who can is asked to pay, just enough to keep us going. That really isn't very much. You see, I used my savings to buy the building and fix it up, and my staff are all Christian women who give two days a week to work with the children. Of course, I'm here every day, and so is Uncle Joe."

"Uncle Joe?"

"Yes, he was in the Congregation when we first were led to this ministry. Since he retired, he gives his time to taking care of the place. And to the children. You should see how they love him! And it's so good for the children to have a man here. Many of them have no father at home, you know."

"Then you only charge those who can pay?"

"Yes. It's better for everyone to feel independent. We never want our mothers to feel they're objects of charity."

"Have you ever run short of money?"

"Yes, we have. But this is the Lord's work, and He provides. More than once some gift has come from one of the Congregations, and it has always been through prayer. You see, we don't advertise our needs. We don't have to."

On our way to the next stop Major told me more of Mary. It had taken all her money to buy Second Home, and she lives very simply on the part of her social security check she doesn't invest in the children. Major also told me that the personal interest Second Home staff members take in the children and their mothers has led to several conversions. "Mary doesn't have the school just to reach the parents," he said. "She cares. And when you care, the Gospel seems to come into it somewhere."

The Gospel and serving go together. There can be no conflict between them. It was the Gospel that created the love these

Christians have, and the love they show in serving others just has to express itself in sharing Christ with them too.

Major now took a road leading into Dunsea. "We're going to a Listening Post," he said without explanation.

Soon we turned into one of Dunsea's four educational/shopping centers, and parked near an attractive cafe. It was fronted with green-tinted glass windows, on which was lettered, LISTENING POST. Inside what seemed a small room at first, opened out into alcoves, dimly lit, that held several comfortable chairs each. At the back is a C-Bar (short for coke and coffee). Several young people were at tables in the central room, and I could hear murmurs of conversation from four or five of the alcoves. Major led me behind the C-bar into a small office, and introduced me to Rick, the manager. There I heard the story of LISTENING POSTS.

Until the Recognized religions swallowed up psychiatric and counseling services in America, and licensing was done through RCR channels, many Congregations had counseling services for alcoholics, drug adicts, marital problems, etc. The opportunity to give such services was cut off when the Recognized clergy gained control of these professions, and many clinics run by Christians were forced to close.

However, our pleasure-oriented culture creates many tensions, especially among the young. And Dunsea's Christians felt a deep responsibility to help. Fortunately, the old pattern of judging has not come into the renewed church. In the old days, the sight of a beard brought a snort of indignation from many a churchgoer, and a very cool reception should anyone who seemed a "hippy" happen into church. Today, in accord with Scripture, we do not judge those outside — but we do care, and show it by accepting each individual, and valuing him as a person. And we want to help.

The problem Dunsea faced was, *how* to help? The LISTENING POST is one answer. Located in educational and shopping centers, they provide a quiet place for talk, where anyone who wants to can find people who will listen. LISTENING POSTS are self supporting, as all businesses are required by law to reach a breakeven point. But they support themselves in a peculiar way. Unable to make enough from sales of coke and coffee, LISTENING POSTS actually charge those who give their time as listeners a "cover charge" for space used! And there are many Christians who pay for this right to serve.

Rick told me the simple rules for Listeners. No one who is not a participant in Home Unit and Congregational life is accepted. All who are accepted spend a minimum of four hours a week at one of Dunsea's six Posts. Each listener is really a *listener*. He is there to care — not to give advice. While he is free to share his experiences with those who drop in, he does not force his views, or the Gospel, unless asked.

Of course, everyone knows that LISTENING POSTS are operated by "the Holys." And that makes it easier, because people who do come in often ask about the Christian way. But everyone who comes also knows the code of the posts: *don't intrude — care*.

Rick gave me a number of illustrations of LISTENING POST ministries. He told of students who were faced with decisions about drugs and personal moral codes, and discouraged about grades. He told of families who had been helped to work out marital problems. He told of suicides that had been averted. And of many who, sensing the love of God in the men and women who listened, were thus drawn to Him. "Don't intrude — care."

So few people really care about others. So few people ever have.

Epilogue

I left Dunsea that night, took a taxi-copter to Chicago, and jetted my way back home.

And I thought about the people I had met, the ever-young church that renewal has created in our modern world. And, in a way, I was glad that I hadn't known the future back in 1970, when my first book on renewal was released. Then it would only have been a dream which I might have felt wistful, or discouraged, about. And I am sure that if I had written then, as I have now, about the church at Dunsea, some of my readers would have misunderstood. They would have dismissed it all as a utopian dream, or, even worse, searched in it for "the" pattern on which to build their congregations. And that would have been impossible to do. For, if you happen to remember that dusty old work, I insisted then that renewal must come step by step. That God must lead each congregation, and that as patterns given in the Word — of mutual ministry, of leadership, of decision-making — were followed, the future would be better than any dream!

I remembered how I ended the book, and said the words over again. "Any of us can dream of the future. But none of us has more than the present in which to live, and in which to do the will of God. And so, while it is today, let those of us who hear His voice harden not our hearts, nor stagger because of unbelief. Let us take His Word as a pattern we can trust. Let us step out in faith to find a future we cannot know today, yet knowing today that we can trust the God who leads us toward it."

Bibliography

The books listed here are those which seem to me of particular value for following up the present text. Inclusion does not mean full agreement with an author's position: it does mean that I believe careful study will stimulate thinking and help the reader develop his own insights and ideas.

Baker, Wesley. *The Split-level Fellowship*. Philadelphia: Westminster Press, 1965.

Bennis, Warren G., Benne, Kenneth D., and Chin, Robert. *The Planning of Change*. New York: Holt, Rinehart and Winston, Inc., 1969.

Berton, Pierre. *The Comfortable Pew*. Philadelphia: J. B. Lippincott, 1965.

Bow, R. *Integrity of Church Membership*. Waco: Word Books, 1968.

Bradford, Leland P., Benne, Kenneth D., and Gibb, Jack R. *T-Group Theory and Laboratory Method*. New York: John Wiley & Sons, 1967.

Casteel, John L. *Spiritual Renewal Through Personal Groups*. New York: Association Press, 1965.
> One of the earliest books to document and discuss the impact of the small group on individuals from a religious perspective. Good insight.

Casteel, John L. *The Creative Role of Interpersonal Groups in the Church Today.* New York: Association Press, 1968.

Clark, M. Edward, ed. *The Church Creative.* Nashville: Abingdon Press, 1967.

Cox, Harvey. *The Secular City.* New York: The Macmillan Company, 1965.

Fischer, Wallace. *From Tradition to Mission.* Nashville: Abingdon Press, 1965.

Glasser, William. *Reality Therapy.* New York: Harper and Row, 1965.
> Extremely important book with insights relevant to the functioning of the small group in the church.

Gulley, Halbert E. *Discussion, Conference and Group Process.* New York: Holt, Rinehart & Winston, Inc., 1968.

Howard, Walden. *Groups That Work.* Grand Rapids: Zondervan Publishing House, 1967.
> Insights from many writers with various theological perspectives; many first-hand experiences and suggestions.

Howard, Walden. *Nine Roads to Renewal.* Waco: Word Books, 1967.
> Illustrations of directions specific churches have taken in their search for renewal.

Larson, Bruce. *Setting Men Free.* Grand Rapids: Zondervan Publishing House, 1967.
> Guidelines and principles for laymen who want to participate personally in renewal. Excellent for discussion groups on renewal and its impact.

Larson, Bruce. *Dare to Live Now!* Grand Rapids: Zondervan Publishing House, 1965.

Larson, Bruce. *Living on the Growing Edge.* Grand Rapids: Zondervan Publishing House, 1968.

Lippit, Ronald, Watson, Jeanne; and Westley, Bruce. *The Dynamics of Planned Change.* New York: Harcourt, Brace & World, Inc., 1958.

Miller, Keith. *A Taste of New Wine.* Waco: Word Books, 1965.

Nederhoed, Joel. *The Church's Mission to the Educated American*. Grand Rapids: Eerdmans Publishing Company, 1961.

Neill, S. C. and Weber, H. R. eds. *The Layman in Christian History*. Philadelphia: Westminster, 1963.

Raines, Robert A. *New Life in the Church*. New York: Harper & Row, 1961.
> Reports of the author's experiences in his own church, particularly helpful in showing how he worked through changes in his own and his people's thinking, with an emphasis on Koinonia groups.

Raines, Robert A. *Reshaping the Christian Life*. New York: Harper & Row, 1964.

Rath, Lewis Edward. *Teaching for Thinking*. Columbus: C. E. Merrill Books, 1967.

Reid, Clyde. *The God-Evaders*. New York: Harper & Row, 1966.

Reid, Clyde. *Groups Alive: Church Alive*. Evanston: Harper & Row Publishers, 1969.

Reitz, Rudiger. *The Church in Experiment*. Nashville: Abingdon Press, 1969.

Richards, Lawrence O. *Creative Bible Teaching*. Chicago: Moody Press, 1970.

Rose, Stephen C. ed. *Who's Killing the Church?* New York: Association Press, 1966.

Rose, Stephen C. *The Grass Roots*. New York: Holt, Rinehart & Winston, Inc., 1966.

Schein, Edgar H. and Bennis, Warren C. *Personal and Organizational Change Through Group Methods*. New York: John Wiley & Sons, 1967.

Schein, Edgar H. *Organizational Psychology*. New York: Prentice-Hall, Inc., 1965.
> Another outstanding secular text on change, with a clear focus on the role of the encounter group (T-Group) in stimulating and guiding change.

Trueblood, Elton. *The Company of the Committed*. New York: Harper & Row, 1961.

Scripture Index